Grains, Beans, Nuts

also by David Scott

The Japanese Cookbook
Recipes for Living

David Scott

GRAINS!
BEANS!
NUTS!

Illustrated by Steve Hardstaff

Rider

London Melbourne Sydney Auckland Johannesburg

Rider & Company

An imprint of the Hutchinson Publishing Group

3 Fitzroy Square, London W1P 6JD

Hutchinson Group (Australia) Pty Ltd
30–32 Cremorne Street, Richmond South, Victoria 3121
PO Box 151, Broadway, New South Wales 2007

Hutchinson Group (NZ) Ltd
32–34 View Road, PO Box 40–086, Glenfield, Auckland 10

Hutchinson Group (SA) (Pty) Ltd
PO Box 337, Bergvlei 2012, South Africa

First published 1980

© David Scott 1980

Set in Bembo
Printed and bound in Great Britain by
Redwood Burn Limited, Trowbridge & Esher

British Library Cataloguing in Publication Data

Scott, David
    Grains, beans, nuts.
    1. Vegetarian cookery
    I. Title
    641.5'636   TX837

ISBN 0 09 141681 7

CONTENTS

GRAINS

Wheat

Rice

Maize or corn

Oats

Barley

Millet and sorghum

Rye

Buckwheat

BEANS

NUTS

ACKNOWLEDGEMENTS

Thanks to:

Home–Grown Cereals Authority, Hamlyn House, Highgate Hill, London N19
   5PR
British Edible Pulses Association, Works Lane, Setchy, King's Lynn, Norfolk
Processors and Growers Research Organisation, The Research Station,
   Great North Road, Thornhaugh, Peterborough PE8 6HJ
IFST, 105–111 Euston Road, London NW1 2ED

INTRODUCTION

There is a renewed awareness among many people of the value of cereal grains, beans (also called legumes) and nuts both as wholesome foods and as cheap alternatives to meat and fish as protein sources. The intention of this book is to give a historical, nutritional and geographical background to each of the important cereal grains, beans and nuts as well as to provide a host of the fascinating and multifarious recipes that man and woman has created around the world and through the ages for cooking these basic and possibly first human foodstuffs.

Beans and grains particularly complement one another nutritionally, and a diet containing moderate amounts of both will provide all the protein we need as well as many of the vitamins and minerals. They contain very little fat and are most useful in diets designed to reduce fat intake, which, for most people, is usually too high. Nuts too are a high-protein food and deserve more than the roasting and salting treatment they are normally allotted.

The book is divided into three sections: Grains, Beans and Nuts. The Grains section is divided into chapters which deal separately with each of the principle grains and each chapter gives a brief history, nutritional information and recipes for a particular grain. In both the Beans and Nuts sections there is a general discussion of the history and nutritional worth of these foodstuffs followed by a short individual description of each of the main beans and nuts. The recipe sections are divided into the usual categories, e.g. soups, salads, main meals, etc., rather than under the name of a particular bean or nut.

Most of the recipes given in the book are for non-meat dishes. Where a traditional bean, grain or nut recipe contains meat as one of the main ingredients this has been included but otherwise where meat is included in a recipe it is normally as a minor ingredient. Some of the cereal grains and wheat in particular are most commonly used in their milled form as flour which is then made into pasta, noodles, bread, couscous etc. Recipes are given for the preparation from basics of these products, and there are a number of recipes which concentrate on less usual ways of using the grain such as in its whole or cracked forms.

NUTRIENT CONTENT OF CEREAL GRAINS.*

	WHEAT (HARD)	WHEAT (SOFT)	RICE	MAIZE	BARLEY	RYE	OATS	SORGHUM	MILLET (FINGER)	MILLET (BULRUSH)
PROTEIN (gms)	13.8	10.5	7.5	9.5	11.0	11.0	11.2	9.7	5.6	10.3
FAT (gms)	2.0	1.9	1.8	4.3	1.8	1.9	7.5	3.4	1.5	5.0
CARBOHYDRATES (gms)	70.0	74.0	77.0	73.0	73.0	73.0	70.0	73.0	78.0	71.0
VITAMINS										
THIAMINE B_1 (mgms)	0.45	0.38	0.33	0.45	0.46	0.41	0.50	0.50	0.30	0.30
RIBOFLAVIN B_2 (mgms)	0.13	0.08	0.05	0.11	0.12	0.16	0.15	0.12	0.10	0.15
NIACIN B_5 (mgms)	5.4	4.3	4.6	2.0	5.5	1.3	1.0	3.5	1.4	2.0
MINERALS										
CALCIUM (mgms)	37.0	35.0	15.0	10.0	33.0	38.0	60.0	32.0	350.0	25.0
IRON (mgms)	4.1	3.9	1.4	2.3	3.6	3.7	5.0	4.5	5.0	3.0

* ALL FIGURES GIVEN ARE PER 100 gms OF GRAIN.

Table 1

The grain family comprises over 5000 species, and amongst these can be found the world's principal cereal crops, i.e. barley, maize (corn), millet, oats, rice, rye, sorghum and wheat. The name given to a particular cereal grass is the same as that given to its edible seeds. Thus we have the plants wheat and rice and the seeds or grain of these plants also called wheat and rice. The discovery by primitive man that he could plant and harvest the seeds of these previously wild grasses led to the formation of the first village communities. They were established in fertile areas where the wild grasses were most abundant, such as the banks of the Nile and the region of Western Asia, later to be called Mesopotamia.

The cultivation of cereals provided ancient communities with a food source that could be stored over long periods without becoming inedible. Thus animals could now be kept and fed through the winter months and large herds could be bred. Further, in conjunction with the sowing of seasonal crops and their storage and trade the sciences of astronomy, mathematics and writing developed, and the earliest civilizations started to grow. The prime importance of cereal grains to these ancient cultures is reflected in many ancient traditions and myths, and the name cereal itself is derived from Ceres, the ancient Greek and Roman goddess who was the giver of grain and life.

Until recently, particular staple grains have been associated with particular areas in the world: rice with East Asia, wheat with the west, maize (corn) with the Americas. Nowadays, with a few exceptions, these divisions are less clear, and rice is as common in Europe as bread is in Japan. The exceptions stand out: sorghum and millet for instance are the staple grains of much of Africa, but sorghum is virtually unknown in the west, and millet is fed here only to budgerigars! I hope the following chapters contribute to breaking down these barriers still further and encourage you to investigate all the cereal grains and to make full use of their distinctive qualities as ingredients in many excellent recipes and as nutritious foods. Table 1 opposite lists the nutrient contents of all the principal grains.

DURUM.   COMMON (BREAD)   SPELT.   CLUB.
          WHEAT.

Introduction

Wheat, which has been called the Queen of Grains, is one of the world's most vital foods, and certainly the most widely cultivated cereal crop. It has been important to mankind since neolithic times, and has become increasingly vital as forms of wheat specifically suited to particular climatic conditions have been developed. Such has been progress that world wheat production has doubled in the last sixty years.

The success of wheat as a food crop is due to a number of factors, but two of them are particularly important. The first is the wide climatic growing range of wheat. It can be grown as far north as Alaska and as far south as the equator, and in fact it now seems possible to develop a hybrid of wheat suited to almost any habitat. The second factor is the unique quality wheat shares with rye of having a protein structure which makes its flour excellently suited to bread-making. Wheat protein has the property of forming an elastic gluten matrix when mixed with water. When yeast and sugar are added to a dough of flour and water the carbon dioxide produced is trapped by this gluten matrix. The matrix is stretched giving a light airy mixture that bakes into beautiful bread. Add to these properties of wheat the compact size and food value of wheat grain and its excellent storage qualities and we have a food suited to most of man's and woman's needs as an explorer and settler.

In this chapter we chart a brief history of wheat which is then followed by a discussion of the nutritional qualities of the various kinds of wheat and the differences between brown and white bread. The recipe section that follows gives recipes for bread-making, pasta and noodles, bulgar wheat, semolina (including couscous) and wholewheat berry dishes.

The small number of meat recipes included in this book are identified by the following symbol: ★. They may be ignored if you wish.

History

The name wheat derives from the Old German word *Weizzi*, which is similar to the Old English word *Hwoete*, both meaning white. This was a description of wheat flour which, compared to other cereal flours in use in earlier times, was light in colour. There is also the English habit of calling wheat, corn. This caused me much confusion as a boy since I could never relate wheat to corn on the cob. This usage stems from the early English word *corne*, which meant staple grain. Thus the staple grain of any country was *corne*, and the first English settlers in America called the cereal crop grown by the Indians 'Indian Corne'. The Americans now call it maize, but of course the English continue to call it corn as well as calling wheat, corn.

There are thousands of species of wheat both wild and cultivated, but they all belong to the plant genus *Triticum* and of these many types, only fourteen are commonly recognized as cereal grasses. One variety *Triticum vulgare*, which is very suited to bread-making, accounts for more than 80% of wheat presently under cultivation. Apart from this, winter or Lammas wheat (*Triticum hybernum*) and spring or summer wheat (*Triticum aestivum*) are the most widely grown for general use, and the hard-grained durum wheat (*Triticum durum*) is cultivated exclusively for the manufacture of pasta and noodles.

Triticum vulgare first evolved, according to archaeological sources, around the third or fourth century B C, but the earliest remains of wheat, dated 6700 B C have been found in the neolithic sites of Jarmo in Northern Iraq. Two species of wheat, Wild Emmer and Wild Einkorn, along with similarly carbonized remains of barley and lentils, were found. Domesticated Emmer is a hard-grained wheat which was cultivated by neolithic peoples throughout central Europe. It is now only grown in a limited way in parts of North Africa and Russia. Domestic Einkorn was once a valuable wheat, since it will thrive on poor ground and makes good flour. However, it gives very low yields of wheat per acre and is now grown only as animal fodder.

The earliest wheats had grains that were enclosed in tight husks; to remove them the early farmer roasted the wheat on hot stones. The grains were loosened and could then be separated from the husks. The parched wheat berries were eaten whole or ground into a coarse meal between two stones. The rough branny meal produced could be mixed with water and cooked over a fire to give what must have been pretty rotten porridge.

Through this parching process the primitive farmer discovered that parched grains could be stored without sprouting, and only grain for seeding had to be left unroasted. Further, he probably discovered that by choosing the best and healthiest-looking grains from his wheat harvest one year and using them as seed the next, he could gradually improve the yield and quality of his crops. By later prehistoric times both the quality of wheat and the way it was milled had been improved. The wheat grain was separated from the chaff by crude threshing, although it would probably have been mixed up with the seeds of weeds and maybe barley growing in the same field as the wheat. This mixture would be ground into flour on a saddle stone. This was a flat-based stone with a hollow in the top to hold the grain and the grinding was done with a ball-shaped rock. The rough flour produced was made into a dough with water and baked on a hot stone near the fire's edge. This was probably man's first bread. Unleavened and coarse, it still made a change from porridge, but it must have been almost inedible by today's standards. Perhaps, as has been suggested, honey or sweet berries and animal fat were later added to the dough to improve its taste and digestibility.

Later, unleavened bread was mentioned in the Bible: 'And unleavened bread, and cakes unleavened tempered with oil, and wafers unleavened anointed with oil, of wheaten flour shalt thou make them' and in much improved forms it is still eaten today as a staple food in parts of the Middle East and throughout India and Pakistan. Recipes for unleavened breads are given later in the book.

With the development of more sophisticated cooking pots, the prehistoric cook was able to start making stews. The grain left unmilled, mixed with seeds and green leaves and boiled with water, gave a nutritious and filling meal, which was possibly improved with meat saved from the last successful kill. Wholewheat pottages have remained popular up to the present day. The Romans introduced a dish called Frumenty to the British Isles in the first century A D. Wholewheat was soaked overnight and then cooked with dried fruit, spices and milk or nut milk. According to some sources Frumenty is still eaten in northern England, although I have never come across it.

The parched-wheat method of making flour used by primitive farmers destroys the enzymes necessary for the leavening process used in risen bread-making, and in earlier times only unleavened bread could have been made. However, with the development of wheats that could be threshed easily, and better milling techniques, conditions were created for the discovery of leavened bread-making. The discovery was made by the ancient Egyptians around 4000 B C, and like many other great discoveries was probably an accident. If a dough of water and flour is not baked immediately, but left for some time in a warm place, wild yeast spores present in the atmosphere will settle on it and initiate a fermentation process which produces the leavening process. From here our curious baker needed only to discover that the addition of a small quantity of fermented dough to a larger amount of fresh dough resulted in leavening in the whole amount. This is the basis of the sour-dough method of bread-making which was used by bakers right up to the nineteenth century. At this time developments in the brewery trade resulted in the discovery that artificial cultures of yeast could be used to speed up the leavening process and yeasted dough replaced sour dough.

By 2500 B C the Babylonians were growing a fine bread wheat and had started what was to become a flourishing wheat trade with other countries. The dry, hot, Assyrio-Babylonian region was perfectly suited for storing wheat over long periods, and the grain merchants built huge silo pits. They stored wheat in the good years and shipped it off by camel and ship to surrounding lands in bad years.

The farmers irrigated their fields using a complex canal system fed by the rivers of the Euphrates and Tigris. Wheat was grown to the exclusion of other crops and Babylonia became the grain basket of the Middle East, as Egypt later became for the Roman Empire.

Meanwhile the Egyptians were also doing well, but they didn't need to work so hard since for them the Nile did all the work. Herodotus writing in the fifth Century B C, had this to say about the farmers in the Nile Delta:

They obtain the fruits of the field with less trouble than any other people in the World, the rest of Egypt included, since they have no need to break the ground with plough, nor to use the hoe, nor to do any work which the rest of mankind finds necessary if they are to get a crop: but the husbandman waits till the river has of its own accord spread itself over the fields and withdrawn again to its bed, and then sows his plot of ground. . . .

Lucky for some! The Egyptians also invented the water mill, something the slaves who pushed the old mills around by hand must have been happy about.

The armies of the Roman Empire were dependent on wheat, and Roman armies encouraged its cultivation wherever they travelled. During their occupation of Britain, wheat production was increased to the point where the Romans were able to export it. Vespasian, who became Emperor of the Roman Empire after the death of Nero, was able to manoeuvre his way into the top job by occupying Egypt and cutting off supplies of wheat to the rest of the Empire.

In Rome itself there were, by the time of Christ, many commercial milling and baking establishments, producing breads of many different types and qualities to suit the tastes and pockets of their various customers. During the time Trajan was Emperor (about 100 A D) the bakers organized themselves into a society which laid down rules and regulations that not only governed the way members ran their businesses, but also the way they conducted their lives. Members had a high social status, and were represented on the Senate. Such was their rank that they were forbidden to mix with gladiators and comedians! So if you respect your baker, no jokes across the counter!

In Britain it wasn't until 1266 that Henry II initiated the Assize of Bread which made it the duty of the Lord Mayor and the sheriffs of each town to arrange inspections of bakers' shops every day to examine the loaves they had for sale. The king was prompted to institute new laws by the way unscrupulous bakers added chalk, lime, alum or even ground-up human bones to their flour. The aim was to make the bread look whiter, which made it more expensive. To protect themselves the bakers formed the first Guild of the City of London and began the long road that ends with our present trade union system. In those days only the rich could afford white bread which in fact was more akin to our 100% wholemeal bread than the packets of white sliced in plastic wrappers we buy today. Poorer people ate bread made from very coarse flour filled with bran.

Under Henry II's charter, any baker who was found selling underweight or contaminated bread was placed in a pillory. There he was subjected to the wrath of his fellow citizens, some of whom, in the event of such a treat, carried with them rotten vegetables for throwing at the poor man.

In country areas the system was different and people baked their own bread with flour milled for them from their own wheat by the local Lord of the Manor. He charged for the service and to ensure he wasn't duped out of his revenue by private enterprise a law was passed banning the milling of grain at home.

Effectively that brings us up to the eighteenth century, since in broad terms (and this includes the time from the Babylonians onwards), there were no radical changes in methods of wheat cultivation, harvesting or milling up to this date. All the significant changes have taken place in the last 150 years. Even now there are many areas in the world where methods used for wheat production are thousands of years old. Improvements in developed countries in agricultural techniques and the application of other scientific methods have resulted in large increases in yields for a fixed area of wheat. The development of strains of wheat particularly suited to the plains of North America and Canada and the pampas of South America has proceeded alongside improvements in mechanization such that now enormous areas of land producing millions of tons of wheat can be farmed by small groups of people. Modern mills have power-driven rollers and the milling, sifting, blending, etc., processes are completely automatic, producing so many different grades of flour our ancestors would be dazzled by the variety. Where though, you may ask, is the progress when we look at the type of bread now being mass-produced? Well, from the point of view of nutrition and taste there seems to be none at all. Although it must be said that attitudes are changing and good bread is now becoming more easily available than at any time in the last thirty years.

Wheat and nutrition

The nutrient content of wheat varies widely, and more so than for other cereal grains. The percentage protein can range from 7% to 20%, although it is usually contained within the limits 9% to 14%. There are many factors which govern the nutritional quality of wheat, e.g. where it grows, when it was sown and harvested, the type and condition of the soil, climate, etc., but the main differences are between soft and hard wheats.

Soft wheat has a lower protein content, and thus less gluten than hard wheat; it is usually winter-sown and grown in moist temperate conditions. The flour it gives is good for making cakes and biscuits. British-grown wheat is normally of this variety.

Hard-grained wheat contains more protein and thus more gluten, which makes it excellent for bread and pasta-making. It is spring-sown, and harvested in warm dry conditions. American and Canadian wheats are often of this type. In practice hard and soft wheats are frequently blended to provide flour for specific purposes and to simplify the following discussion as to the types and quantities of nutrients present in wheat, the figures given are for an 'average wheat' and for most purposes this is a completely satisfactory approximation.

Protein in wheat

Compared with some other common foods like meat, fish, pulses, cheese and eggs, wheat does not have a high protein content. However, it does have protein of high biological value, that is a high percentage of the protein present can be utilized by the body (Table 2). Further the protein value of a food not only depends on its biological value but also on the amount of that protein that is actually used by the body for protein jobs such as growth, maintenance and repair of the body. If a food is very high in protein and low in carbohydrate, the body will use up protein for calorie production in place of the missing carbohydrate. When all these factors have been taken into account we discover that whole wheat, except during periods of growth, can satisfy human protein requirements. A scale based on the unit (NDp Cals%) (Net Dietary Protein Calories per cent), on which the average adult protein requirement is 5, shows the average figure for wheat is 6.

The factor limiting the biological value of wheat is its shortage, in comparison to the other amino acids present, of lysine. If this deficiency is corrected by supplementing wheat with other foods richer in lysine an excellent balance can be achieved. Thus a 70/30% mixture of wheat and pulses gives an almost perfect protein combination for the needs of the human body. Table 2 compares the available protein in wheat with that in other foods.

Vitamins and minerals in wheat

Apart from protein and calorie needs, a balanced food must also provide vitamins and minerals. Wholewheat grain is a rich source of B complex and E

THE STRUCTURE OF A WHEAT GRAIN.

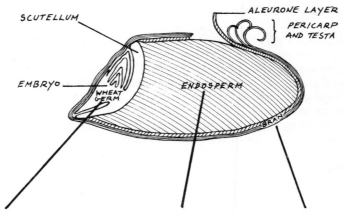

WHEAT GERM (3% BY WEIGHT OF WHOLE GRAIN).

CONSISTS OF THE EMBRYO OR GERM THAT CONTAINS ALL THE NUTRIENTS NEEDED TO SUSTAIN A NEW PLANT, AND THE SCUTELLUM WHICH CONNECTS THE EMBRYO TO THE ENDOSPERM. WITH THE INTRODUCTION OF STEEL ROLLERS TO FLOUR MILLING AND LATER BECAUSE OF THE NEED FOR LONG SHELF LIFE FLOURS, WHEAT GERM IS NOW OFTEN REMOVED FROM THE GRAIN DURING MILLING. THE UNSATURATED OILS PRESENT IN THE GERM CLOG UP THE STEEL ROLLERS AND CAUSE THE FLOUR TO GO RANCID. THIS PRACTICE PRODUCES A FLOUR LACKING IN NUTRIENTS SINCE THE WHEAT GERM IS PARTICULARLY RICH IN VITAMIN E, AND THE B COMPLEX VITAMINS, AND A GOOD SOURCE OF THE MINERALS CALCIUM AND IRON (SEE TABLE 3). IN SOME CIRCLES WHEAT GERM HAS A REPUTATION AS SOMETHING OF A WONDER FOOD FOR FERTILITY AND REJUVENATION!

ENDOSPERM (82% BY WEIGHT OF WHOLE GRAIN).

THIS IS THE MAIN PART IN MASS OF THE GRAIN (80%). IT IS PRINCIPALLY STARCH WITH SOME PROTEIN AND SMALL AMOUNTS OF VITAMINS AND MINERALS. THE OUTER PART OF THE ENDOSPERM BENEATH THE ALEURONE LAYER IS RICHER IN NUTRIENTS THAN THE CENTRE. THE ENDOSPERM IS USED TO MAKE WHITE FLOUR AND SEMOLINA FROM WHICH COUS-COUS AND PASTA PRODUCTS ARE MADE.

BRAN (15% BY WEIGHT OF WHOLE GRAIN).

CONSISTS OF THE TOUGH OUTER PERICARP LAYER. THE PERICARP LAYER CONTAINS LITTLE PROTEIN OR VITAMINS, BUT IT DOES PROVIDE ROUGHAGE WHICH IS NOW BEING RECOGNISED AS A NECESSARY REQUIREMENT OF A GOOD DIET. THE ALEURONE LAYER IS MOST IMPORTANT, IT CONTAINS 80% OF THE NIACIN PRESENT IN THE GRAIN, SUBSTANTIAL AMOUNTS OF THE OTHER B VITAMINS, MANY MINERALS AND A SIGNIFICANT AMOUNT (20%) OF GOOD VALUE PROTEIN (SEE TABLE 3). THE ALEURONE LAYER IS REMOVED IN VARYING AMOUNTS DURING MILLING, AND BRAN CONTAINING MUCH OF THIS LAYER WAS ONCE SOLD ONLY AS ANIMAL FOOD.

vitamins and many minerals. The protein, vitamins and minerals are distributed throughout the grain, but as you can see from the drawing of a wheat grain, a substantial proportion of them are contained in its outer edges. It is this portion of the grain that is removed when the grain is milled to produce white flour. The lower the extraction rate of a flour, the more of this outer layer is removed, and generally, the quantities of nearly all nutrients fall off rapidly as the extraction rate decreases. If you enjoy white bread but still want to benefit from the goodness of wheat, you can buy bran and wheat germ, which are removed during the production of white flour, and contain much of the goodness, and add them to your diet in other ways. Table 3 gives the nutrient contents of wheat bran and wheat germ.

FOOD	% PROTEIN PRESENT THAT IS USABLE BY THE BODY.
Whole Egg	90~95%
Meat and Brown Rice	75%
Whole Wheat	70%
Maize (Corn)	60%
White Flour, low extraction	50%
Pulses	40~50%

Table 2

NUTRITIONAL CONTENT OF WHEAT BRAN AND WHEAT GERM.

	WHEAT BRAN	WHEAT GERM
mg PER 100 gm		
PROTEIN	4·5	7·6
CARBOHYDRATE	17·6	13·3
FAT	1·3	3·1
FIBRE	2·6	0·7
MINERALS mg PER 100g		
PHOSPHOROUS	365	320
CALCIUM	34	21
IRON	4·2	2·7
SODIUM	2·6	0·9
POTASSIUM	320	236
MAGNESIUM	—	96
VITAMINS mg PER 100gm		
B_1	0·6	0·6
B_2	0·2	0·2
B_5	6·0	1·2
E	0·1	4·5

FIGURES UNDERLINED INDICATE QUANTITIES OF NUTRIENT PRESENT IN SIGNIFICANT AMOUNTS RELATIVE TO HUMAN DAILY NEEDS.

Table 3

Brown and white bread

To get the best out of the nutritional value of wheat via bread-eating, we should buy or make bread from 100% wholemeal flour milled on stone rollers. Although this of course does not take into account the question of taste or appe-

NUTRITIONAL CONTENT OF FLOURS OF DIFFERENT EXTRACTION RATES.

| EXTRACTION RATE (TYPE OF FLOUR) | PROTEIN | FIBRE | CARBOHYDRATE | B_1 | B_2 | NIACIN | IRON | CALCIUM |
	(gms PER 100 gms FLOUR)			(mg PER 100 gms FLOUR)				
100% (WHOLEMEAL FLOUR)	12·2	2·00	64·1	0·37	0·12	5·70	3·50	36·0
81% (BROWN BREAD)	11·7	0·21	70·2	0·24	0·06	1·60	1·65	–
70%	11·3	0·10	72·0	0·08	0·05	0·80	1·25	–

Table 4

tite, and on some occasions we may prefer a lighter, blander tasting but less nutritious bread than the wholemeal variety (for instance, who can resist a freshly baked French loaf?).

The nutritional qualities of different breads are illustrated in Table 4, which shows the nutrient contents of flours of various extraction rates. White bread is made from flour of 65% to 70% extraction, and brown breads from flours of 80% to 100% extraction. Incidentally, be careful to check when buying brown bread that it is not made from white flour dyed brown. Because of the growing popularity of brown bread, manufacturers are finding it worth while to make more of it; however, their production methods are such that it is simpler for them to add colourants to white flour than to use high-extraction-rate brown flour.

WHEAT RECIPES

The ways of cooking wheat and wheat flour are numerous and diverse. The variety of methods has resulted from regional differences in cooking methods, types of wheat available, cultural traditions, the extent to which technological changes have influenced ideas, and of course the most important reason, human inventiveness.

The recipes are divided into six sections. The first three – 'Unleavened bread', 'Leavened bread' and 'Pasta and noodles' – contain recipes which use wheat flour. These are followed by a section on 'Bulgar wheat', the roasted and cracked wheat-grain product used all over Eastern Europe, Western Asia and North Africa. The fifth section is devoted to 'Semolina' recipes, which include the preparation of couscous; and finally, under the heading 'Wholewheat', a selection of recipes which use the wholewheat grain or berry.

UNLEAVENED BREAD

Unleavened bread is made by mixing flour, salt and water to form a dough which is shaped into a loaf or rolled out into a flat round and baked. In the past, since it can be cooked more quickly than leavened bread, this type of bread has been more common in areas of the world where fuel was not easily available. In recent times it has become more widely popular, and is particularly recommended by the macrobiotic movement.

In India and Pakistan the most common form of bread is the flat, round, unleavened chapatti. The wheat grain is ground locally on stone mills, and the flour produced is quite coarse. In the West special chapatti flour can be obtained from Indian provision stores. Puris are made in the same way as chapattis, but they are cooked by frying in oil rather than baking or dry frying. Parathas, another unleavened Indian bread, are similar to chapattis, but with the addition of oil to the dough.

Tortillas are a Mexican unleavened bread prepared with a cornflour and wheat flour mixture.

Matzoth, the Jewish bread, baked to commemorate the exodus of the Jews from Egypt, and eaten during the Passover, is also unleavened.

The recipes in this section also include sour dough bread which in preparation, texture and taste lies between unleavened and leavened breads.

Chapattis

This Indian bread is normally eaten with curried food or other Indian-style savoury dishes. If rice is served with the meal it is customarily eaten before or after the chapattis, but never with them. This recipe makes 6 to 8 chapattis.

8 oz (2 cups) 100% wholewheat flour   4 oz (1 cup) 100% wholewheat flour
or   pinch salt
4 oz (1 cup) stoneground strong white   water
    flour *and*

Combine the flour and salt in a bowl. Stir in the water slowly until you have made a fairly stiff dough that comes away from the sides of the bowl. Cover the bowl with a damp cloth and leave for up to 2 hours (the longer the better). Knead the dough again and then break off small pieces the size of golf balls. Flatten the balls and on a floured board roll them out thinly into approximately 8 inch circles. Heat an ungreased, heavy frying pan over a high flame or very hot electric plate. Place in a chapatti, cook for about 1 minute and turn over. Press the edges of the chapatti with a spatula, and they should puff up slightly. Continue cooking until the underside is just mottled with brown spots. Remove the chapatti from the pan and store in a warm oven or wrap in a clean cloth to keep warm while the others are cooked.

Alternatively, the chapattis may be baked on a greased baking sheet in an oven at 350°F (gas mark 4) for 15 minutes.

Puris

Puris are made from the same ingredients and in the same way as chapattis, but the dough is deep-fried rather than dry-fried to give a light puffed-up bread. Ingredients as for chapattis plus vegetable oil for deep frying.

Prepare the dough as for chapattis. Pinch off small pieces the size of golf balls and roll out on a floured board into rounds about 5 inches in diameter. Heat the oil in a deep pan until it just begins to smoke (360°F). Deep-fry the puris one at a time. After dropping a puri into the deep fat it will puff up, at this stage turn it over and continue frying until it is golden brown. Drain on absorbent paper and store in a warm oven until all the puris are cooked. Serve.

Parathas

Parathas are prepared from a chapatti dough with the addition of butter. They are filling and delicious. This recipe makes 6 to 8 parathas.

8 oz (2 cups) 100% wholewheat flour
or
4 oz (1 cup) stoneground strong white
    flour *and*

4 oz (1 cup) 100% wholewheat flour
pinch salt
water
2 oz melted butter

Prepare a dough and roll out into 8 inch rounds as instructed in the recipe above for chapattis. Brush the top of a dough round with butter and fold it into a half circle. Brush with more butter and fold it into a quarter circle. Roll this out into a fan shape. Repeat for each of the rounds. Very lightly grease a heavy frying pan with any butter you may have left and heat over a high flame or very hot electric plate. Place in the pan one or two of the parathas and fry quickly on each side two or three times. Serve at once or store in a warm oven until all the parathas are cooked.

Stuffed parathas

A particular filling is not specified since this recipe is well suited to using up left-over cooked food.

8 oz (2 cups) 100% wholewheat flour
or
4 oz (1 cup) stoneground strong white
    flour *and*
4 oz (1 cup) 100% wholewheat flour
1 teaspoon salt

3 oz (⅜ cup) butter
water
4 oz (1 cup) mixed, cooked and spiced
    vegetables
or other filling of your choice (e.g.
    cooked beans)

Combine the flour and salt, and blend in a third of the butter. Add water slowly, beating until you have formed a soft, more sticky dough. Cut the dough into eight equal portions and roll each into a ball shape. Roll out into eight thin rounds each of the same diameter. Spread four of them with filling, cover with another round and press the edges together. Gently roll out each of the filled parathas on a floured board to seal the edges together. Heat half the remaining butter in a heavy frying pan, put in two stuffed parathas and cook gently, turning once or twice, until lightly browned on both sides. Repeat with remaining butter and parathas.

Tortillas

Tortillas are served with hot, spicy dishes and especially bean dishes like Chili con carne.

4 oz (1 cup) 100% wholewheat flour
or
4 oz (1 cup) stoneground strong white
    flour

4 oz (1 cup) cornmeal
pinch salt
water

Combine the flour, cornmeal and salt and mix well. Add water slowly to form a firm dough that does not stick to the sides of the bowl. Pinch off pieces of dough and roll into balls about the size of a small egg. Flatten them and roll out on a floured board into rounds about 6 inches in diameter. Heat an ungreased frying pan over a moderate flame or electric hot plate and cook 2 or 3 tortillas at a time. Turn frequently until they are flecked with brown on both sides. Remove to a moderate oven to keep warm and cook the remaining tortillas.

Basic unleavened bread

Unyeasted bread is heavier than the risen variety so cut it in thin slices and chew it well. The recipe given is a very simple one but it can be made more interesting by replacing half the wheat flour with other flours (e.g. buckwheat, cornmeal, rice, soya, millet or rye flour, etc.) or combinations of them (see below). For a sweet bread add chopped nuts and dried fruit to the ingredients. To make a bread that will double as a meal try adding left-over cooked vegetables or grains to the dough mix and then serve slices of the baked bread with a spicy sauce.

1 lb (4 cups) 100% wholewheat flour
2 teaspoons salt
warm water

Combine the flour and salt in a mixing bowl and slowly stir in the warm water until you have a firm dough that comes away from the sides of the bowl. Knead the dough on a floured board for as long as you have the patience (at least five minutes). The more you knead the dough the better will be the texture of the finished bread. Shape the dough into a loaf and place in a 2 lb bread tin. Cover with a damp cloth and leave in a warm place for up to 24 hours (2 hours is a minimum time). Preheat oven to 300°F (gas mark 2). Place bread in the oven and bake for 2 hours at this temperature. Now turn the heat up to 400°F (gas mark 6) and bake for a further 30 minutes. The times given are only an indication, because times will vary depending on the type of flour and other ingredients you have used. Basically you want a well-baked bread with a crust on top; thus cook slowly until the bread is cooked through and then increase oven temperature to brown the crust.

Suggestions for unleavened bread flour mixtures

8 oz (2 cups) 100% wholewheat flour *or*
4 oz (1 cup) rye flour
4 oz (1 cup) cornmeal flour

8 oz (2 cups) 100% wholewheat flour
4 oz (1 cup) bulgar wheat flour
4 oz (1 cup) cornmeal flour

Quick cinnamon and caraway seed bread

This is a dense, closely textured bread and should be cut into thin slices before serving. The caraway seeds are a great aid to digestion.

1 lb (4 cups) 81% wholemeal flour
1 teaspoon salt
1 tablespoon caraway seeds
1 teaspoon cinnamon

4 tablespoons vegetable oil (sesame oil is best)
about 1 pint (2½ cups) water

Preheat oven to 325°F (gas mark 3). Combine the flour, salt, caraway seeds and cinnamon and mix thoroughly. Add the oil and rub it evenly into the mixture by hand. Now slowly beat in the water and add a little more than given if the dough is too stiff. Lightly grease a 2 lb bread tin and turn the dough into it without too much pressing. Bake for about 1½ hours or until nicely browned on top. Remove from oven, turn out of tin and leave to cool before eating.

Matzo bagels

Jewish dietary laws forbid risen bread and other leavened flour products during Passover, and to overcome this problem Jewish bakers have devised some delicious unleavened breads using Matzo meal (a type of wheat flour). The following recipe is for bagels, but the dough could be just as readily used to make rolls or other shapes.

8 fl oz (1 cup) water
1 teaspoon salt
4 fl oz (½ cup) vegetable oil

6 oz (1½ cups) matzo meal
4 eggs

Preheat oven to 400°F (gas mark 6). Combine water, salt and oil in a saucepan and bring to the boil. Remove pan from the heat and stir in matzo meal. Return to the heat and continue cooking and stirring for a further 2 to 3 minutes. Remove from the heat and allow to stand for 10 minutes. Stir in the eggs 1 at a time making a homogeneous mixture with the dough. Now lightly oil your hands and pinch off a small ball of dough. Roll it into a rope 5 inches long and press the ends together to form a circle. Repeat for the remainder of the dough. Arrange the circles on a greased baking tray and bake for 35 to 40 minutes or until golden brown.

Sour dough bread

This type of bread is the predecessor to yeasted breads. The method depends on the fact that if a dough made of wheat flour is allowed to stand for a few days in a warm place it will begin to rise. This natural leavening is a result of the action of wild yeast spores carried to the dough by the air. If some of this dough is now added to another fresh batch of dough the rising process will be quicker than the first batch of dough. This is the basis of sour dough bread making. To speed up the process and to provide a continuously available source of sour dough, a sour dough start or 'plant' is prepared. In making the starter we cheat a little by using artificially cultured yeast rather than depending only on wild yeast spores.

Sour dough starter

8 oz (2 cups) unsifted, unbleached
  white flour
1 oz fresh yeast
or

2 teaspoons dry yeast
2 tablespoons sugar
1 pt (2½ cups) warm water

Mix the ingredients in a large bowl (preferably glass) using a wooden spoon. Cover the bowl with a damp cloth and leave in a warm place for 5 days. Keep the cloth damp and stir the mixture daily with a wooden spoon. At the end of the 5th day add 1 oz flour and 3 tablespoons water, mix well and leave to ferment one more day. The starter is now ready for use. Store in a tightly sealed container in the fridge. After using a portion always replace what is removed by equal amounts of flour and warm water. If the starter is not used more than once a week, feed it once a week with 1 teaspoon sugar.

Sour dough bread recipe

12 oz (3 cups) wholewheat flour
8 oz (2 cups) unbleached white flour
10 fl oz (1¼ cups) water
10 fl oz (1¼ cups) sour dough starter

1 teaspoon salt
2 tablespoons vegetable oil
2 tablespoons honey (optional)

Combine the ingredients and mix well until the dough no longer sticks to the bowl. It should be a firm and workable dough. If it is not, adjust the flour or water as necessary. Place the bowl in warm spot (80°F) cover and leave the dough to rise until doubled in size (2½ hours). Pinch the dough down and shape into two loaves, place in greased bread tins. Cover and allow to rise until doubled in size (2 hours). Pre-set oven to 400°F (gas mark 6). Bake the bread at this temperature for 15 minutes, then reduce heat to 325°F (gas mark 3) for another 30 minutes or until the bread is baked. The leavening process can be speeded up by adding a little dry yeast (or fresh yeast) to the dough. The sour dough starter gives the bread its characteristic and delicious flavour.

LEAVENED BREAD

Leavened bread can be made from any sort of wheat flour, but to make bread with a fine texture and a good satisfying taste it is best to use a hard (also called strong) flour. These are flours with a high gluten content and they give a firm, elastic dough. You may use either strong brown or strong white flour, depending upon your preferences and the type of bread you wish to make. Stoneground 100% wholemeal flour makes the most nutritious and filling bread. For a lighter and less chewy bread, but one which still retains most of the goodness of the wheat, use wheat meal flour of 81% to 85% extraction. For the times when you wish to make a light-textured bread use a strong white flour of low extraction rate.

Factory made bread is normally prepared with a very low extraction rate flour made from a combination of hard and soft flours. For the factory baker this has particular advantages. The bread produced is of uniform quality, it has a long shelf life, the flour suits mass production techniques, and, most important, in recent years it has been the type of bread most people wanted to buy. Fortunately, nowadays many independent bakers are baking and selling as much brown bread as they can make, and the large manufacturers are being persuaded to move in that direction themselves.

There is no magic attached to bread making, and as long as you know what you are doing and why, there is no reason why every home baking session shouldn't be a success. Below is a simple description of the various stages involved in making bread and why they are needed.

Yeast is mixed with water and to initiate the process that produces the gas carbon dioxide which causes the dough to rise, it is fed some sugar. The yeast/ sugar mixture starts to bubble and it is then mixed with flour, a little salt and enough water to give a firm dough. The yeast enzymes start to feed on the sugar in the flour itself, the water hydrates the protein in the flour to give gluten and the salt encourages enzyme activity. The gluten forms a matrix which is expanded by the carbon dioxide to give a spongy dough full of air. After the dough is made it is kneaded which has a two-fold purpose. Kneading improves the elasticity of the gluten and re-distributes the yeast evenly throughout the dough producing fresh sites for enzyme activity. The dough is now shaped into a loaf or loaves and placed in a tin to rise one more time. The timing here is important since if it goes on too long the dough loses its elasticity and the texture of the bread is uneven. If it is stopped too soon the gluten remains unstretched and the bread will be heavier than it should be. In the final stage of the operation the bread is placed in the oven to bake. The heat kills the yeast and stops further activity, expands the gas in the dough and sets the starch and proteins. This combined activity produces a firm but airy bread.

Well, that's the theory behind bread making and now you can test it out on the wholemeal bread recipe given below. Both this recipe and the recipes for the quick unkneaded bread and the soda bread have been used in another cookery book I have written. However, no excuses for using them again since they are proven and time-tested recipes.

Wholemeal bread

This bread keeps well, and it can be used up to one week after baking. All wholemeal flours do not bake in the same way, so do experiment with different brands of flour (and with the given recipe) until the bread you make is exactly to your liking. This is a basic bread recipe; other variations are given below. To make four 1 lb (500 g) loaves:

1 teaspoon brown sugar	1 tablespoon salt
1½ oz fresh yeast	1 tablespoon vegetable oil
or	1½ pt (4 cups) slightly warm water
3 level teaspoons dried yeast	cracked wheat or sesame seeds
3 lb (12 cups) wholewheat flour	

Mix the sugar, yeast and a little of the water into a smooth paste and set aside in a warm place until the mixture has frothed up (approximately 15 to 20 minutes). Put the flour and salt into a large mixing bowl (a plastic washing-up bowl is perfect) and mix well. Now add the yeast mixture, oil and remaining water. Mix until you have a smooth dough that comes away from the sides of the bowl. Turn the dough onto a floured board and knead well for about 5 minutes (longer if you have strong arms). Wash, dry and slightly grease the bowl, place the dough in it, cover the top with a damp cloth and set aside in a warm place for 1 to 1½ hours or until the dough has risen to double its original size. Re-knead the dough for 5 minutes and then divide it into 4 equal parts. Shape the dough pieces and place into lightly greased bread tins. Sprinkle the cracked wheat or sesame seeds on to the top of each loaf, cover the tins with a damp cloth and leave in a warm place for 30 to 45 minutes, or until the dough has risen to the top of the tins. Preheat the oven to 450°F (gas mark 9) place the tins in the centre of the oven and bake for 40 minutes. Remove the bread from the oven, tip the loaves out of the tins and knock the underside, if the bread sounds hollow like a drum it is cooked. If the bread does not sound hollow, return the loaves, upside down, to the oven and bake for a further 10 minutes at 375°F (gas mark 5). Leave the bread to cool on a wire rack, or resting across the top of the empty bread tins.

Other breads

To prepare a variety of different breads you may partially replace the whole-wheat flour in the above recipe with the following substitutes. Do experiment and invent your own favourite bread recipes.

1 lb to 2 lb (4 to 8 cups) unbleached white flour

8 oz to 1 lb (2 to 4 cups) cornflour

4 oz to 8 oz (1 to 2 cups) arrowroot flour

1 lb to 1½ lb (4 to 6 cups) rye flour

8 oz to 1 lb (2 to 4 cups) potato flour

8 oz to 1 lb (2 to 4 cups) rice flour

8 oz to 1 lb (2 to 4 cups) soy flour

1 lb to 1½ lb (4 to 6 cups) buckwheat flour

8 oz to 1 lb (2 to 4 cups) oatmeal or rolled oats

Also try adding raisins or other dried fruit.

Unkneaded brown bread

15 fl oz (2 cups) warm water

2 level teaspoons dried yeast

or

1 oz fresh yeast

1 tablespoon honey

3 lb (12 cups) 100% wholemeal flour

2 teaspoons salt

2 tablespoons vegetable oil

Combine water, yeast and honey, mix well and leave to stand for 10 minutes. Add this mixture to flour and salt and mix to a smooth dough. Cover with a damp cloth and leave in a warm place for 2 to 3 hours. Grease four 1 lb bread tins with oil. Divide dough into four and press into bread tins. Place on the middle rack of a cold oven. Set oven to 350°F (gas mark 4) and bake for 50 to 60 minutes. Remove the bread from tins and leave to cool on a rack.

Irish soda bread

This recipe is useful if you have run out of yeast or if you do not have the time to make 'proper' bread. It makes one very large round loaf.

2 lb (8 cups) unbleached strong plain white flour

1 lb (4 cups) wholewheat flour

2 teaspoons salt

2 teaspoons bicarbonate of soda

4 oz (½ cup) margarine (vegetable based)

4 eggs

1 pt (2½ cups) thick sour milk (milk can be soured by squeezing a little lemon juice into it)

Sift all the dry ingredients into a large mixing bowl and then rub in the margarine. Beat the eggs and sour milk and mix into the bowl. Knead the mixture gently for a few minutes and then form it into a flattish round pat. Cut a cross into the top and place the loaf on a floured baking sheet. Preheat the oven to 425°F (gas mark 7), place the baking sheet in the centre of the oven and bake for 30 minutes.

Slightly sweet wholemeal fruit bread

1 oz fresh yeast	1 lb (4 cups) wholewheat flour
or	2 teaspoons salt
2 level teaspoons dry yeast	4 oz (1 cup) sultanas or currants
2 fl oz (¼ cup) warm water	2 tablespoons table oil
4 oz (½ cup) honey or brown sugar	15 fl oz (2 cups) water

Mix the yeast, warm water and honey into a smooth paste and leave the mixture to stand in a warm place for about 15 to 20 minutes or until frothed up. Combine the flour, salt, dried fruit and oil and mix thoroughly. Stir in the yeast mixture and slowly add the water to form a quite soft dough. Turn the dough onto a floured board and knead for 2 to 3 minutes. Place the dough in a clean bowl, cover with a damp cloth, set in a warm place and leave to rise for 1½ to 2 hours. Grease two 1 lb bread tins, divide the dough between them, and press into tins. Cover again and leave to rise again for 45 minutes to 1 hour. Preheat oven to 350°F (gas mark 4). Bake bread for 50 minutes or until it forms a nice golden brown crust. Turn loaves onto a wire rack and leave to cool.

Yeasted bread rolls

1 oz fresh yeast	*or*
or	8 oz (2 cups) strong white flour *and*
2 level teaspoons dried yeast	8 oz (2 cups) 100% wholewheat flour
approximately 3 fl oz (¼ cup) warm water	2 tablespoons vegetable oil or butter
	8 fl oz (1 cup) milk
1 tablespoon brown sugar	1 egg, beaten
1 teaspoon salt	
1 lb (4 cups) strong white flour	

Mix yeast, warm water and sugar into a smooth paste and set aside in a warm place for 15 to 20 minutes or until the mixture has frothed up. Combine salt, flour, oil and milk in a mixing bowl, add yeast mixture and mix into a fairly soft dough which easily comes away from the sides of the bowl. If necessary add extra water. Turn the dough onto a floured board, cover with a damp cloth and leave to rest for 10 minutes. Now knead for 5 minutes to form a smooth elastic dough. Place in a clean greased bowl, cover with a damp cloth and leave to rise in a warm place for 45 minutes to 1 hour.

Preheat oven to 425°F (gas mark 6). Turn dough onto a floured board, shape into a long cylindrical roll and cut into 18 portions. Shape each into a roll and place them at least 1 inch apart on a greased baking sheet. Leave to rise for 10 to 15 minutes, brush the tops with beaten egg and bake for 15 to 20 minutes until nicely browned.

Fruited bread rolls

Ingredients as for Yeasted bread rolls plus 4 oz (⅔ to 1 cup) mixed dried fruit. Proceed as for yeasted bread rolls, but before forming the dough into a cylindrical roll, sprinkle the dried fruit over the top. Do not knead the fruit into the dough since this affects the texture. Now continue to follow the recipe for yeasted bread rolls.

Pita bread

Pita bread is round and flat with a hollow in the middle. The texture is soft, even on the outside and it is delicious for eating with dips such as hummus or for mopping up sauces. In the Middle East, where pita bread is a staple food, it is served stuffed with salads and/or cooked food. A very popular dish available from street corner stalls is pita bread filled with falafel (page 191) and topped with a spicy sauce.

Pita dough is leavened but baking time is very short and at a high temperature. During baking the dough magically separates, giving the important pouch or hollow in the middle of the bread. In Jerusalem I visited a small pita bakery run by a Syrian where he made the very large and slightly crisp Syrian pita bread. They were baked in a dome-shaped oven with a wood fire in the bottom. The rolled–out flat dough rings were stuck onto the inside surface of the domed oven roof and baked for 2 to 3 minutes by which time they were just about to fall into the flames below. Just in the nick of time the Syrian would reach into the oven with a long spatula, catch them and deliver them to the counter truly freshly baked.

½ oz fresh yeast	1 lb (4 cups) strong white flour
or	½ teaspoon salt
1 level teaspoon dried yeast	10 fl oz (1¼ cups) water
2 fl oz (¼ cup) warm water	(approximately)
1 teaspoon sugar	

Mix yeast, warm water and sugar into a smooth paste and set aside in a warm place for 15 to 20 minutes or until the mixture has frothed up. Combine flour and salt in a mixing bowl and pour in the yeast mixture. Knead by hand and slowly add water to form a firm dough, neither too hard or too soft. Turn onto a floured board and knead for 10 to 15 minutes. This is vital if the bread is to have the right texture. Lightly grease a large bowl, place the dough in it and leave in a warm place for 2 to 3 hours. Knead the dough again for 2 to 3 minutes then pinch off lumps the size of a large egg. Roll them into ¼ inch thick, 5-inch diameter circles on a floured board. Dust each round with flour and set to rise again on a floured cloth in a warm place for about 20 minutes. Meanwhile pre-set the oven to maximum temperature. After 10 minutes place 2 ungreased baking sheets in the oven to warm up. Lightly sprinkle the dough rounds with cold water and load them onto the hot baking sheets. Place in the oven and bake for about 8 minutes. Do not open the oven door during this time. The finished pita bread should be soft and white with a hollow in the middle. Serve as they are, or cut crosswise at the middle or top and stuff with whatever filling you have ready. Store uneaten bread in plastic bags in the freezer or refrigerator. To reheat place in a 350°F (gas mark 4) oven for about 3 minutes. Serve and eat immediately: uncovered pita bread goes stale quickly.

PASTA AND NOODLES

Both pasta and noodles are made from a dough of flour and water. This is shaped into any one of 100 or more shapes and then dried before cooking in water. Eggs are sometimes added to the dough to give the Italian pasta *al uovo* or Chinese egg noodles. To produce green pasta (lasagne verde) spinach is added. The Japanese also make green noodles using powdered green tea as the colouring agent.

The best pasta and noodles are made from hard-grained wheats, particularly durum wheat. The wheat grain is milled down to the endosperm, the starchy centre of the grain, which is then ground into a fine flour. Many of the nutrients in the wheat are lost in this process, but since pasta and noodles are normally eaten with a meat or vegetable or cheese sauce, the loss is to some extent compensated for. Nowadays wholefood manufacturers are making pasta from a finely ground wholewheat flour. For me this type of pasta is a little heavy although the taste and texture are good. For a change and in small amounts, it is, however, an excellent alternative to normal pasta.

In the East, particularly in China and Japan, noodles have been a staple food for thousands of years and tradition has it that Marco Polo introduced pasta to Italy after his travels in China. The Italians, quite naturally, think this idea is absurd and to them of course must go the credit for the creation of spaghetti, lasagne, cannelloni, vermicelli, etc., but if the Italians are great inventors of pasta dishes, the Chinese and Japanese are great eaters of them and to them must go the prize for the fastest noodle-eaters in the world. With the help of one pair of chopsticks and much noise, the average East Asian noodle-eater can finish off a huge bowl of long noodles in a shorter time than it takes a Lancashire man to eat a bag of fish and chips or an American a McDonald's hamburger. They do, of course, make excellent noodles (as well as some awful but big-selling fast-cooking noodles called Instant Raman) from both buckwheat and wheat flour, and recipes for both these varieties are given in the recipe section (pages 36 and 153).

The following recipes are for simple pasta dishes that can be prepared from home-made and hand-shaped pasta and noodles. You may of course substitute bought pasta, but if you do, always try to buy the best pasta, since the difference in price between good pasta and the cheap varieties is small compared to the difference in quality. For a more nutritious and filling pasta buy the 100% wholewheat variety.

Preparation and cooking of hand-made pasta

Making the dough is easy, and if you have the time and patience, so is the rolling out, but for a faster job you can now buy domestic kitchen-size pasta rolling and cutting machines. They are efficient, quite cheap and worth buying if you eat a lot of pasta.

Basic dough

Pasta for 4 people

4 large fresh eggs
4 tablespoons cold water
1 lb (4 cups) strong white flour

or
8 oz (2 cups) strong white flour *and*
8 oz (2 cups) 100% wholewheat flour

Break the eggs into a mixing bowl, whisk in the water, add one quarter of the flour and beat to a smooth paste. Add nearly all of the rest of the flour and work the mixture with your hands into a soft dough. Add remaining flour if the dough is still sticky. Turn the dough onto a floured board and knead for 5 to 10 minutes. Put the dough back in the mixing bowl, cover with a damp cloth and leave for 20 to 30 minutes. Now flour a large board or work surface, cut the dough into 2 pieces and roll 1 piece out into a sheet of ⅛ inch thickness. Fold it up and roll out again. Repeat 1 or 2 times and finally end up with a sheet of dough approximately 20 inches long and ⅛ inch thick. Repeat for the other piece of dough.

Shaping the pasta

For cannelloni cut the sheet into 4 inch squares. For lasagne cut the sheet into 4 inch × 10 inch rectangles. For tagliatelle roll the sheet up like a roll of lino and cut ½ inch thick slices off the end. Unroll ready for use. For fettucine cut as for tagliatelle, but in ¼ inch thick slices. Store all pasta shapes you make on a well-floured surface and use as quickly as possible.

Cooking pasta

The important rule when cooking pasta is to use a large pot and plenty of water. Generally 1 lb pasta needs 8 pints (20 cups) water. For salt, 2 tablespoons per 1 lb pasta is an average amount and it is added after the water has boiled and before the pasta is put in. Finally to prevent the pasta sticking to itself during cooking, a little butter or oil is added to the water. Thus the water is brought to a rolling boil, salted, a little oil is added and the pasta is then carefully fed into the pot and boiled, uncovered, until it is soft on the outside but with a slight resistance at the centre or *al dente* as it is known. Cooking times vary depending on the type of pasta, and whether it is bought or home-made. Shop-bought pasta will have cooking times on the packet and below are approximate cooking times for fresh home-made pasta.

> Cannelloni — 4 minutes
> Lasagne   — 4 minutes
> Tagliatelle — 5 to 6 minutes
> Fettuccine — 5 to 6 minutes

After cooking, drain the pasta and serve or mix with sauce as directed in the recipe.

Fettucine with butter and cheese

4 oz (½ cup) butter
8 fl oz (1 cup) cream
6 oz (1⅔ cups) cheese, grated
(parmesan if possible)

salt and freshly milled black pepper to
taste
1 lb fettuccine, cooked and drained

Melt the butter in a heavy pan. Remove from the heat and stir in the cream, add
the cheese and return to a very low heat. Stir the sauce and cook without boiling
until the cheese is all melted. Season to taste. Combine the noodles and sauce in a
serving bowl and serve with a fresh salad.

Lasagne with wholewheat breadcrumbs

This is a useful and exciting way of using up stale bread.

5 fl oz (⅝ cup) vegetable oil
(olive oil is best, followed by sesame
seed or cornflour oil)
4 oz (1 cup) wholewheat
breadcrumbs, lightly toasted
1 teaspoon salt

½ teaspoon freshly milled black
pepper
1 tablespoon fresh parsley, finely
chopped
1 lb lasagne
3 oz (⅔ cup) parmesan cheese (or a
tangy, strong cheese, grated)

Place a small pan with the oil in it on the stove. Place alongside two bowls, one
containing the breadcrumbs already seasoned with the salt and black pepper,
and the other containing the parsley. Start to cook the lasagne (see cooking
method above) and while doing this, heat the oil until it just starts to smoke.
Drop the breadcrumbs into the oil and remove from the heat. Drain the lasagne,
pour over the oil and breadcrumbs and sprinkle with parsley. Serve immediately with the parmesan cheese.

Cannelloni

1 lb basic pasta dough, cut into 4 inch
squares (see above)
or
1 lb bought cannelloni shells
2 eggs

1 lb cheese, grated or cottage
1 pt (2½ cups) béchamel sauce (see
overleaf)
4 tablespoons parmesan or other
grated cheese

Preheat oven to 400°F (gas mark 6). Cook the pasta in lots of boiling water
until just soft. Drain and cool under cold water. Beat the eggs and cheese together. Grease a shallow baking dish. Place a square of pasta in the dish, spoon
on a portion of the cheese and egg mixture, and roll up, leaving the seam side
down. Repeat for each square of pasta. If you are using pre-prepared cannelloni
shells, carefully stuff each one with the filling. Pour béchamel sauce over the
stuffed pasta rolls and sprinkle parmesan or grated cheese over the top. Bake for
15 to 20 minutes or until the cheese topping is nicely browned.

Béchamel sauce

1 oz (⅛ cup) butter   salt and black pepper to taste
2 oz (½ cup) white flour   pinch of nutmeg
10 fl oz (1¼ cup) milk

Melt the butter in a heavy saucepan over a moderate heat. Stir in the flour to form a smooth paste and cook for 2 to 3 minutes. Add the milk to the pan slowly with constant stirring. Continue cooking and stirring until the mixture thickens. Season with salt and black pepper to taste, add the nutmeg and simmer over a very low heat for 10 minutes. Stir now and again.

★Tagliatelle with fish and tomatoes

2 tablespoons vegetable oil   1 lb fresh tomatoes, chopped
2 cloves garlic, crushed   *or*
1 medium onion, diced   1 lb (2 cups) tinned tomatoes
1 green pepper, cut into long strips   1 lb white fish, filleted and cut into
1 teaspoon oregano   cubes
salt and freshly milled black pepper to   1 lb tagliatelle cooked and drained
    taste

Heat the oil in a heavy pan, add the garlic and sauté for 1 minute. Add the onion and green pepper and cook until just soft. Season with oregano, salt and pepper, drop in the tomatoes and fish and cook uncovered until the fish is just tender. Combine fish sauce with tagliatelle and serve.

Noodles

Traditionally in the East, flour has been used to prepare noodles – not to make bread. Flour in noodle form is easily digestible, and noodles made with some or all wholewheat or buckwheat flour are nutritious as well as delicious.

Preparation and cooking of home-made noodles

One pound of noodles serves 5 to 6 people.

Wheatflour noodles   *or*
4 oz (1 cup) wholewheat flour *and*   1 lb (4 cups) plain white flour
12 oz (3 cups) strong, plain white flour   1 teaspoon salt
                                       5 fl oz (½ cup) water, approximately

Mix flour and salt in a large bowl, then gradually add water to form a slightly dry dough. Knead for 10 to 15 minutes. Flour a board and roll out dough into a thin (approximately ⅛ inch thick) rectangular sheet. Fold the two narrow ends of the sheet into the middle, fold again at the middle to divide dough into quarters.

With a sharp knife, cut folded sheet crosswise into ⅛ inch strips. Unroll noodles and spread on floured board to await cooking. Boil 4 pints of water, carefully lower in noodles and return water to boil. Add 8 fl oz (1 cup) cold water and bring to the boil a second time. Reduce heat and simmer until noodles are cooked but still just hard at the core (approximately 10 minutes). This method of cooking ensures that both the inside and outside of the noodle are evenly cooked. Drain noodles and rinse under cold running water separating any noodles that are stuck together. To reheat pour boiling water over the noodles. Note: the water in which the noodles were cooked may be reserved and used for preparing soup stock.

To cook dried noodles

For 4 people

12 oz (1½ cups) dried noodles
5 pt (12½ cups) water

Either follow instructions on the packet or use the following method: bring water to boil, add noodles and stir gently. Return to the boil, reduce heat until water is just bubbling. Cook uncovered until noodles are cooked, but still just hard at the core (approximately 5 minutes). Drain, and if not to be used immediately, rinse under cold running water. Stand to drain. Use as required. If storing add a little soft butter or oil to stop the noodles sticking together. To reheat, pour boiling water over noodles.

Noodles in soup with topping

12 oz (3 cups) noodles, cooked and drained
2 pt (5 cups) hot soup stock
2 tablespoons chives or spring onions, chopped

and/or
other garnishing (see below)
soy sauce to taste

Divide noodles among 4 bowls, pour over soup stock and garnish with chives or spring onions.

Other possible toppings are: parboiled carrot slices; bamboo shoots or lotus root slices, cooked; fresh or frozen garden peas or other vegetables; slices of mushroom or soaked shiitake (dried mushrooms) sautéed in oil; pieces of cooked chicken or pork; whole shrimps; hardboiled-egg slices; abalone slices.

Fried noodles

There are two ways of frying noodles: soft fried in a little oil or deep fried. In each case the noodles are pre-cooked, drained and cooled before frying. To soft fry noodles, heat 2 to 3 tablespoons oil, per 8 ounce (2 cups) cooked noodles, in a heavy frying pan. Add the noodles and sauté with constant stirring for 4 to 5 minutes. To deep fry, separate the cooked noodles into single strands, fill heavy pan or deep frying pan with 3 to 4 inches (7 to 10 centimetres) oil and heat to 350°F (175°C). Drop in the noodles, a handful at a time, and fry until medium brown in colour. Remove with chopsticks and drain on absorbent paper.

Soft fried noodles and vegetables

This is a basic recipe; more elaborate additions are suggested below.

4 tablespoons vegetable oil
1 clove garlic, minced
1 oz (1 tablespoon) of ginger root, grated (optional)
½ medium carrot, grated
4 oz (1 cup) chinese cabbage, chopped

1 medium green pepper, diced
12 oz (3 cups) noodles, cooked and drained
black pepper to taste
soy sauce to taste

Heat the oil in a heavy frying pan, sauté the garlic and ginger for 2 to 3 minutes, then add the other vegetables. Fry until just soft cooked. Stir in the noodles, heat through, season with black pepper and soy sauce.

Other ingredients that can be fried with noodles are:

1: 2 paper-thin omelettes, cut into 1 inch strips
2: 4 oz (1 cup) french beans, cut into 1 inch pieces
3: 2 stalks celery, chopped
4: 1 medium onion, diced
5: 2 spring onions, chopped
6: 4 oz (1 cup) bean sprouts
7: 4 oz (½ cup) cooked meat, sliced
8: 4 oz (½ cup) cooked fish, whole or sliced
9: 1 medium lotus, sliced, or bamboo shoots
10: 2 oz (⅓ cup) mushrooms, sliced
11: 4 shiitake (dried mushrooms), soaked for 20 minutes, hard stems removed, sliced
12: 6 oz (⅔ cup) tofu, 1 inch cubes
13: 6 oz (⅔ cup) fried tofu
14: 4 oz (½ cup) cheese, grated
15: 4 oz (¾ cup) beans (soya, aduki, kidney, etc.) cooked. Combine with 2 tablespoons soy sauce, separate beans into equal portions, mash one portion, salt, recombine
16: 4 oz (¾ cup) shrimps or prawns, shelled, de-veined and cooked or tinned

★Curried noodles

2 tablespoons vegetable oil
8 oz (1 cup) chicken, lean pork or beef, diced into small cubes
1 medium onion, thinly sliced
2 medium potatoes, diced
1 medium carrot, thinly sliced
4 fl oz (½ cup) water
1 to 2 teaspoons mild curry powder

pinch of salt
12 oz (3 cups) noodles, cooked and drained
1 oz (1 tablespoon) ginger root, grated
or
2 tablespoons finely chopped spring onion
chutney

Brown the meat or chicken in oil in a heavy pan, add the vegetables and sauté until soft. Make a paste with a little of the water and curry powder and add it with remaining water to pan. Add salt and ginger and cook, stirring, for 5 to 10 minutes. The consistency should be quite thick; simmer to reduce liquid if necessary. Either stir in the noodles and warm through or heat noodles by pouring boiling water over them and serve curry sauce over the noodles. Garnish with chutney or, more authentically, with chopped spring onions.

BULGAR WHEAT RECIPES

Bulgar, also known as burghul and cracked wheat is still something of a mystery in the West, although nowadays it can be bought in most wholefood shops. It is a wheat product that has been made from ancient times in parts of Western Asia, Eastern Europe and North Africa. It has excellent nutritional qualities, a fine taste and lends itself to many ways of cooking.

Bulgar is prepared by parboiling whole wheat grains in a minimum amount of water. The wheat is then spread thinly on a cloth or tray, dried out (traditionally in the sun) and finally cracked between stone rollers. The starch in the grain is gelatinized by the boiling water and after drying and cracking this results in a hard, vitreous product. The boiling process also has the affect of diffusing part of the wheat germ and bran into the starchy centre of the wheat and if the wheat is then cracked or milled the product retains almost all the goodness of the whole grain.

Bulgar wheat is cooked by steaming or boiling, and sometimes it is dry roasted first. It is bought in various grades ranging from fine to coarsely cracked. Sometimes the makers parboil and roast the bulgar before packaging it to give a fast cooking product.

Bulgar flour can be substituted for some of the regular flour in bread making. The resultant dough needs more kneading than ordinary wheat dough but it does bake into beautiful bread. Because of the nutritious wheat germ in bulgar flour it doesn't keep too well, except under refrigeration. Thus, buy enough flour for your immediate needs only, or best of all, if you have a hand mill at home, grind your own as needed.

Bulgar has a special place in the cooking of the Middle East, and is the basis of Kibby, the great traditional dish of Syria and Lebanon. It also has a long culinary tradition in Jewish cooking and is even mentioned in the Bible where it is described as a food particularly attractive to young men (see Zachariah 9:17). So ladies, young or old, if you want to seduce a young man, bulgar is the food to serve him.

Plain bulgar wheat

Bulgar may be served instead of rice with meat, vegetables, or sauces, etc., or as the basis of a cold salad. The methods given below prepare enough bulgar for 3 to 4 servings.

Method 1

8 oz (1 cup) bulgar wheat
16 fl oz (2 cups) water
salt

Dry roast the bulgar in a heavy saucepan over a medium heat for 2 to 3 minutes stirring constantly. Remove from the heat, allow to cool for a couple of minutes and then add the water. Bring to the boil, reduce the heat, cover and simmer for 25 to 30 minutes or until all the water is absorbed. Salt to taste towards the end of cooking time.

Method 2

4 tablespoons vegetable oil   16 fl oz (2 cups) water or stock
1 clove garlic, crushed   salt, black pepper and cayenne to taste
8 oz (1 cup) bulgar wheat

Heat the oil in a heavy pan, add the garlic and lightly sauté. Add the bulgar and gently fry, stirring, for 2 to 3 minutes. Pour in the stock or water and simmer over a very low heat for 30 to 45 minutes or until all the water is absorbed. Towards the end of cooking time season to taste with salt, pepper and cayenne.

Pine nuts make a really delicious addition to bulgar. In Method 2, fry 1 oz pine nuts in the oil along with the garlic and then proceed with the recipe as directed.

Method 3

3 tablespoons vegetable oil   16 fl oz (2 cups) boiling water
1 medium onion, finely chopped   salt
8 oz (1 cup) bulgar

Heat the oil in a heavy pan over a high heat, add the onion and sauté until well browned. Reduce heat and pour in the bulgar and boiling water. Stir well, add salt to taste, cover and cook over a low heat until all the water is absorbed (30 to 45 minutes).

Simple bulgar stew

2 tablespoons vegetable oil   1½ pt (4 cups) water
1 medium onion, chopped   ½ teaspoon thyme
3 medium green peppers, diced   ½ teaspoon oregano
8 oz (2 cups) cabbage, finely shredded   salt and black pepper to taste
8 oz (1 cup) bulgar wheat

Heat the oil in a heavy pan, add the onion and sauté until just soft, add the peppers and cabbage, stir well and sauté until nearly soft. Stir in the bulgar and continue cooking and stirring for 2 to 3 minutes. Add the water and herbs, bring to the boil, reduce the heat, cover and simmer for 30 minutes. Towards the end of cooking time season to taste with salt and black pepper.

Winter vegetables and bulgar

12 oz (1½ cups) bulgar wheat
1¼ pt (3 cups) water
1 teaspoon salt
2 tablespoons vegetable oil
1 small onion, diced

1 carrot, cut in matchsticks
1 medium parsnip, thinly sliced
½ small turnip, finely diced
1 tablespoon sesame seeds, roasted
   (optional)

Dry roast the bulgar in a heavy saucepan over a medium heat for 2 to 3 minutes, stirring constantly. Remove from heat, cool and pour in the water. Bring to the boil, reduce heat to very low, cover and simmer for 25 to 30 minutes. Add salt towards the end of cooking time. Meanwhile heat the oil in another pan, add the onion and sauté until soft and translucent. Now add the carrot, parsnip and turnip, stir well, reduce heat, cover and leave to cook in their own juices for 25 to 30 minutes. Now and again check and add a little water if needed. Combine the cooked bulgar and vegetables, sprinkle with sesame seeds and serve.

Stuffed bulgar

Bulgar wheat is cooked, bound with flour and formed into dumplings which are then stuffed with a filling. The stuffed dumplings are fried or cooked in a boiling soup.

Dumplings
8 oz (1 cup) bulgar wheat
16 fl oz (2 cups) water
salt
flour
oil

Filling
8 oz (1 cup) cooked rice
4 oz (½ cup) tinned tomatoes
1 small onion, finely chopped
1 tablespoon parsley, finely chopped
½ teaspoon ground cinnamon
salt and black pepper to taste

Cook the bulgar wheat by Method 1. Put it into a mixing bowl and stir in enough flour to give a mixture stiff enough to hold its form when pressed into a ball shape. Shape the mixture into about 12 dumplings. Take each dumpling and push your forefinger into its centre, working the dumpling around your finger to form a jacket. Combine the filling ingredients and stuff the dumplings with the mixture. Seal off the filling by pressing wheat over the top of the hole. Fry the stuffed dumplings in an oiled frying pan over a high heat, turning once or twice during cooking. Alternatively, drop the dumplings in a boiling soup or stock, reduce the heat and simmer for 15 to 20 minutes before serving.

Variation
Paint the dumplings with beaten egg, roll in breadcrumbs and deep fry.

Alternative filling
3 oz (½ cup) chick peas
1 oz (¼ cup) walnuts
1 tablespoon chopped parsley
1 small onion, minced

6 tomatoes, thinly sliced
2 tablespoons olive oil
1 small green pepper, diced
salt and black pepper to taste

Combine all the ingredients and mix well.

Bulgar wheat and chick-peas

1 medium onion, chopped
2 tablespoons vegetable oil
4 oz (½ cup) chick-peas, cooked
8 oz (1 cup) bulgar wheat

16 fl oz (2 cups) boiling water
8 oz (1 cup) tomato purée
salt and black pepper to taste

Sauté the onion in a heavy pan in the oil until just lightly browned, add chick-peas, reduce heat, cover pan and simmer for 5 minutes. Add the bulgar and cook for 2 minutes with constant stirring over a medium heat. Add the boiling water, stir in the tomato purée, reduce heat, cover and simmer for 25 minutes or until all the water is absorbed. Season to taste and serve.

Bulgar wheat pilaff

Serves 6 to 8

2 pt (5 cups) stock
1 lb (2 cups) bulgar wheat
1 teaspoon salt
½ teaspoon black pepper

4 oz (½ cup) butter
1 medium onion, diced
4 oz (1 cup) breadcrumbs
2 tablespoons fresh parsley, chopped

Preheat oven to 350°F (gas mark 4). Boil the stock in a large pan. Add the bulgar wheat and seasoning and simmer covered for 30 minutes. Melt half the butter in a frying pan, add the onion and fry until golden brown. Stir this into the cooked bulgar and transfer the mixture to an ovenproof casserole. Bake uncovered for 30 minutes or until all the liquid is absorbed. Combine the parsley and breadcrumbs and sprinkle the mixture over the baked wheat. Dot the surface with the remaining butter. Return to the oven and bake for a further 5 minutes. Serve.

Variation
Add mushrooms and green peppers and replace breadcrumbs with cheese.

Lentils with bulgar

This is a Lebanese dish and consequently a little oily for some tastes. Reduce the quantity of oil in the recipe by half if you wish.

8 oz (1 cup) brown or green lentils,
    washed, picked over, soaked 4 hrs
    or more, drained
1½ pt (4 cups) *plus*
8 fl oz (1 cup) water

2 medium onions, diced
4 fl oz (½ cup) oil
8 oz (1 cup) bulgar wheat
1 small carton plain yoghurt

Bring lentils (in 2 pints of water) to the boil in a heavy pan. Meanwhile fry the onions in the oil until golden brown. Drain the oil into the boiling lentils and water, reduce heat and gently boil the lentils. Pour 8 fl oz (1 cup) of water over the onions and simmer over a low heat for 10 minutes. Pour the onions and water into the lentil pot and continue cooking another 10 minutes. Now add the bulgar to the pot and return to the boil. Reduce the heat, cover and simmer for 25 to 30 minutes or until all the water is absorbed. Serve hot topped with natural yoghurt and a fresh crispy green salad.

Bulgar gratin

8 oz (1 cup) bulgar wheat
1 clove garlic, crushed
4 tablespoons vegetable oil
16 fl oz (2 cups) water or stock
salt, black pepper and cayenne to taste
2 tablespoons oil

1 medium onion, diced
1 medium green pepper, diced
4 oz (1 cup) mushrooms, sliced
8 fl oz (1 cup) béchamel sauce (see
  index)
4 oz (½ cup) cheese, grated

Preheat oven to 375°F (gas mark 5). Cook the bulgar wheat by Method 2. Meanwhile heat 2 tablespoons oil in a heavy pan, sauté onion and green pepper until just soft, stir in mushrooms and cook a further 2 to 3 minutes. Prepare béchemal sauce. Place bulgar wheat in a casserole dish, cover top with onion, pepper and mushroom mixture, pour over béchemal sauce, sprinkle on grated cheese and bake in the oven for 30 minutes or until nicely browned.

Tabbouleh (bulgar salad)

Tabbouleh is a beautiful salad. It has a sharp refreshing flavour and is perfect for a hot summer day. In its simplest form its served in individual lettuce lined bowls or stuffed in pita bread. Here we serve it piled high on a large dish and garnished with cucumber, tomatoes and olives.

8 oz (1 cup) bulgar wheat, fine grade
1 medium onion, finely diced
2 oz (1 cup) parsley, finely chopped
salt and black pepper to taste
1 oz (½ cup) fresh mint, finely
  chopped

or

2 tablespoons dried mint
4 tablespoons lemon juice
4 tablespoons vegetable oil (olive oil if
  possible)
4 oz (½ cup) tomatoes, thinly sliced
¼ cucumber, thinly sliced
2 oz (¼ cup) olives

Cover bulgar wheat in water, leave to soak for 30 minutes and drain. Thoroughly mix bulgar wheat and onion, stir in parsley and season to taste with salt and freshly milled black pepper. Mix the mint, lemon juice and oil together and pour over the bulgar. Carefully stir it in and finally adjust taste to suit with the addition of more seasoning or lemon juice. Pile the wheat on a serving dish and decorate with tomatoes, cucumber and olives and serve.

*Persian meat and bulgar casserole

This is a really delicious dish, it has a moist but firm texture and a smell that summons up images of veiled concubines and sultans.

3 tablespoons vegetable oil or butter
8 oz (1 cup) minced beef
1 large onion, diced
4 oz (2 cups) spinach, washed and
  chopped
1 medium leek, including green part,
  chopped

4 oz (½ cup) bulgar wheat fine grade,
  soaked 30 minutes, drained
1 teaspoon salt
1 teaspoon curry powder
½ teaspoon cinnamon
½ teaspoon black pepper
4 eggs, slightly beaten

Preheat oven to 325°F (gas mark 3). Heat the oil in a frying pan, add the meat and onion and sauté together for 15 minutes over a moderate heat, then transfer to a mixing bowl. Cook the spinach next in a little water and add to the beef. Add the remaining ingredients and mix well. Grease a 9 inch pie dish or shallow gratin dish and pour in the mixture. Bake for 30 minutes. Serve with a fresh salad and natural yoghurt.

★Fried meat and wheat cakes

Serves 6 to 8

1 lb (2 cups) bulgar wheat, fine grade
8 oz (1 cup) mutton or lamb, minced
2 medium onions, diced
2 tablespoons flour

2 teaspoons salt
1 teaspoon ground cumin
1 teaspoon black pepper
oil for frying

Cover bulgar wheat with water, leave to soak for 30 minutes and then drain and squeeze out excess water. Mix all the ingredients together and form into 8 to 10 circular cakes. If the mixture doesn't bind too well add 1 or 2 beaten eggs. Heat oil in a heavy frying pan and fry the cakes over a low heat for about 2 minutes each side or until nicely browned. Serve.

Kibby

Kibby, sometimes spelt kibbeh, is the national dish of Syria and Lebanon. It is a mixture of fine bulgar wheat, diced onion and minced lamb or beef pounded to a paste and eaten raw, fried or grilled. Alternatively, the Kibby is formed into oval cakes, stuffed and then baked or deep fried. A mincer or blender or pestle and mortar is needed for the correct preparation of this dish although they are not absolutely essential.

★Kibby neeyee (raw kibby)

This may not be to your liking (even though it doesn't taste uncooked). If this is the case you can either fry the dish or use one of the following recipes for cooked kibby.

Serves 6 to 8.

6 oz (⅔ cup) bulgar wheat, fine grade
1 lb (2 cups) lean minced lamb or beef
1 medium onion, diced

salt and black pepper to taste
4 fl oz (½ cup) water
2 oz (¼ cup) butter melted
2 tablespoons lemon juice

Cover the bulgar with water and leave to stand for 30 minutes. Drain and squeeze dry. Add the meat, onion and seasoning to taste. Put the mixture through a mincer or grinder at the finest setting, or blend small amounts at a time, in an electric blender. Now add the water to the ground mixture and knead by hand to form a smooth moist kibby.

Serve the kibby on an attractive dish accompanied by a bowl of lettuce leaves or celery sticks. To eat, scoop a little kibby onto a lettuce leaf and sprinkle with melted butter and lemon juice.

*Stuffed kibby

Serves 6 to 8.

Raw kibby, made as above, plus *filling* as follows:

2 oz (¼ cup) pine nuts or English walnuts (chopped)
6 oz (¾ cup) minced lamb or beef
6 tablespoons butter
½ teaspoon salt
½ teaspoon pepper
½ teaspoon cinnamon
iced water
oil for frying

Preheat oven to 350°F (gas mark 4). Heat 3 tablespoons butter in a heavy frying pan. Add the nuts and the beef and lightly brown the meat. Season with salt, pepper and cinnamon, mix well and leave to cool. Now take a portion of raw kibby the size of an egg and roll it between your palms into an oval shape about 5 inches long. Dip one finger into iced water and make a hollow in the oval cake by pushing your finger down one end whilst holding the outside wall together with the palm of your other hand. Seal any cracks with a wet finger. Place 1 tablespoon of the meat and nut mixture in the hollow and seal over the end. Grease a baking tray and place the stuffed kibby side by side in the tray. Melt the remaining butter and brush the kibby with it. Now put the tray in the oven and bake for 20 minutes or until golden brown.

*Kibby baked in a tray

Serves 6 to 8

This is a simpler method of preparing Stuffed kibby than the one given above. Ingredients as for Stuffed kibby (above). Prepare the raw kibby and filling as directed. Preheat oven to 350°F (gas mark 4). Grease a 9 inch circular baking tin or square equivalent and spread half the raw kibby on the bottom, layer all the filling on top cover with the remaining kibby and pour over 3 tablespoons melted butter. Bake for 45 minutes or until nicely browned and crisp. Slice the top diagonally to form diamond patterns and serve.

*Fish kibby

Serves 6 to 8

1 lb fish, filleted and skinned
½ teaspoon ground coriander
grated skin of small orange
½ small onion, diced
salt and black pepper to taste
12 oz (1½ cups) bulgar wheat, fine grade
3 tablespoons vegetable oil
1 medium onion, diced
2 oz (¼ cup) pine nuts
2 oz (¼ cup) butter

Preheat oven to 375°F (gas mark 5). Grind the fish with coriander, orange skin and onion in a pestle and mortar or pass through a mincer. Season to taste with salt and pepper. Soak bulgar in water for 30 minutes, drain and squeeze. Mix fish with bulgar and mince again. Lightly brown the onion in oil, add nuts and fry another 2 to 3 minutes. Grease a 9 inch round baking dish or square equivalent and layer half the fish and bulgar mixture on the bottom. Spread on this the onion and nut mixture and cover with remaining wheat and fish. Dot the top with butter and bake until golden brown (about 45 minutes).

SEMOLINA (INCLUDING COUSCOUS)

Semolina is produced from the starchy endosperm of the wheat grain. This part of the wheat is milled in various grades to give fine, medium or course semolina. Fine semolina is used to make puddings and in the production of pasta, while coarse grade semolina is used to make couscous. Semolina may also be substituted for ordinary flour in cake recipes where a crumbly texture is required.

Savoury semolina dumplings

1 pt (2½ cups) milk	1 teaspoon salt
8 oz (1 cup) semolina	4 eggs, beaten
2 oz (¼ cup) butter	8 oz (1 cup) cottage cheese

Bring the milk to the boil in a heavy saucepan or double boiler, reduce heat to a simmer and slowly whisk in the semolina. Add the butter and salt, stir the mixture well and cook over a low heat, stirring continuously, until the mixture thickens. Remove from heat, allow to cool for 2 to 3 minutes, stir in the eggs and cheese and leave to cool another 5 minutes. Shape the mixture into dumplings. Boil them in lightly salted water for 20 to 25 minutes, drain and serve with a fresh salad. Alternatively add the dumplings to a boiling soup or stew, cook through and serve with the soup.

Sweet semolina dumplings

Ingredients as for Savoury semolina dumplings plus 3 tablespoons sugar. Prepare the dumplings as for Savoury semolina dumplings with the addition of sugar to the butter and salt. Boil the dumplings in unsalted water for 20 to 25 minutes. Drain and serve with sour cream and honey for a genuine Rumanian sweet dish.

Semolina soup dumplings

1 egg	a pan of your favourite soup
2 oz (¼ cup) semolina	

Separate the egg white from the yolk. Beat the egg white stiff and fold in the yolk. Now add enough semolina to form a soft, light dough. Pull off enough dough to form 1 inch diameter balls. Bring the soup to a gentle boil and drop in the dumplings. Leave to cook for 2 to 3 minutes then remove pan from the heat and stand for 2 to 3 minutes to give the dumplings time to swell up before serving.

Gnocchi a la romana

An Italian dish pronounced 'knocky'. Serve as a main dish with salad and vegetables.

1 pt (2½ cups) milk	6 oz (¾ cup) cheese, grated
4 oz (½ cup) semolina	1 egg
2 oz (¼ cup) butter	salt and black pepper to taste

Bring the milk to the boil in a heavy pan or double boiler, reduce the heat and slowly stir in the semolina. Add the butter, stir, cover and leave to simmer for 10 minutes. Remove from the heat and mix in half of the cheese and the egg. Season to taste, cover and leave to simmer for another 10 minutes or until the mixture thickens. Sprinkle a large shallow dish with water and pour in the mixture to a thickness of ¼ inch to ½ inch. Leave it to cool, and if you have the time place the tray in the refrigerator for an hour or two. Now cut the solidified mixture into 2 inch squares (or into circles with a scone cutter) and transfer them to a shallow greased baking dish. Preheat oven to 375°F (gas mark 5). Sprinkle the remaining cheese over the top of the squares and bake them for 25 minutes or until nicely browned. Alternatively, they may be grilled in a gratin dish.

Roasted semolina and potatoes

1 lb (3 cups) potatoes, peeled and cubed	3 oz (⅜ cup) vegetable fat or bacon dripping
1 medium onion, diced	salt and black pepper to taste
8 oz (1 cup) semolina	water

Boil the potatoes until just cooked and drain. Heat ⅓ of the fat in a frying pan, add the onions and sauté until brown. Store the cooked potatoes and onion in a low oven. Clean the frying pan and place dry, over a low heat. Pour in the semolina and dry roast, stirring continuously until it starts to brown. Season with salt and pepper, remove from heat for a moment, and start to add water slowly, giving the semolina time to swell up. Return to the heat as it cools. Stop addition when the mixture has a crumbly, just dry, texture. Transfer the semolina to a serving dish, stir in cooked potatoes, decorate with fried onions and serve.

Semolina noodles

1 lb noodles (see index)	4 oz (½ cup) vegetable oil
4 oz (½ cup) semolina	water and salt

Heat the oil in a frying pan. Add the semolina and cook over a moderate heat, stirring continuously. As it starts to brown add water, 1 tablespoon at a time until you have a crumbly mixture in which each of the grains are separate. Meanwhile cook the noodles in plenty of boiling water and drain. Transfer the noodles and semolina to a mixing bowl and mix well. Return to the frying pan and stir over a low heat until heated right through. Serve. A cheese sauce goes well with this dish.

Semolina halva

This is an Indian sweet. It makes an excellent dessert.

1 pt (2½ cups) water
4 oz (½ cup) white or brown sugar
4 oz (½ cup) butter
4 oz (½ cup) semolina

1 oz (⅛ cup) almonds, blanched and
  chopped
1 oz (⅛ cup) raisins

Bring the water to a boil, pour in the sugar and boil until it is all dissolved. Melt the butter in a frying pan or heavy saucepan over a moderate heat, add the semolina and cook, stirring continuously. As the semolina starts to brown, add the almonds and raisins and cook a further few minutes. Carefully pour in the sugar solution and cook, stirring, until the semolina is thick and doesn't stick to the sides of the pan. Pour into a shallow dish and allow to cool. Cut into squares while still just warm.

Couscous

Before we start, to avoid confusion, it should be explained that couscous is the name of a product made from semolina, and also the name of a dish which includes couscous as a main ingredient. This dish is the traditional meal of the countries of North Africa. Cooked couscous has the look of large white grains of buckshot. It is served in a mountainous heap with meat and vegetables layered on top and the whole dressed with a rich sauce.

The basic steps in the preparation of the dish couscous are as follows:
1: Prepare or buy couscous grains.
2: Prepare the meat and vegetable sauce.
3: Steam the couscous over the sauce until cooked (couscous grain is never cooked in the sauce). There is a special pot called a couscousier available for this job. It is basically a saucepan with a snug fitting colander on top. A type of saucepan/colander arrangement or a regular double boiler will do just as well as a couscousier.
4: Finally, the couscous grains are piled on a large serving dish, the meat and vegetables are lifted out of the sauce and arranged over the grains. Some of the cooking broth is poured over the top and the whole is served with the remaining broth and hot pepper sauce.

Nowadays it is possible to buy prepared couscous grain, although for most cooks, in the countries where it is popular, it is still a job to tackle by hand. It is made from water, flour and coarsely milled semolina. For the more adventurous and proficient among you a recipe for the preparation of couscous grain is given, but initially it may be wise to buy the prepared variety.

Preparation of couscous grains

This recipe gives enough couscous for 12 servings. Store unused grain in a dry container.

1½ lb (3 cups) coarse semolina
3 tablespoons salt

up to 8 oz (1 cup) flour
water

Place the semolina in a large bowl and form a well in the middle. Now with a tablespoon, sprinkle some water into the centre, and with the same spoon lightly push the semolina into the well. Sprinkle the salt and 1 tablespoon flour over the grains and then mix it well together by stirring with your fingers in one direction only. Gradually some of the semolina forms into large grains the size of pearl barley. They are the couscous. With a coarse sieve sift out these large grains and return the small grains and large globules of grains to the bowl. Repeat the first process adding only 1 tablespoon of flour at a time. Continue repeating the process using a maximum of 8 oz (1 cup) flour. The finished couscous is steamed in a colander over boiling water, spread on a dry cloth in an airy warm place to dry (about 24 hours) and then stored ready for use.

*Algerian couscous

Serves 6 to 8

This is a recipe that you may add to or change to include any suitable vegetables, meat or poultry you have available. In order to get the timing of the preparation correct, please read the whole recipe before starting it.

1½ lb meat, cut into 1½ inch cubes	4 medium carrots, thinly sliced
1 medium onion, coarsely diced	lengthwise
4 tablespoons vegetable oil	2 small turnips, thinly sliced
4 tablespoons fresh parsley, chopped	lengthwise
1 tablespoon salt	4 oz (½ cup) chick-peas, soaked
1 teaspoon black pepper	overnight
1 tablespoon cinnamon	4 oz (½ cup) raisins
½ teaspoon saffron (or turmeric)	1 lb (3 cups) couscous
2 pt (5 cups) water	

Put the first 8 ingredients in the base of the couscousier or one of the alternative arrangements suggested above and stir. Fry over a medium heat for 10 to 15 minutes. Add the water, bring to the boil, reduce heat and simmer for 1 to 1½ hours or until meat is tender. Adjust the seasoning to taste, and then drop in the carrots and turnips. Continue cooking until the vegetables are cooked, when the sauce will be ready. While preparing the sauce cook the chick-peas in lightly salted water until tender (1 to 1½ hours). While the sauce is cooking the couscous is also prepared and cooked. Place the couscous in a large bowl and gently stir in 1 pint (2½ cups) cold water, immediately drain and allow the wet grains to stand for 10 to 15 minutes. As they swell up rake them with your fingers to prevent lumps forming. Turn the grains into a colander or steamer and place them over the cooking sauce. Let them steam for 30 minutes by which time the cooked grains should be soft but not mushy. If they are still hard, remove the steamer from over the sauce, sprinkle ¼ to ½ cup of water over the grains and stir with a wooden spoon. Return them to the top of the pan and steam until cooked. Whilst the couscous is steaming, boil the raisins in lightly salted water for 10 minutes and then leave to stand.

The couscous is now ready to be served. Pile the grains onto a large serving dish. On top of the mound place the meat (removed from the sauce with a slotted spoon) and then decorate the sides with carrots and turnips. Sprinkle chick-

peas and raisins over the grains and pour on some of the sauce. Serve with the
remaining sauce and a small bowl of hot pepper sauce.

Alternative suggestions

1: Replace the meat with filleted fish
2: Replace the chick-peas with blanched almonds
3: Add tomato purée to the sauce
4: Make a separate hot sauce by boiling some of the liquid from the sauce with
½ teaspoon hot red peppers

Couscous with sweet Moroccan sauce

4 oz (½ cup) butter
2 medium onions, diced small
2 tablespoons cinnamon
½ teaspoon saffron (or turmeric)
1 teaspoon ginger
½ teaspoon black pepper

1 teaspoon salt
12 fl. oz (1½ cups) water
4 oz (½ cup) sugar
8 oz (1 cup) raisins, soaked overnight,
drained
1 lb (3 cups) couscous

Melt the butter in a heavy pan, add the onion and seasoning and sauté until the
onion is soft and golden. Pour in the water, sugar and raisins, bring to the boil,
reduce heat, cover and cook for 25 to 30 minutes. The sauce should be quite
thick by this time, but if it isn't, remove the cover and reduce the liquid a little
over a moderate heat. Meanwhile steam the couscous over a pan of boiling
water for 30 to 35 minutes. If by this time it is not cooked, sprinkle ¼ pint (½
cup) of water over it and stir with a wooden spoon. Continue steaming until
cooked. Piled the cooked grains on a serving dish, make a hollow in the top, fill
with sweet sauce and serve.

WHOLEWHEAT

Cooked wholewheat grains (sometimes called berries) make surprisingly tasty
and satisfying dishes, and eating the whole grain ensures you get all the nutritious goodness of the wheat. They also make excellent salads if mixed with salad
vegetables and dressing or with cooked beans. The latter mixture is an especially rich protein combination.

The grains are prepared for cooking by soaking in water for 3 to 4 hours.
They are then cooked in the same way as brown rice. Wholewheat is more
fibrous than rice, however, and never cooks to the same softness. For this
reason it is much harder to overcook wholewheat than rice. In most dishes
where you would use brown rice, wholewheat can be substituted.

Plain boiled wholewheat

2 pt (5 cups) water
1 lb (2 cups) wholewheat berries,
soaked and drained
1 teaspoon salt

Bring the water to a rolling boil. Add the wheat to the boiling water, return mixture to the boil, reduce heat and simmer for 1 to 1½ hours or until the wheat is cooked to the softness you require. Add salt towards the end of cooking time.

To speed up the cooking time dry roast the wheat in a hot frying pan for 2 to 3 minutes before adding to the boiling water.

Chinese-style wholewheat

2 eggs
1 tablespoon butter
4 tablespoons vegetable oil
1 medium onion, finely chopped
3 sticks celery, diced

2 peppers, diced
1 lb (2 cups) cold, cooked wholewheat
4 oz (1½ cups) mushrooms, diced
4 teaspoons soy sauce
salt and black pepper to taste

Beat the eggs together, heat butter in a large frying pan, and prepare two thin omelettes. Cut the omelettes into thin strips and set aside. Heat the oil in the frying pan. When it is hot, add the onion, celery and peppers and sauté until just tender. Now add the wholewheat and mushrooms and cook for a further 5 minutes. Just before serving, mix in the egg strips, soy sauce, salt and black pepper. Serve immediately.

Baked vegetable and wholewheat

8 oz (1 cup) wholewheat
1 large onion, sliced
8 oz (1 cup) potatoes, peeled and cubed
4 oz (1½ cups) mushrooms, sliced
   (optional)
8 oz (1½ cups) carrots, finely chopped
2 medium green peppers, de-seeded

1 tablespoon tomato purée
4 oz (1 cup) wholemeal flour or brown
   breadcrumbs
4 tablespoons vegetable oil
1 teaspoon thyme
salt and black pepper to taste
4 oz (1 cup) cheese, grated

Boil the wholewheat in plenty of water for 15 minutes. Drain. Preheat oven to 400°F (gas mark 6). Combine partially cooked wheat with the remaining ingredients, except cheese, mix well and season to taste. Place mixture in deep baking dish or bread tin, sprinkle cheese on top and bake for 50 to 60 minutes or until a knife pushed into the centre of the bake comes out clean.

Wholewheat pilaff

8 oz (1 cup) wholewheat, soaked and
   drained
4 tablespoons vegetable oil
1 medium onion, chopped
2 to 3 cloves garlic, crushed
3 sticks celery, chopped
1 pt (2½ cups) hot water

2 oz (⅜ cup) sultanas
4 oz (1½ cups) mushrooms, sliced
4 oz (1 cup) unsalted peanuts
1 teaspoon nutmeg
1 teaspoon ground ginger
salt and black pepper to taste

Fry the wheat in oil in a heavy pan for 5 minutes. Add the onion, garlic and celery and cook for 5 minutes longer. Add the water, sultanas and mushrooms. Cover and simmer until all the liquid is absorbed and the wheat is just tender (about 45 minutes). You may need to add more water. Stir in the rest of the ingredients and adjust the seasoning as necessary. Serve immediately.

Wholewheat and rice mix

This mixture of rice and wholewheat may be served in place of rice or whole-wheat alone.

4 oz (½ cup) wholewheat, soaked   2 pt (5½ cups) water
   overnight   ½ teaspoon salt
8 oz (1 cup) brown rice

Place all the ingredients in a heavy saucepan and bring to the boil. Reduce the heat and simmer for 1½ to 2 hours. The rice will be very soft in contrast to the chewy wheat.

★Wholewheat bean and beef casserole

This is a Persian recipe that's slightly complicated to follow, but the casserole is delicious and it makes an unusual and exotic meal.

Serves 6 to 8

2 pt (5 cups) water   8 fl oz (1 cup) hot water
4 oz (½ cup) lentils, soaked overnight,   8 oz (1 cup) white rice
   drained   8 oz (1 cup) wholewheat cooked and
4 oz (½ cup) red beans, soaked   drained
   overnight, drained   2 teaspoons salt
2 medium onions, diced   1 teaspoon black pepper
12 oz beef or lamb cut into 1 inch   6 oz (¾ cup) butter
   cubes   6 oz (1 cup) pitted dates

Bring half the cold water to the boil, add the lentils and red beans and cook, covered, over a moderate heat for 45 to 60 minutes. Melt ⅓ of the butter in a frying pan, add the onions and meat and fry gently until nicely browned. Pour in the hot water, cover and leave to cook slowly for 30 minutes. Place the rice and wholewheat in a large, heavy pan, add the remaining water and 8 fluid ounces (1 cup) of the bean and lentil cooking liquid. Season with salt and pepper and drop in half the remaining butter, stir, cover and bring to the boil. Now add meat, onions and cooking liquid and cook gently, uncoverd, until all the liquid is absorbed (about 15 to 20 minutes). Drain the beans and lentils and stir them into the pot. Melt the remaining butter in a frying pan, add the pitted dates and fry for 2 to 3 minutes. Transfer the contents of the casserole to a serving dish, decorate with fried dates and serve. Traditionally any rice/wheat mixture that sticks to the bottom of the pan is carefully removed and served on a separate plate.

Introduction

Rice and wheat are the world's most important foodstuffs. Nearly half the world's population depend on rice as their staple food, and a fair proportion of this number rely almost solely on rice for their nutritional needs. Most rice is grown and consumed in Asia, particularly the Far East, and a substantial amount of this rice is consumed by the farmers and families that grow it. Much of the remainder of the world's rice crop is produced in the U S A, Brazil, Spain and Italy.

In Britain most of the rice is imported from America, and more recently there has been a certain amount from Australia. This unexpected rice source is the result of the Second World War, when the Australians had their rice supplies cut off by the Japanese and were prompted to start cultivating their own.

Rice is an excellent crop for populous areas short of space. It gives a better yield and requires less seed per acre than other cereal grains, and under the right conditions two crops a year may be cultivated. Further, natural, unpolished rice (brown rice) is of good nutritive value with an excellent balance of vitamins, minerals, protein, fat and carbohydrate. Finally, and perhaps most important of all, rice is easy to cook, satisfying to eat and easy to digest.

A predominant characteristic of rice-eating peoples is their great preference for rice over other foods, and given extra spending power they normally prefer to buy more rice than add other grains to their diets. In a small way I understand this desire for rice, having spent a year in Japan, and during this time eaten rice with every meal. On my return to England I was surprised to discover I was longing for rice, even for breakfast!

The history of rice

The botanical name for rice (*Oryza*) is derived from the Latin *oryzon*, which some scholars suggest derives from the even earlier Tamil word *arisi*, meaning 'rice without husks'. Another theory is that the name was given by the Chinese Emperor Chin-nung. He ruled in about 2800 B C and was responsible for the first clear written record of rice. Rice did not, however, originate in China but in India. By piecing together tiny fragments of evidence historians believe that domesticated rice was developed from the seeds of a wild Indian grain called *Newaree*. From India rice spread eastwards to China and Japan and westward to Persia and the Middle East. The Persians introduced it to the Greeks, and the Greek poet Sophocles (495–406 B C) mentioned it as a 'God bestowed' food. During the medieval wars between Moslems and Christians, the Moors (Moslems) occupied Spain and took rice with them. It became very popular, and by the sixteenth century had spread to Italy (although some suggest Marco Polo introduced it there in the thirteenth century) and from there to the south of France.

Rice never grew wild in the Americas (so-called wild rice indigenous to that continent is not the same species), although in 1647 an Englishman, Sir William Buckly, tried to cultivate it in Virginia. He was unsuccessful in his efforts, and it was to be another fifty years before rice was finally introduced to America. The captain of a ship bound for Liverpool from Madagascar, was blown off course, and he decided to put into Charleston in Carolina for repairs. Among the colonists who visited the ship was a man with the fine name Landgrave Thomas Smith. He discovered that the ship was carrying unhulled rice, and asked for a small bag to use as seeds. He planted them in some local swampy fields, and they grew well. Four years later Carolina exported its first shipment of rice to England. Although most rice now grown in the U S A is from states other than Carolina, the French still call long-grain rice *riz Caroline*.

The rice plant

Many varieties of rice have been developed to suit the climate, soil and methods of cultivation of particular areas and rice is grown within a range which includes the northern and southern limits of the temperate zone, although optimum yields are obtained in the humid tropical and subtropical zones of the world. These many types have their origins in two species. The most important is *Oryza satiya*, a white-grain rice originally cultivated in the monsoon belt of South East Asia, and the other is *Oryza glaberrima*, a red-grain rice first grown in Central Africa.

Rice plants grow to between 2 and 5 feet tall depending on the variety. They have a central stalk to which long, smooth, narrow leaves are attached. While the rice plants are growing in the fields and before husking, they are known as paddy rice.

· Rice plants can be broadly divided into *indica* or long-grain rices, and *japonica* or short-grain rices. Strangely, although *japonica* plants give higher yields per acre than *indica*, there is normally a definite preference for *indica* in areas of the world where rice is a staple crop. These long-grain rices remain in separate grains when cooked, and become light and fluffy. *Japonica* rices, popular in Japan and parts of China, are soft cooking and the cooked grains tend to stick to one another.

Rice is the only major cereal crop that is planted in water (there are dry land-growing rice varieties, but they are not as common as the aquatic). The plant likes abundant supplies of fresh water, and it is estimated that it requires 300 gallons of water to grow 1 lb of rice! It grows with its roots constantly submerged but with the leaves above the surface of the water taking in oxygen and transporting it to the roots. Unfortunately, this peculiar characteristic of rice requires that its cultivation, unless mechanized, involves many man and woman hours of back-breaking work.

In the first stage of rice growing, a seed bed is planted. The seedlings are allowed to grow a few inches and then the bed is flooded. The rice plants are now grown to nearly a foot high, the bed is drained, and they are then carefully transplanted by hand, one by one, to a flooded paddy field. The plants are given time to establish themselves before the field is drained for weeding and hoeing. Finally the field is flooded again and the rice ripens ready for harvest. In modern rice-growing countries, all these operations are mechanized and the rice is even sown by air straight into the fields. In primitive areas nature controls the process and the farmers have to wait for the monsoon rains to flood their fields. Many of

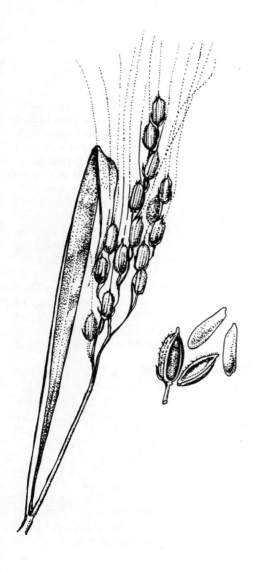

these farmers grow a fascinating variety of rice called *floating rice*, which can grow very fast, up to a foot a day, and so keep its head above the flood waters.

Humanity seems to thrive on adversity and, despite all the hard work involved in cultivating rice, the flowering paddy fields have inspired Eastern poets through the centuries. The Chinese poet Sun Tung-po writing in the eleventh century about his own rice growing efforts, started one of his poems like so:

> I planted rice before Spring Festival
> And already I'm counting joys,
> Rainy skies darken the Spring pond;
> I chat with friends by green bladed paddies.
> Transplanting takes till the first of Summer,
> Delight growing with wind-blown stalks.
> The moon looks down on dew-wet leaves
> Strung one by one with hanging pearls.

Rice and nutrition

After the paddy rice has been harvested, it's dried and threshed, and the unhulled rice grains are separated from the rice stalks. This rough rice is then hulled by gentle crushing and the thick woody husk surrounding the grain is removed, by winnowing or other methods, leaving the whole rice grain. As with wheat this wholegrain (or brown) rice contains all the nutriments naturally present in the grain. Again, as with wheat, it has become normal to mill off the outer layers of the grain to give white rice. In so doing many of the vitamins, minerals and much of the protein present in the rice are lost, since they are collected in the outer shells or bran of the rice grain. This practice developed for many reasons. White rice, which was once eaten only by the rich, (who didn't need the lost nutrients, since they had a rich mixed diet) became a status symbol. It was seen to be more attractive and its bland flavour considered more appealing than the more distinctive-tasting brown rice. With improvements in milling techniques, white rice became as cheap and as generally available as brown rice, and it was what people wanted. Further, rice as a commodity for export is easier to deal with in its milled form. Its natural oils are removed during the milling, and it consequently stores better. Thus white rice became the norm. This had, and is still having, disastrous consequences in areas of the world where rice is relied upon for most nutritional needs.

The difference in nutritional content of brown and white rice is illustrated in the following table, which also compares the two with whole and refined wheat and whole corn. As you will see, the nutritional worth of rice is comparable with the other grains, and it is an excellent source of B complex vitamins, vitamin E, and calcium and phosphorus.

Thus we have the choice of eating nutritious brown rice or refined white rice. In the west this choice is not so important, since most of us have a mixed diet that probably supplies our nutritional needs. There is, however, one element that may be missing from our diet, and that's roughage or bran, and if your diet is heavily dependent on refined foods you would be wise to start including in it some wholefoods like brown rice.

There are of course some dishes that are best prepared with white rice (e.g. sushi rice, page 80), but for my taste I prefer brown rice. To me it looks more

NUTRITIONAL CONTENT OF BROWN AND WHITE RICE COMPARED TO OTHER GRAINS.

COMPONENTS	RICE		WHEAT		CORN
	BROWN	WHITE	WHOLE	WHITE	WHOLE
PROTEIN%	8·9	7·6	11·1	9·3	10
FAT %	2·0	0·3	1·7	1·0	4·3
CARBOHYDRATE%	77·2	79·4	75·5	77·2	73·4
FIBRE	1·0	0·2	2·4	0·4	2·3
VITAMINS (PARTS PER MILLION)					
VITAMIN C	0	0	0	0	0
THIAMINE (B$_1$)	3-5	0·6-1·0	3·2-7·7	0·87	4·4
RIBOFLAVIN (B$_2$)	8-1·0	0·28	1 -1·2	0·40	1·3-1·5
NIACIN (B$_5$)	55	15-20	53	10·00	21
MINERALS (PER CENT × 1000)					
CALCIUM	84	9	500	20	15
PHOSPHOROUS	290	96	400	92	430
IRON	2	0·9	4	0·8	3
POTASSIUM	342	79	480	—	400

FIGURES FROM F.A.O. NUTRITIONAL STUDIES No 1 LONDON H.M.S.O 19.

Table 5

wholesome and appetizing and tastes better than white rice and I cannot really understand why it's not more popular. It's clear that my view is not shared by everyone, and Fran Lebowitz in her funny book *Metropolitan Life* describes brown rice as 'ponderous, overly chewy, and possessed of unpleasant religious overtones'!

The rice grain and types of rice

Brown rice
Rice minus its hull or husk with the germ pericarp and aleurone layers intact. Contains all nutrients naturally present in the grain.

Converted or parboiled rice
Rice prepared from unhulled rice that has been soaked in water, steamed and dried before hulling and milling. Contains most of the original nutrients.

White rice
Rice with its outer layers of pericarp, aleurone, and germ removed by milling. Considerable loss of natural nutrients. These are sometimes re-added artificially to give enriched white rice.

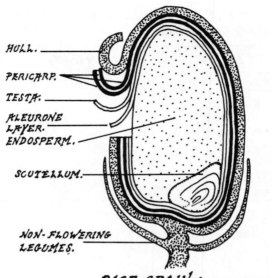

HULL.

PERICARP.

TESTA.

ALEURONE
LAYER.
ENDOSPERM.

SCUTELLUM.

NON-FLOWERING
LEGUMES.

RICE GRAIN (CROSS SECTION)

Rice bran
This consists of the aleurone, testa, pericarp and germ removed to make white
rice. An excellent source of B vitamins, minerals and protein. Add it to sweet
dishes, breads, biscuits (cookies), pancakes, etc.

Rice polishings
The inner bran layers and part of the endosperm removed when white rice is
polished. Milled fine and sold as flour, used to make noodles, thicken soups,
etc.

Rice flakes
White rice flaked in a power mill. Prepared for its quick cooking properties.
Used in soups and puddings. Brown rice flakes now available.

Rice flour
White rice ground into flour and used in puddings, sauces, confectionery, pasta
and bread–making (mixed with wheat flour).

Long-grain rice
This is often called patna rice, since it was thought to have originated from
Patna in India. The grain is from 4 to 5 times as long as wide, and if milled it is
milky white in appearance. When cooked, the grains separate and become light
and fluffy. Excellent for serving on its own as well as in pilaffs, risottos and
other savoury dishes.

Medium-grain rice
This is the type of rice first grown in Carolina, America. It's shorter than patna
rice, but the grains are a little more plump. Basmatti rice from India is of
medium length but much thinner, even than patna rice.

Short-grain (or round-grain) rice

This is a short plump grain rice, most popular in Japan and parts of China. It's quite sticky when cooked and in the west is usually reserved for making puddings. It is, however, well suited to being eaten with chopsticks, which may account for its popularity in Japan, where it is always served plain and unsalted as an accompaniment to a savoury dish.

Italian rice

This is another short-grain variety, and as its name implies, it's cultivated mainly in Italy. The grain absorbs more water than other types of rice, and is used for making dishes such as risotto in which the sauce is cooked in with the rice.

Wild rice

Wild rice is a cereal grain native to North America, China and Japan. It belongs to the same broad family as the rice plant, but is not an ancestor in that the rice we cultivate today did not develop from this particular wild grass. It is a very beautiful plant growing in areas of abundant fresh water. The Red Indians would collect the grain by floating alongside the ripe plants and then gently pulling them over the boat while they knocked the delicately held grains into the hull. The plant is difficult to grow domestically, and is consequently expensive. Nutritionally it's very rich and contains more protein and vitamins than regular rice. Raw wild rice is brown, but it acquires a faint purplish colour when cooked. It has a delicate nutty flavour.

Cooking Plain Rice

There are almost as many ways of cooking rice as there are countries that grow it, but below I have given only the principal methods. Whichever method you use there is still the question of whether to wash the rice before cooking or not. Too much rinsing will wash away some of the water soluble vitamins and minerals, whereas not enough may be unhygenic. I would suggest that with European or American packed rice, only the lightest rinse is necessary. If you buy loose rice or Asian-packed rice, then it should be washed but not excessively. Brown rice should be picked over for small stones and well rinsed. Having washed the rice before cooking, it is not necessary to do so again afterwards. Also it's important to learn to judge how much cooking water you need for a particular amount of rice. If the cooked rice needs draining you will lose important nutrients and flavour with the water.

General method of cooking rice

Methods given below are more precise, but a general rule is 1 volume of rice to just over 1½ volumes of water for white rice, and 2 volumes of water for brown rice. Bring rice and water to the boil, cover with a heavy lid and simmer for 20 to 40 minutes for white rice, and up to 50 minutes for brown rice. The cooked rice should be dry and puffed up. Note: in a number of Asian countries they do not add salt to cooking rice.

   Where the following recipes do not stipulate long or short-grain rice, cooking methods and times will be about the same for both. But remember the cooking qualities of rices differ even within the same general type.

   The following approximate figures may help you in your rice cooking:
2 to 3 oz uncooked rice per person is an average serving
1 cup uncooked rice weighs about 8 oz and gives about 1½ lb cooked rice
1 cup cooked rice weighs about 8 oz
1 volume uncooked rice gives 2½ to 3 volumes of cooked rice
   All the recipes that follow are for 4 servings.

Brown rice (boiled)

12 oz (1½ cups) brown rice
32 fl oz (4 cups) water
pinch of salt

Wash the rice thoroughly in cold water. Drain and transfer to a heavy pot, add the water and bring to the boil. Add a pinch of salt, cover, reduce heat and simmer for 50 minutes. Remove from heat and allow to stand for 10 minutes. Mix gently with a wooden spoon or rice paddle and serve.

Brown rice (pressure cooked)

12 oz (1½ cups) brown rice
24 fl oz (3 cups) water
pinch of salt

Wash the rice thoroughly in cold water. Drain and transfer to a pressure cooker. Cover and bring to full pressure over a high heat. Reduce heat to very low and gently simmer for 40 minutes. Remove from heat, allow pressure to drop to normal, uncover pan, add salt, gently mix rice with wooden spoon or rice paddle, cover again and allow to stand for five minutes. Serve.

Brown rice (baked)

12 oz (1½ cups) brown rice
28 fl oz (3½ cups) boiling water
pinch of salt or 1 tablespoon soy sauce

Preheat oven to 350°F (gas mark 4). Wash the rice thoroughly in cold water and drain well. Place the rice in a heavy frying pan and dry roast over a medium heat until the rice is dry, deepened in colour and beginning to pop. Transfer to a casserole dish, add the boiling water and salt, cover and bake for 50 to 60 minutes. Mix gently with a wooden spoon or rice paddle and serve.

General method for boiled white rice

1¼ pt (3 cups) water
1½ teaspoons salt
12 oz (1½ cups) rice

Bring the water to the boil in a heavy saucepan. Toss in the salt and add the rice. Return to the boil, reduce heat, cover and simmer for 15 to 20 minutes or until the rice is puffed up and dry (exact times will depend on the rice). The rice should be just tender when cooked; if not, simmer a little longer.

Chinese boiled rice

Place 12 oz (1½ cups) of rice in a heavy bottomed pan and add water to a level of 1 inch above the surface of the rice. This is the rule of thumb method used by the

Chinese. You may if you wish use 12 oz (1½ cups) of rice to 1¼ pint (3 cups) of water. Bring the rice and water to a fast boil, reduce the heat and gently boil for 5 minutes. Now cover the pot, reduce the heat to as low as it will go and leave to simmer for 20 minutes. Stir once whilst simmering. If you prefer a softer rice, add more water or vice versa for a harder rice.

Chinese steamed rice

12 oz (1½ cups) rice
1 pt (2½ cups) water

Bring the rice and water to the boil and cook for 2 minutes. Strain off the water and put the rice in a rice steamer or colander over boiling water. Steam for 40 to 50 minutes or until the rice is fluffy and tender.

Indian boiled rice

This is only one of many methods the Indians use for cooking rice. Nutritionally it's not a very good method, since it involves draining the cooked rice. It is, however, useful if you wish to pre-prepare the rice so that you can devote the last stages of the preparation of a meal to something else.

12 oz (1½ cups) rice
4½ pt (10 cups) water

Place rice and water in a saucepan, cover and bring to the boil. Remove cover and boil moderately fast for 15 minutes or until the rice is just tender. Drain rice in a colander and place the colander over a pan of hot water. Gently heat the pan and leave the rice until it is puffed up and dry (about 10 minutes).

Middle Eastern boiled rice

Two methods are given, both use oil in the ingredients, but in the second the rice is fried before boiling, and in the first the oil or fat is added after cooking.

12 oz (1½ cups) long grain rice   salt to taste
1¼ pt (3 cups) water   3 oz (⅓ cup) butter or vegetable oil

Method 1
Wash and drain the rice. Bring the water to the boil, toss in the salt and rice and return to the boil, boil fairly rapidly until all the water has evaporated. Remove from heat, cover and allow to stand for 5 to 10 minutes. Melt the butter and pour evenly over the rice, re-cover and allow to stand for 3 to 5 minutes or until the butter has been absorbed.

Method 2
If the rice is good quality do not wash it; if it isn't, rinse it and leave to dry out in a warm place. Heat the butter or oil in a heavy saucepan, add the rice and fry, stirring, for a minute or two. Pour in the water, add the salt and bring to the boil. Cover tightly, reduce heat to simmer and leave for 20 minutes. Do not remove the lid during this time. Remove from heat, allow to stand for 5 minutes

and serve. For the preparation of parboiled rice, needed in some recipes, remove the pan from heat after 10 minutes of the simmering time and stand in a basin of cold water until cooled.

Japanese boiled rice

The Japanese use short-grain rice and cook it until it's just sticky enough to pick up mouthful amounts with chopsticks.

12 oz (1½ cups) short-grain rice
1¼ pt (3 cups) water

Wash the rice well by stirring it vigorously in lots of water. Let the rice settle and carefully pour off all the milky residue. Repeat the process until the water remains almost clear. Drain and place the rice in a heavy bottomed pan with a good lid. Add the cooking water, cover the pan and bring to the boil quickly. Turn the heat right down and allow to simmer for 15 minutes (longer for brown rice). Finally, turn the heat off and allow the rice to stand for 5 to 10 minutes.

RICE DISHES

Cooked rice is, of course, served on its own as an accompaniment to savoury dishes, but it can also be used as a major ingredient in the preparation of main meals, desserts, salads, soups, etc., and the following recipes are for these types of dishes. There are many ways in which the recipes could have been arranged, but I have decided to collect them under headings that reflect the style of cooking (e.g. Middle Eastern, Indian, wholefood, etc.) rather than the ingredients. If the recipes specify white rice and you wish to use brown, extend cooking times by 15 to 20 minutes or use parboiled brown rice in place of uncooked white rice. All the recipes are for 4 generous servings unless otherwise specified. Other rice recipes can be found in the sections on bean dishes (see index).

Wholefood rice dishes

Brown rice with mushrooms

2 tablespoons vegetable oil (sesame oil if possible)
2 medium onions, chopped
8 oz (3 cups) mushrooms, chopped
12 oz (1½ cups) brown rice, washed and drained
1½ pt (3¾ cups) water
1 tablespoon soy sauce
¼ teaspoon salt

Preheat oven to 325°F (gas mark 3). Heat the oil in a heavy frying pan, add the onions and fry until they are just soft. Stir in the mushrooms and cook a further 2 minutes. Combine the onions and mushrooms with rice in an ovenproof casserole and mix in the water, soy sauce and salt. Cover and bake for 1 hour or until the rice is tender.

Brown rice croquettes

This is a good recipe for using left-over cooked rice and/or cooked vegetables. Serve with a crisp salad.

1 lb (2 cups) cooked brown rice
2 medium onions, diced fine
2 medium carrots, diced
or
1 lb (2 cups) mixed cooked vegetables
4 oz (1 cup) wholewheat flour
salt and black pepper to taste

1 egg, beaten
oil for deep frying
6 oz (1½ cups) breadcrumbs
or
wholemeal flour
or
semolina

Combine the rice with the onions and carrots or mixed cooked vegetables. Add the flour and mix well. Season to taste with salt and black pepper. Stir in the beaten egg. Form about 12 croquettes (cakes) from the mixture. Pour oil into a deep pan or deep fryer to a depth of about 3 inches. Heat the oil to 320°F or until it just begins to smoke. Roll the croquettes in the breadcrumbs or other coating, and then deep fry for 2 to 4 minutes, as many as the pan will hold comfortably. Drain on absorbent paper and keep warm in a moderate oven until all the croquettes are fried. Serve.

Variations
Serve sprinkled with parmesan cheese and chopped parsley.
Shallow fry the croquettes in a lightly greased heavy frying pan over a moderate heat instead of deep frying.

Baked cabbage and brown rice

1½ lb (3 cups) cooked brown rice
1 oz (1 tablespoon) fresh ginger root, grated
1 tablespoon soy sauce

1 small or ½ medium cabbage, finely shredded
salt and black pepper to taste
2 oz (¼ cup) butter
4 oz (½ cup) cheese, grated

Preheat oven to 350°F (gas mark 4). Combine the rice, ginger root and soy sauce and mix well. Use half the butter to grease a heavy casserole and put in the bottom half the shredded cabbage. Sprinkle lightly with salt and black pepper. Layer this with half the rice mixture and then repeat with the remaining cabbage and then the rice mixture. Dot the top with the rest of the butter, and then sprinkle with cheese. Cover casserole and bake for 45 to 50 minutes.

Variations
Replace cabbage with 8 oz of finely chopped spinach.

Baked rice and aubergines (eggplant)

salt
1 large aubergine (eggplant), thinly
   sliced
4 tablespoons vegetable oil
1 medium onion, diced
8 oz (1 cup) tinned tomatoes

1 lb (2 cups) cooked brown rice
1 tablespoon dried basil
8 oz (1 cup) cheese, grated
salt and black pepper to taste

Salt the aubergine slices liberally and leave under light pressure in a colander for 30 minutes. Meanwhile heat two tablespoons of oil in a heavy pan and lightly sauté the onion. Pour in the tomatoes and leave to simmer. Preheat oven to 350°F (gas mark 4). Rinse the aubergines under plenty of cold water and pat dry on absorbent paper. Fry them lightly in the remaining oil. Now layer half of each of the rice, aubergine, basil, onion and tomato mixture and cheese into a lightly greased heavy casserole. Sprinkle black pepper and salt to taste over the top. Repeat with the remaining ingredients and bake for 30 to 40 minutes.

Vegetable fried rice

Use a wok or a heavy frying pan
2 tablespoons vegetable oil (sesame if
   possible)
1 medium onion, finely diced
1 medium carrot, finely diced

4 oz (½ cup) fresh or tinned green peas
5 oz (1 cup) water chestnuts, sliced
   (optional)
1 lb (2 cups) cooked brown rice
2 tablespoons soy sauce

Heat the oil in a wok or heavy frying pan, add the onion, carrot, peas (if fresh) and water chestnuts. Stir fry over a high heat for 2 to 3 minutes. Add the peas if you are using the tinned variety and stir in the cooked rice. Reduce heat to medium and cook with constant stirring for 3 to 4 minutes. Sprinkle with the soy sauce and serve.

Variations
Add chopped celery or bean-sprouts to the vegetables. Garnish the finished dish with toasted sesame seeds.

Rice tempura

8 oz (2 cups) wholewheat flour
8 fl oz (1 cup) water
1½ lb (3 cups) cooked brown rice
pinch salt

oil for deep frying
2 lemons, quartered
and/or
soy sauce

Combine the flour and water into a smooth batter. Add the rice and salt and mix well. Pour the oil 2 to 3 inches deep into a deep pan or frying pan and heat to 320°–350°F or until the oil just begins to smoke. Drop tablespoonful amounts of the rice batter mixture into the hot oil and deep fry for 3 to 4 minutes or until golden brown. Remove the rice tempura from the oil with chopsticks or a slotted spoon, shake off excess oil and drain on absorbent paper. Repeat for remaining mixture and keep the cooked tempura in a moderate oven until they are all ready. Serve with slices of lemon, salt and/or soy sauce.

Cheese and brown rice bake

4 eggs, beaten
6 fl oz (¾ cup) milk
1 lb (2 cups) cooked brown rice
8 oz (1 cup) cheese, grated

1 small green pepper, diced
1 medium onion, diced
4 oz (1 cup) mushrooms, sliced
salt and black pepper to taste

Preheat oven to 350°F (gas mark 4). Mix together the egg and milk in a large bowl, and stir in the remaining ingredients. Season to taste with salt and black pepper. Lightly grease a heavy casserole and tip in the rice mixture. Bake uncovered for 40 to 45 minutes or until firm and nicely browned on top.

Brown rice and herbs

This dish is excellent in the summer, served cold or hot with a crisp salad. If you do not have fresh herbs available, use dried, but remember to halve the quantities of the herbs recommended in the recipe.

2 oz (¼ cup) butter
1 medium onion, diced
8 oz (1 cup) brown rice
1 teaspoon salt
½ teaspoon black pepper

1¼ pt (3 cups) water, boiling
1 tablespoon basil, chopped
1 tablespoon tarragon, chopped
1 tablespoon parsley, chopped

Heat the butter in a heavy pan. Add the onion and sauté until soft and lightly browned, add the rice, salt, black pepper and water, cover and simmer over a very low heat for 30 minutes. Now add the herbs, adjust the seasoning, cover and simmer for a further 10 to 15 minutes. Add a little water if the rice is drying out. Serve or allow to cool and then serve.

Nut and vegetable brown rice casserole

Serves 4 to 6

2 tablespoons vegetable oil
1 medium onion, diced
1 small carrot, grated
4 oz (1½ cups) chinese cabbage, shredded

or
spinach
2 oz (1 cup) bean sprouts
2 oz (½ cup) walnuts, chopped
soy sauce to taste
1 lb (2 cups) cooked brown rice
2 eggs, beaten

Preheat oven to 350°F (gas mark 4). Heat the oil in a large, heavy pan. Add the onion and sauté until soft, stir in the carrot and cook over a moderate heat a further 2 minutes. Add the cabbage or spinach, mix well, cover pan and cook until the greens are wilted. Stir in the bean sprouts, walnuts, soy sauce and cooked rice, mix well and then stir in the beaten egg. Turn contents of pan into a lightly greased casserole, cover and bake for 20 to 30 minutes. Serve.

*Brown rice with shrimps

1 lb (2 cups) brown rice, rinsed and
   drained
1¼ pt (3 cups) water
3 tablespoons vegetable oil
1 medium onion, minced

8 oz (2 cups) raw shrimps, boiled in
   salted water, peeled and cut in half
salt and black pepper to taste
2 eggs, beaten

Add the rice to the water in a heavy pan and bring to the boil. Reduce the heat, cover and leave to simmer for 20 minutes. Heat 2 tablespoons oil in a heavy pan, sauté the onions for 2 to 3 minutes, add the shrimps and sauté together for 2 minutes more. Turn off the heat and sprinkle in the soy sauce. Gently stir this mixture into the cooking rice, season to taste with salt and black pepper, cover again and leave to simmer a further 10 to 15 minutes. Meanwhile heat the remaining oil in the frying pan and prepare an omelette from the beaten egg. Allow to cool a little and then cut into strips. Serve the rice and shrimps topped with egg strips.

*Brown rice and beef loaf

Serves 6 to 8

1½ lb minced beef
'1 lb (2 cups) cooked brown rice
1 medium carrot, grated
1 medium onion, diced
2 eggs, beaten
4 oz (1 cup) brown breadcrumbs

2 tablespoons tomato purée
1 teaspoon dried thyme
or
1 tablespoon fresh thyme
1 tablespoon fresh parsley, chopped
salt and black pepper to taste

Preheat oven to 325°F (gas mark 3). Combine all the ingredients and season to taste (if it seems a little dry, stir in some water). Lightly oil 2, 2 lb bread tins or suitable casserole dish, and spoon the mixture in. Place the tins or dish in a water bath and bake for 1½ to 2 hours or until firm and nicely browned on top. Serve hot with a cheese sauce.

Variations
Line the bread tin with thin rashers of bacon and put strips over the top of the mixture before baking.

Middle Eastern rice dishes

Rice stew with yoghurt and vegetables

Yoghurt is served in many forms all over the Middle East, sometimes cooked in dishes sometimes with them, in hot soups in the winter and in cold soups in the summer. Genghis Khan is said to have lived on yoghourt during his marches through Mongola and the Persian Empire.

This particular stew can be served as a starter or served with pita bread and hummus (see index) as a main meal. Lemon juice may be used in place of the yoghurt for a sharper, less creamy stew.

4 tablespoons vegetable oil	1 teaspoon powdered coriander
3 medium onions, thinly sliced	1 tablespoon fresh parsley, chopped
3 tablespoons split red lentils	salt and black pepper to taste
8 oz (1 cup) rice	8 fl oz (1 cup) natural yoghurt
2 pt (5 cups) water	1 medium onion, diced
1 lb spinach, chopped	1 teaspoon dried mint

Heat 3 tablespoons oil in a heavy pan, add the sliced onions and sauté until lightly browned. Stir in the lentils and the rice, add the water and bring to the boil. Reduce the heat, cover and simmer for 20 minutes. Now add the spinach, coriander, parsley and salt and pepper to taste, and continue cooking a further 30 minutes. Meanwhile fry the diced onion in the remaining oil until well browned, sprinkle on the mint and fry a further minute. Pour the stew into a serving bowl, beat in the yoghurt, garnish with mint and fried onion and serve.

Nut and fruit rice

This dish reflects the Middle Eastern enjoyment of sweet things. You can, if you wish, make it more savoury by replacing the sugar with 1 teaspoon of salt. It's a very nourishing and economical dish.

1 lb (2 cups) cooked rice (brown or white)	grated peel of 1 orange
4 fl oz (½ cup) milk	2 oz (¼ cup) brown sugar
8 oz (1 cup) mixed dates and raisins	3 tablespoons butter, melted
4 oz (¾ cup) blanched almonds or walnuts, chopped	

Preheat oven to 325°F (gas mark 3). Place ⅓ of the rice in the bottom of a heavy casserole and pour on the milk. Sprinkle half the fruit, nuts, orange peel and sugar over the top. Cover with half the remaining rice and layer again with remaining fruit, nuts, orange peel and sugar. Top with the last of rice and pour melted butter evenly over. Cover casserole and place in shallow dish containing 1 inch of water. Place in the oven and bake for 50 minutes to 1 hour.

Savoury pilaff

This is a famous dish in Middle Eastern countries. It's called either pilaff or pilau from the Persian *pilaw*. The recipe given below is a basic one and can be improvised upon using your own ingenuity. There is no meat in the ingredients, but if you wish, you may add 8 ounces of liver or minced meat at the onion-frying stage. The pine nuts required may be difficult to buy, but they are an important ingredient, so do find some if you can. Otherwise use chopped almonds.

4 oz (½ cup) butter
2 large onions, finely diced
2 oz (¼ cup) pine nuts
1 lb (2 cups) brown or white rice
½ teaspoon mixed spice
½ tablespoon fresh sage
or
1 teaspoon dried sage
½ tablespoon fresh parsley

or
1 teaspoon dried parsley
salt and black pepper to taste
2 oz (¼ cup) sultanas or raisins
2 medium tomatoes, quartered
1½ pt (4 cups) boiling water or stock

In a large, heavy saucepan melt the butter and sauté the onions until soft, but not brown. Add the pine nuts and rice and fry, stirring, for 4 to 5 minutes. Add the mixed spice, sage, parsley and season to taste with salt and freshly milled black pepper. Stir in the dried fruit, tomatoes, and then pour in the water or stock. Stir well, bring to the boil, reduce heat, cover and simmer until all the liquid is absorbed (45 to 50 minutes for brown rice, 20 to 30 minutes for white rice). Now allow to stand away from heat for 10 minutes and then serve.

Rice with spinach

Serves 6 to 8

½ lb spinach, washed, chopped
4 tablespoons butter
1 medium onion, diced
4 fl oz (½ cup) natural yoghurt
1 teaspoon cinnamon

salt and black pepper to taste
1 lb (2 cups) parboiled, long-grain rice
  (use Middle Eastern Method 2,
  p. 62)
1 egg, beaten

Preheat oven to 350°F (gas mark 4). Boil the spinach in a little water (1 or 2 tablespoons) for 6 to 8 minutes. Drain and squeeze out excess water. Heat the butter in a heavy frying pan and sauté the onion for 2 minutes. Add the spinach and sauté, stirring, a further 2 to 4 minutes. Pour the mixture into a bowl and stir in the yoghurt and cinnamon. Season to taste with salt and black pepper. Combine ⅓ of the rice with the beaten egg and cover the bottom of a 9 inch casserole with the mixture. Now make alternate layers of the spinach/yoghurt mixture and the remaining rice ending up with a layer of rice. Cover and bake for 30 minutes. Alternatively this dish can be steamed. Prepare the layers of rice and spinach mixture in a heavy pan. Cover with a tight-fitting lid and cook for 45 to 60 minutes over a very low heat. This is the more genuine way to cook the dish.

Variation
Rice with spinach and lamb: fry 1 pound of lamb chops in butter until browned on both sides. Sprinkle with a little saffron and use as a middle layer in the method described above.

Rice stuffed aubergines (eggplant)

The rice filling used in this recipe may also be used to stuff green peppers, vine leaves, cabbage leaves, etc.

Stuffing
8 oz (1 cup) cooked rice (brown or
    white)
4 oz (½ cup) tinned tomatoes
1 medium onion, finely diced
1 tablespoon parsley, finely chopped
½ teaspoon cinnamon

salt and black pepper to taste
plus
4 medium aubergines (eggplant)
salt
2 tablespoons vegetable oil
4 tablespoons cheese, grated

Combine all the stuffing ingredients and mix well by hand. Cut the aubergines in half lengthways. Score across the top and around the edge of each half and sprinkle with salt. Leave for 30 minutes. Meanwhile preheat oven to 425°F (gas mark 7). Rinse the aubergines in lots of water and pat dry. Scoop out the centres leaving a ½″ thick shell, chop pulp small and fry gently in oil for 4 to 5 minutes. Add the pulp to the stuffing and stuff the aubergines with the mixture. Place the stuffed vegetables on a lightly greased baking tray, sprinkle with cheese and bake for 15 minutes.

Sweet rice (shirini polo)

This type of Iranian rice dish is normally served with meat balls or surrounding a leg of lamb or chicken breasts. It is, however, excellent as an accompaniment to a savoury vegetable dish or served on its own with a bowl of lightly fried or boiled vegetables. For those of you who wish to serve it in the traditional way a recipe follows for meat balls.

3 oz (⅓ cup) butter
1 medium onion, diced
2 medium carrots, grated
2 oz (¼ cup) almonds, chopped
    (optional)
grated peel of 1 orange

1 tablespoon sugar
salt and black pepper to taste
2 lb (4 cups) parboiled long-grain rice
    (use Middle Eastern Method 2,
    p. 63).

Heat 2 oz of the butter in a heavy frying pan, add the onion and sauté until soft. Add carrots and gently sauté for 8 to 10 minutes. Stir in the almonds, orange peel, sugar and salt and black pepper to taste. Cook and stir for a further 2 minutes. Coat the bottom of a heavy pan with the remaining butter and spread alternate layers of the onion and carrot mixture and rice. Cover the pan with a heavy, tight-fitting lid and simmer over a very low light for 25 to 30 minutes.

★Meat balls

1 lb minced beef
½ green pepper, finely diced
¼ teaspoon nutmeg

½ teaspoon cinnamon
salt and black pepper to taste
oil or butter for frying

Mix all the ingredients and knead into a smooth mixture. Form into walnut size balls and fry them in oil or butter until browned all over and cooked through. Serve with the sweet rice or bury in the rice along with the carrot and onion mixture as in the recipe above.

Rice with noodles (reshte polo)

3 oz (⅓ cup) butter
1 large onion, finely chopped
2 oz (¼ cup) raisins
6 oz (2 cups) fine egg noodles (chinese
  or vermicelli type)

12 oz (1½ cups) white rice, washed
  and drained
1 pt (2½ cups) water
salt to taste

Heat the butter in a heavy pan, add the onions and sauté until soft and golden. Add the raisins and sauté a further 2 to 3 minutes. Stir in the noodles and fry until lightly coloured. Add the rice and stir fry over a low heat until all the grains are coated in oil. Pour in the water, season to taste with salt. Bring to the boil, reduce heat, cover with tight-fitting lid and simmer until all the water has been absorbed and the rice is tender and fluffy (about 20 minutes). Add a little more water if needed. Serve with a fresh salad and yoghurt.

★Rice with chicken (morg polo)

This is an Iranian dish usually prepared for special occasions such as weddings or birthdays. For very special days the chicken may be marinated first, and a recipe for a traditional marinade is given. However, if you wish to prepare the dish immediately, miss this stage out.

Serves 4 to 6 people

4 oz (½ cup) butter
and
1 tablespoon butter
1 large onion, finely diced
1 teaspoon turmeric
1 teaspoon salt
1 teaspoon cinnamon
1 teaspoon black pepper
2 to 3 lb roasting chicken, jointed
or
4 to 6 pieces of chicken
4 oz (½ cup) diced apricots, washed
  and drained

2 lb (4 cups) parboiled long-grain rice
  (use Middle Eastern Method 2,
  p. 63).

Marinade
1 medium onion, finely diced
juice of 2 lemons
2 cloves garlic, crushed
3 tablespoons verve or sesame oil
1 teaspoon salt
½ teaspoon black pepper

Marinade: crush the onion with the back of a wooden spoon or with a pestle and mortar and then mix it with the remaining marinade ingredients. Place the chicken pieces in a shallow dish and pour over or paint on the marinade. Cover and leave overnight.
Melt 3 oz (⅓ cup) butter in a heavy frying pan and sauté the onion until golden. Sprinkle in the turmeric, salt, cinnamon and black pepper and mix well. Now add the chicken and sauté over a moderate heat while turning until both sides are well coloured by the seasoning and the chicken is almost tender. Meanwhile soak the apricots in water for 5 minutes, drain, pat dry and sauté in 1 tablespoon of butter for 2 to 3 minutes. In a large heavy pan, melt the remaining butter and pour in half the parboiled rice. Spread evenly and then place on top the chicken

pieces and apricots. Cover with remaining rice. Stretch a clean cloth taut across the top of the pan, press on the lid and simmer (steam) over a low heat for 30 to 45 minutes. Serve.

*Rice, lamb and aubergine (eggplant) casserole

This dish neatly combines 3 of the most common ingredients in Middle Eastern cooking. If you wish to make it even more typical add 2 to 3 ounces of soaked chick-peas and some fried pine nuts or almonds to the casserole.

1 large aubergine (eggplant), thinly sliced
salt
4 oz (½ cup) butter
2 cloves garlic, crushed
1 medium onion, diced
4 lamb cutlets (total weight 1 to 2 lb)

1 teaspoon cinnamon
1 teaspoon allspice
4 oz (½ cup) tomato purée
1½ pt (4 cups) water or stock
8 oz (1 cup) long-grain rice (brown or white)

Place aubergine slices in a colander, sprinkle generously with salt and leave for 30 minutes to 1 hour. Rinse and pat dry on an absorbent cloth. Melt half the butter in a heavy frying pan, sauté the garlic until soft, add the onion and sauté golden. Place the cutlets in the pan and brown on both sides. Arrange the onion and cutlets in the base of a heavy casserole. Preheat oven to 325°F (gas mark 3). Melt remaining butter in frying pan and gently brown the aubergine slices on both sides. Layer the aubergine slices over the cutlets, and sprinkle over the cinnamon and alspice. Combine the tomato purée with the water or stock and pour into the casserole. Lastly, add the rice and then season to taste with salt and black pepper. Cover the casserole and bake for 1½ to 2 hours.

Indian rice dishes

The Indian cook like his Arab counterpart, tends to use a lot of oil or butter in his or her rice cooking. The rice is fried in ghee (a sort of clarified butter) before cooking and this seals the starch in the rice inside the grain. The result is that the cooked rice remains unsoggy and in separate grains. If you are on a fat-reducing diet you would be advised to concentrate on rice dishes other than the Indian ones or alternatively modify the recipes given here to suit your needs. Indian food is beautifully spiced and shouldn't be missed.

Yellow rice

Yellow cooked rice is an excellent accompaniment to curries. For a more elaborate dish that will serve as a main meal serve the yellow rice with some or all of the garnishings suggested below the recipe.

3 oz (⅓ cup) butter or oil
12 oz (1½ cups) rice (brown or white)
1 teaspoon turmeric powder

1 teaspoon coriander powder
1½ pt (3½ cups) water, boiling
salt to taste

Heat the butter or oil in a heavy pan and stir in the rice. Fry over a low heat for 5 minutes. Sprinkle in the turmeric and coriander powders and mix well. Pour in the water, season to taste with salt. Cover pot, reduce heat to as low as possible and leave to simmer until all the liquid is absorbed and the rice is tender and fluffy (45 to 50 minutes for brown rice and 25 to 30 minutes for white rice).

Suggested garnishings

1 medium onion, thinly sliced and fried
1 hard-boiled egg, sliced
1 oz (⅛ cup) roasted almonds
2 oz (⅜ cup) sultanas

1 tablespoon freshly chopped parsley
or
coriander leaves
2 medium tomatoes, sliced
¼ medium cucumber, sliced .

Tomato rice

This is another basic rice dish. It may be made more elaborate by serving it with some of the garnishings suggested for Yellow rice. One of the ingredients in the dish is garam masala which is a combination of spices used frequently in Indian cooking. It can be bought in Indian food shops but if you wish to prepare your own a recipe is given below.

Serves 4 to 6

2 oz (¼ cup) butter or oil
2 medium onions, thinly sliced
2 cloves garlic, crushed
½ teaspoon powdered ginger
¼ teaspoon chili sauce
or
shredded fresh chili

½ teaspoon garam masala
12 oz (1½ cups) rice (brown or white), washed, drained and dried
1½ pt (3½ cups) water, boiling
4 oz (½ cup) tomato purée
salt to taste

Heat the butter or oil in a heavy pan and sauté the onions until golden brown. In a mortar or small bowl crush the garlic, ginger and chili into a paste and stir into the onions. Sprinkle in the garam masala and continue cooking for 1 or 2 minutes. Now put in the rice and fry, stirring, over a low heat for 5 minutes. Add the water and tomato purée and mix well. Season with salt, cover, reduce heat and simmer until all the liquid is absorbed and the rice is tender and fluffy (45 to 50 minutes for brown rice, 25 to 30 minutes for white rice).

To prepare garam masala

2 oz cumin seeds
1 oz cloves
1 oz cardamon seeds
4 oz coriander seeds

1 oz cinnamon
pinch mace
pinch nutmeg

Grind the ingredients together with a mortar and pestle or in the coffee grinder (clean well afterwards). Store in an airtight jar.

Vegetable kichiri

The English breakfast dish kedgeree (page 85) was derived from an Indian dish called kichiri, in which lentils (or other pulses), rice and other ingredients are cooked together in one pot. Kichiri is in fact nothing like kedgeree, which contains fish, but it did inspire the English.

3 oz (⅜ cup) butter or vegetable oil
1 medium onion, thinly sliced
1 medium carrot, grated
8 oz (1 cup) brown rice, washed,
    drained
4 oz (½ cup) green or brown lentils,
    soaked overnight, drained

2 tablespoons dessicated coconut
    (optional)
1 teaspoon cumin seeds
1 teaspoon powdered cinnamon
½ teaspoon turmeric
¼ teaspoon powdered cloves
1½ pt (3½ cups) water, boiling
salt to taste

Heat the butter or oil in a heavy pan and sauté the onions until just soft, add the carrots and continue sautéeing until the onions are coloured light brown. Put in the rice and lentils and fry, over a low heat, stirring, for 5 minutes. Add the coconut (if used) and spices, mix well and cook, stirring for a further 2 minutes. Pour in the water, mix, season to taste with salt. Reduce heat to as low as possible, cover pan and simmer for 45 to 50 minutes or until all the liquid is absorbed and the rice and lentils are tender. Serve with natural, unsweetened yoghurt.

Pilau (or pulao) dishes

This is the Indian equivalent of the Arab pilaff or the Spanish paella. There are as many varieties of pilaus as cooks who make them, and they can be as simple or as elaborate as you wish. Below are some suggested recipes that you can follow directly or use as a basis for your own improvisations.

Cauliflower and potato pilau

3 oz (⅓ cup) butter or oil
1 medium potato, peeled and diced
½ small head cauliflower, in sprigs
1 medium onion, finely sliced
2 cloves garlic, crushed
12 oz (1½ cups) rice (brown or white)
½ teaspoon cloves

½ teaspoon turmeric
½ teaspoon ginger
1 teaspoon cumin seeds
½ teaspoon garam masala
1 teaspoon cinnamon
1½ pt (3½ cups) water, boiling
salt to taste

Heat the oil in a heavy pan, add the potatoes and fry until they are half-cooked, remove from the pan and set aside. Add the cauliflower sprigs and fry until they are half-cooked. Remove from the pan and set aside. Add the onions and garlic and sauté until golden brown. Put in the rice and fry, stirring, for 2 to 3 minutes. Sprinkle in the spices, mix well and stir fry for another few minutes. Pour in the water, stir and season to taste with salt. Cook, uncovered, over a moderate heat until half the water in the pot has been absorbed or evaporated. Add the part-cooked potatoes and cauliflower. Now tightly cover the pot. For a really tight-fitting cover, place a double folded clean cloth over the pot and then put the lid on. Reduce heat and leave to simmer until the rice is tender and fluffy (15 to 20 minutes for white rice, 30 to 40 minutes for brown rice). Serve with unsweetened yoghurt or some of the garnishings suggested for Yellow rice (page 74).

Okra and green pepper pilau

Replace the potato and cauliflower in the above by 8 oz okra (ladies fingers) boiled for 2 minutes and drained, and 2 medium green peppers, thinly sliced.

Cashew and almond pilau

In this recipe some of the spices are left whole. They are not removed after cooking, but neither are they eaten!

3 oz (⅓ cup) butter or vegetable oil
1 inch piece cinnamon
3 cloves
3 cardamom seeds
6 pepper corns
½ teaspoon cumin seeds

12 oz (1½ cups) rice (brown or white)
1½ pt (3½ cups) water, boiling
2 oz (⅓ cup) almonds, blanched
2 oz (⅓ cup) cashews, lightly roasted
2 oz (⅓ cup) sultanas

Heat the oil in a heavy pan and fry the cinnamon, cloves, cardamoms, pepper corns and cumin seeds for 2 to 3 minutes. Add the rice and stir fry for 5 minutes. Pour in the water, reduce the heat, cover and simmer until the rice is nearly tender (20 to 25 minutes for white rice, 40 to 45 minutes for brown rice). Now stir in the nuts and sultanas, re-cover pot and cook until the rice is tender.

*Korma (meat) pulao

Spicy fried rice and spicy fried minced meat are cooked separately, combined, baked in the oven and served with a garnish of tomatoes, cucumber and boiled egg.

6 oz (⅔ cup) butter or oil
1 medium onion, diced
¾ lb minced beef or mutton
1 teaspoon ginger
1 teaspoon coriander
½ teaspoon turmeric
½ teaspoon chili sauce

or
shredded chili
12 oz (1½ cups) rice (brown or white)
6 cloves
1 inch piece cinnamon
1½ pt (3½ cups) water
salt to taste
2 medium tomatoes, thinly sliced
½ small cucumber, thinly sliced
2 boiled eggs, shelled, sliced

Heat half the butter or oil in a heavy frying pan and sauté the onion until golden brown. Add the beef, ginger, coriander, turmeric, chili and fry until the beef is nicely browned. Remove from the heat, cover and set aside. Heat the remaining half of the butter in a heavy pan, put in the rice, cloves and cinnamon and stir fry for 5 minutes. Pour in the boiling water, mix well and season to taste with salt. Reduce heat, cover and simmer until the rice is almost cooked (25 to 30 minutes for white rice, 45 to 50 minutes for brown rice). Meanwhile preheat an oven to 300°F (gas mark 2). Carefully combine the meat and rice mixture, and turn into a casserole. Cover and bake for 30 minutes. Serve garnished with the tomatoes, cucumber and egg, and a bowl of chilled yoghurt.

*Fish pulao

Follow the recipe for korma pulao, but replace the meat by 1 pound of filleted fish cut into 1 inch squares. For added flavour substitute fish stock for the rice water. Prepare the stock from the bones, skin and head of the filleted fish.

Zarda or sweet rice

This pudding depends on a long, slow cooking time on top of the oven to give a soft creamy texture to the rice. Serve hot or cold, sprinkled with cinnamon or the saffron milk described below.

8 oz (1 cup) short grain rice (white or brown)
2 pt (3 cups) milk
2 oz (⅓ cup) raisins

2 oz (⅓ cup) almonds, blanched and chopped
2 inch piece cinnamon
4 cardamom seeds (optional)
sugar to taste

Put the ingredients in a heavy saucepan and slowly bring to the boil. Reduce heat to as low as possible or stand pan on an asbestos pad, cover and simmer for at least 2 hours. Remove cinnamon and cardamoms and serve, or chill and serve cold. In either case serve with saffron milk if you wish.

Saffron milk

2 teaspoons saffron strands
¼ pt (½ cup) milk, hot

Toast the saffron gently under the grill and then crumble into the hot milk. Sprinkle this coloured saffron milk over the rice pudding before serving.

Chinese rice dishes

Rice, plain boiled, is served as an accompaniment to every Chinese meal, but sometimes it is used as an ingredient in a dish and in this case it is normally cooked in one of three ways. In the first method the rice and other ingredients, e.g. vegetables, meat or fish, etc., are cooked or steamed together. In the second they are stir fried together and in third a watery rice porridge is mixed with vegetables or meat or fish and then slowly simmered. This is known as congee rice.

Green pepper and mushroom rice

4 oz (1½ cups) small mushrooms
2 medium green peppers, sliced
1 lb (2 cups) brown or white rice

1½ pt (3½ cups) water
1 tablespoon soy sauce
2 tablespoons butter
salt to taste

Preheat oven to 350°F (gas mark 4). Layer the bottom of a casserole dish with the mushrooms and peppers and place the rice over the top. Pour in the water, add the soy sauce and butter and bring to the boil. Remove from the heat and season to taste with salt. Cover and bake in oven for 15 to 20 minutes for white rice or for 45 to 50 minutes for brown rice.

Variations
Cook the dish on top of the stove using a heavy pan and an asbestos pad for slow cooking. Add or substitute shelled or tinned peas, diced carrot, diced cucumber to the ingredients.

Simple fried rice

This well-known Chinese dish is really an excellent way of using up any left-over rice or vegetables you may have. It's best cooked very fast in a wok, but if you haven't got one use a large, heavy frying pan over a high heat.

2 tablespoons vegetable oil
1 lb (2 cups) cooked rice (white or
  brown)

2 eggs, beaten
few spring onions, chopped
soy sauce

Heat the oil in a heavy frying pan or wok over a high heat. Put the rice in the pan and stir fry for 2 to 3 minutes. Reduce the heat and pour in the eggs. Stir fry for 4 to 5 minutes. Transfer from pan to serving dish, sprinkle over spring onions and soy sauce to taste. Serve.

Vegetable fried rice

4 oz (½ cup) vegetable oil (sesame
  seed or peanut oil are best)
1 medium onion, diced
2 oz (½ cup) mushrooms, sliced
4 oz (½ cup) cooked peas
4 oz (½ cup) sweet corn (tinned)

2 eggs, beaten
1½ lb (3 cups) cooked rice (white or
  brown)
4 tablespoons soy sauce
salt to taste

Heat half the oil over a high heat, add the onion and stir fry for 1 minute. Add the mushrooms, peas and sweet corn and stir fry another 2 minutes. Transfer these vegetables to another container. Pour the eggs into the wok or frying pan and make an omelette (or scramble the eggs just before they set). Cut omelette (or scrambled egg) into pieces and combine with the fried vegetables. Add the remaining oil to the wok or frying pan and put in the rice. Stir fry for 2 to 3 minutes, then add the egg and vegetable mixture, soy sauce and salt to taste. Stir fry until the mixture is thoroughly heated through. Serve garnished with finely chopped spring onions or scallions. See p. 78 for Pork fried rice.

Congee

This is an economical and nourishing dish midway between a soup and a porridge. The recipe given uses only vegetables, but you may add pieces of pork or chicken on or off the bone.

8 oz (1 cup) rice (brown or white)
  washed
4 pt (10 cups) water
1 medium carrot, grated
and/or
6 oz (1 cup) water chestnuts

4 oz (1 cup) unsalted peanuts
4 oz (1 cup) bean sprouts
and/or
4 oz (1 cup) watercress
soy sauce to taste
salt to taste

Put the rice and water in a heavy saucepan, and bring to the boil. Cover and reduce heat to as low as possible. Simmer for 30 minutes, stir, add carrots and/or water chestnuts, peanuts and stir again. Simmer a further 30 minutes, add bean sprouts and/or watercress, stir well, season with soy sauce and salt. Cover pot and leave to simmer another hour. Serve garnished with chopped spring onions or parsley.

*Pork fried rice

This recipe uses cooked pork, but cooked chicken or prawns may be substituted.

4 oz (½ cup) vegetable oil (sesame or peanut oil are best)
1 medium onion, diced
2 eggs, beaten
8 oz (1 cup) cooked pork, diced
4 oz (1 cup) cooked peas

4 oz (1 cup) bean sprouts
1½ lb (3 cups) cooked rice (white or brown)
salt to taste
4 tablespoons soy sauce

Heat half the oil in a wok or heavy frying pan and stir fry the onion until golden brown. Drop in the beaten egg and scramble just before it sets. Remove to another container. Add the remaining oil to the wok or pan. Now add the pork and stir fry until nicely browned over a high heat. Drop in the peas and beansprouts and stir fry another minute. Put the rice and egg and onion mixture into the wok, season with salt and stir fry until the whole mixture is thoroughly heated through. Sprinkle with soy sauce and serve.

*Steamed chicken and brown rice

In this recipe the chicken is cleverly steamed over the rice whilst it's cooking. Do not restrict yourself only to the vegetables suggested but experiment with other combinations.

1 small chicken, jointed
or
4 pieces chicken, total weight 1½ lb
1 green pepper, thickly sliced
2 sticks celery, 1 inch pieces
4 spring onions, 1 inch pieces

1 tablespoon cornflour
2 tablespoons soy sauce
8 oz (1 cup) brown rice
1½ pt (3½ cups) water
salt to taste

Lightly coat the chicken and vegetables with a paste made from the cornflour and soy sauce. Set aside. Put the rice and water in a large, heavy pan and bring quickly to the boil, reduce the heat and gently boil the rice until firm enough to support the chicken and vegetables rested on top. At this point salt the rice to taste and then place in the chicken and vegetables. Cover the pot, reduce the heat to minimum and simmer until the rice and chicken are tender, and all the liquid has been absorbed (about 50 to 60 minutes). To improve the steaming process place a double folded clean cloth across the top of the pan before placing on the lid.

Japanese rice dishes

The following recipes are from *The Japanese Cookbook*, written by myself, published by Barrie & Jenkins.

It's unusual to find brown rice used in Japan, but it can be used in any of the following recipes except for the sushi rice recipe. In this dish the sticky starchiness of well-cooked white rice is required.

Red rice

This dish, in which red colouring is given to the rice by cooking it with aduki beans, is usually made with a variety of rice, called mochi, which is sweeter than the regular kind. It is known as Sekihan when made with mochi, and is a great favourite for festive occasions, especially Hina Matouri or Girls' Day. Mochi rice is not readily available in the West, and the recipe given here will be for regular rice. If you cannot obtain aduki beans, use red or kidney beans instead.

Rice and aduki beans eaten together provide a rich protein source as well as a colourful dish.

4 oz (½ cup) aduki beans, soaked in water six hours or more
2 pt (5 cups) water

1 lb (2 cups) rice, washed and drained
1 teaspoon salt
2 tablespoons sesame seeds, toasted

Drain the soaked beans. Place in pot with water, bring to the boil, reduce heat and simmer until cooked (about 1½ hours). Drain and reserve liquid. Put rice in pot, add the bean cooking liquid, plus, if necessary, enough water to make the volume up to 1½ pints (4 cups). Cover and bring to the boil. Add beans, mix and continue to simmer until rice is cooked. Combine salt and toasted sesame seeds. Serve red rice hot or cold, garnished with sesame seed and salt mixture (this mixture is called 'gomashio').

Deep-fried rice balls with barbecue sauce

Deep-fried food seems to have universal appeal, and this rice-ball dish is no exception. You may add other ingredients to the recipe than those suggested, e.g. minced beef, flaked fish, chopped vegetables, etc.

1½ lb (3 cups) cooked rice
1 medium leek, finely chopped
2 tablespoons vegetable oil
2 tablespoons miso
2 cloves garlic, crushed
1 oz (1 tablespoon) ginger root, grated
2 oz (½ cup) plain flour, sieved

oil for deep frying (including, if possible, 25% sesame seed oil)

Barbecue sauce
4 fl. oz (½ cup) soy sauce
4 fl. oz (½ cup) mirin or sweet sherry
1 tablespoon sugar

Combine barbecue sauce ingredients and gently simmer uncovered, until reduced to half original volume. Meanwhile, thoroughly mix all the other ingredients except the flour. Lightly wet hands and shape mixture into small balls (1 inch to 2 inches). Heat deep frying oil in wok or other pan, to about 350°F, roll rice balls in flour and deep fry (6 to 8 at a time) until brown and crisp. Drain well. If you are making a large quantity, keep the fried balls hot in a medium oven. Serve with barbecue sauce. Dip the hot rice balls in sauce before eating.

Donburi

Donburi dishes are large bowls of rice or noodles combined with vegetables or meat, and served topped with egg and perhaps a sauce. Alternatively, the vegetables and meat are mixed with the egg and the whole is fried, before topping the rice. Donburi means 'big bowl'. They can be rich dishes filled with many ingredients or simply cooked rice combined with left over vegetables topped with an omelette.

Vegetable donburi

1 lb (2 cups) rice washed and drained
2 tablespoons vegetable oil
2 small leeks, sliced
or
2 spring onions, thinly sliced
1 medium carrot, grated
4 leaves spinach, chopped

2 sticks celery, chopped
4 oz (1½ cups) mushrooms, sliced
2 tablespoons soy sauce
2 teaspoons sugar
salt to taste
pinch of black pepper
3 eggs, beaten

Cook the rice by the basic method. Meanwhile, heat the oil in a heavy pan and sauté the vegetables and mushrooms until just soft. Add the soy sauce, sugar and salt to taste. Pour over the beaten eggs, add a pinch of black pepper, stir and cook until eggs just set. Put cooked rice in serving bowl, top with egg and vegetables. Serve.

*Chicken donburi

For 4 to 6 people

1 small chicken or chicken pieces
    weighing 1 to 2 lb
1 lb (2 cups) rice, washed and drained
1½ pt (3½ cups) water
8 fl oz (1 cup) chicken stock
2 tablespoons mirin or sweet sherry
    (optional)

2 tablespoons soy sauce
8 oz (3 cups) mushrooms, sliced
4 oz (1 cup) peas (fresh, frozen or
    tinned)
3 eggs, beaten
1 teaspoon salt

Cut the chicken into 4 or 5 pieces and boil in the minimum of water until tender. Strain and reserve liquid. Remove the bones and skin from the chicken pieces and cut the flesh into small pieces. Cook rice by the basic method. Place part of the reserved chicken stock in a large pan and add the mirin or sherry, soy sauce, mushrooms and peas. Cook until vegetables are just soft. Gently mix into the pan the rice and chicken. Combine the egg and salt and pour over rice mixture. Stir well and maintain low heat until egg is just set. Serve in a 'big bowl'.

Sushi rice

Sushi is the word used to describe a variety of dishes in which cooked rice, seasoned with vinegar and sugar, is the basic ingredient. The recipe here is for nigiri-sushi in which the vinegared rice is moulded into an oval, round or square, shape and topped with one of a number of garnishes.

Sushi rice

For 4 people

1 lb (2 cups) white rice, washed and drained
1½ pt (4 cups) water
2 to 3 tablespoons sushi dressing

Sushi dressing
4 fl oz (½ cup) vinegar
6 oz (¾ cup) sugar
1 tablespoon salt

Dressing: combine vinegar, sugar and salt and bring to the boil. Turn off heat and leave. Use hot or cold, either way it gives the same result.

Cook the rice by the basic Japanese method (p. 63) for plain rice, then turn it into a wooden or non-metallic bowl. Pour the sushi dressing over the hot rice until a little will continue to remain unabsorbed in the bottom of the bowl. Now stir the rice gently with a wet rice paddle or wooden spoon, while with the other hand fanning the rice with a flat pan lid or rolled-up newspaper. This cools the rice quickly and gives it an authentic shine.

Nigiri-sushi

Prepare the Sushi rice by the basic method, and while it is still warm, prepare rice patties as follows: wet your hands and using about 1 heaped tablespoon of sushi rice, form a shape (e.g. oval, ball, square, etc.) in the palm of your hands. Continue until all the rice is used up. Wet your hands as necessary to prevent the rice sticking to them. Arrange the rice shapes on a serving dish and garnish with one or more of the suggested toppings below.

Garnishings for nigiri-sushi

Quantities have not been given, since the amount needed will depend on how much Sushi rice you have prepared, and how many different toppings you want to use.

1: Thin egg omelette cut into strips and brushed with soy sauce.
2: Smoked salmon in small pieces, sprinkled with fresh lemon juice.
3: Anchovies.
4: Cooked shrimps.
5: Sardines.
6: Prawns, shelled: leave tail intact and lightly cook.
7: Mussels, cooked.
8: Sliced pickled herring.
9: Fresh cucumber, sliced and sparingly spread with english mustard.
10: Sliced mushrooms, lightly cooked in equal parts of soy sauce and sugar.
11: Cooked vegetables, cut into suitable shapes.
12: Cooked chicken or meat, thinly sliced.
13: Sesame seeds, toasted.
14: Fish paste: grind cooked fish and garlic in a mortar and spread on sushi.

Variation
You may mix the garnishing with the Sushi rice before moulding into shape. The filled sushi is then garnished with toasted sesame seeds.

European rice dishes

Rice wasn't introduced into Europe until around the thirteenth century when Arab invaders carried it with them into Spain where it became very popular. Later it spread to Italy and since those times rice has been cultivated in these countries. It is from Italy and Spain that most European rice dishes have originated: the most famous examples being risotto and paella. Perhaps the major contributions European cooks have made to rice cooking is the introduction of cheese to the ingredients with which rice is cooked and the creation of baked rice dishes.

Risotto

An Italian dish, very similar to pilau and pilaff, but using short-grain Italian rice instead of the long-grain variety. The rice grains in the risotto should be moist but separate. The Italians never wash their rice either before or after cooking and normally boil it in stock not water.

Risotto Milanese

4 oz (¼ cup) butter or olive oil
2 cloves garlic, crushed
1 medium onion, diced
12 oz (1½ cups) rice (Italian short
  grain if possible) brown or white
2 pt (5 cups) stock or water, hot
4 oz (1½ cups) mushrooms, chopped

2 tablespoons white wine or sherry
  (optional)
1 teaspoon basil
½ teaspoon turmeric
salt and black pepper to taste
4 oz (½ cup) cheese grated (parmesan
  if possible)

Heat the butter or oil in a heavy saucepan or casserole, add the garlic and onion and sauté until they start to colour. Add the rice and stir over a low heat for 8 to 10 minutes. Pour in the hot stock or water, mix well and cook over a low heat for 5 minutes. Now add the wine, mushrooms, basil, turmeric and season to taste with salt and black pepper. Cover and continue cooking until all the liquid is absorbed (about 20 to 25 minutes for white rice and 45 to 50 minutes for brown rice). Remove from the heat, stir in the cheese and transfer to a hot serving dish. Pass around more cheese when serving the risotto if desired. Serve with a fresh tomato salad.

Variations
Thinly sliced chopped ham, pieces of chicken, chicken livers, beef, pork, fish, shell fish, etc., may be added to the risotto. Follow the above recipe and fry whichever ingredient you decide to add with the onion and garlic before the addition of the rice.

Ratatouille and rice

8 oz (2 cups) courgettes (zucchini),
  sliced
2 small aubergines (eggplant), sliced
salt
4 tablespoons vegetable oil
2 medium onions, sliced
2 cloves garlic, crushed

2 medium green peppers, sliced
8 oz (1 cup) tinned tomatoes
black pepper to taste
1 lb (2 cups) rice (white or brown)
2 pt (5 cups) water or stock
parmesan cheese, grated

Salt the courgette and aubergine slices and set aside for 30 minutes, then rinse and dry. Heat the oil in a saucepan and fry the onion rings and garlic for 2 to 3 minutes. Add the courgettes and aubergines and fry for 2 to 3 minutes on each side (you may need to add more oil). Add the sliced peppers and tomatoes and season the mixture. Cover the pan and cook slowly for an hour or more. Meanwhile bring the rice and water to the boil, reduce heat, cover and simmer until cooked. Time the rice so that it is just tender when the ratatouille is cooked.

Put the rice in a hot serving bowl, gently stir in the ratatouille and serve with grated cheese.

Italian baked rice

Serves 6

2 lb (4 cups) cooked rice (brown or white)
½ teaspoon black pepper
2 teaspoons salt
4 oz (½ cup) tomato purée

8 fl oz (1 cup) stock or water
1 medium green pepper, diced
8 oz (1 cup) cheese, grated
4 oz (1 cup) brown breadcrumbs
2 oz (¼ cup) butter

Preheat oven to 350°F (gas mark 4). Combine all the ingredients except the breadcrumbs and butter. Turn the mixture into a lightly greased casserole dish. Cover with breadcrumbs and dot the top with butter. Bake for 30 minutes. Serve with a fresh lettuce and tomato salad.

Rice stuffed green peppers

Serves 4 to 6

4 oz (½ cup) vegetable oil
1 medium onion, diced
4 oz (1½ cups) mushrooms, sliced
2 oz (1 cup) chopped nuts
or
cooked beans (e.g. chick-peas, red beans, etc.)

1½ lb (3 cups) cooked rice, (white or brown)
4 oz (½ cup) cheese, grated
salt and black pepper to taste
6 large green peppers

Preheat oven to 375°F (gas mark 5). Use part of the oil to grease a baking dish and pour the rest into a heavy frying pan. Add the onion and sauté until golden, add mushrooms and cook until tender. Remove from the heat and stir in the nuts or beans, rice, cheese and mix well. Season to taste with salt and black pepper. Cut the tops off the peppers and remove seeds and core. Stuff with the rice mixture. Separate the outer rings of the pepper tops from the inner stalks and put them back on top of the stuffed peppers. Put the peppers into the greased baking dish, pour into the bottom of the dish ½ inch to 1 inch of water and bake for 40 to 45 minutes or until peppers are cooked. Serve with a tomato sauce or grated parmesan cheese.

Paella

This famous Spanish dish is named after the large, flat pan with two handles in which it is cooked. The pan doubles as a serving dish. You may equally well use a heavy frying pan and a serving dish. Paella is traditionally cooked with meat and fish together, but you can make a delicious paella with vegetables alone. 2 recipes are given.

★Traditional paella

Serves 6 to 8

4 oz (½ cup) vegetable oil (olive oil if possible)
2 cloves garlic, crushed
2 medium onions, diced
2 medium green peppers, sliced
2 to 3 lb chicken, jointed into 8 pieces
8 oz garlic sausage, sliced

2 medium tomatoes, chopped
4 oz (½ cup) green peas
12 oz (1½ cups) rice (brown or white)
1½ pt (4 cups) stock or water
salt and black pepper to taste
4 oz (½ cup) cooked shrimps or prawns

Heat the oil in a heavy frying pan and sauté the garlic and onion until they start to colour, add the peppers and sauté a further 2 minutes. Add the chicken and brown on both sides, then add the sausage, tomatoes and peas and continue frying for a few minutes. Stir in the rice and cook, stirring, until the rice begins to brown. Pour in the stock, season with salt and black pepper and cook rapidly for 5 minutes. Reduce heat and simmer until rice and chicken are cooked and liquid is absorbed. Add more water if needed. Towards the end of cooking time stir in the shrimps or prawns. Simmering time for white rice will be 15 to 20 minutes and for brown rice 40 to 45 minutes.

Vegetable paella

4 oz (½ cup) vegetable oil
2 cloves garlic, crushed
2 medium onions, sliced
2 medium green peppers, sliced
2 medium tomatoes, chopped
12 oz (1½ cups) rice (brown or white)
1½ pt (4 cups) water or stock
salt and black pepper to taste

4 oz (1 cup) cucumber, peeled and diced
2 sticks celery, chopped
1 tablespoon parsley, chopped
2 oz (¼ cup) chopped nuts (optional)
2 oz (¼ cup) olives
4 oz (½ cup) cheese, grated

Heat the oil in a heavy frying pan and sauté the garlic and onions until they start to colour. Add the pepper and sauté a further 2 to 3 minutes. Stir in the tomatoes and rice and cook over a low heat until the rice starts to brown. Pour in the water or stock, season to taste with salt and black pepper and boil rapidly for 5 minutes. Add the cucumber, celery, parsley and chopped nuts, reduce heat to simmer and cook until the rice is tender and all the liquid is absorbed. Simmering time for white rice is 20 to 25 minutes, and for brown rice 40 to 45 minutes. Add more water as needed if it dries up. Serve garnished with olives and cheese.

Cheese rice cakes

Make these rice cakes with brown rice, it gives them a chewy texture which contrasts well with the soft cheese.

12 oz (1½ cups) cooked brown rice
8 oz (1 cup) cheese, finely grated
or
cottage cheese
1 small onion, finely diced
2 eggs, beaten
salt and black pepper to taste

1 tablespoon wholemeal flour or
   cornmeal
pinch nutmeg
pinch cinnamon
4 oz (1 cup) breadcrumbs
oil for frying

Combine the rice, cheese, onion and half the beaten egg and mix well. Stir in the flour and seasoning and add a little more flour or water, whichever is needed, to form a firm mixture that will hold its shape. Form into 10 to 12 cakes. Dip the cakes in the remaining beaten egg and roll in breadcrumbs. Heat the oil in a heavy frying pan and brown cakes on both sides. Serve.

Variations
Dip the cakes in flour and then parmesan cheese instead of breadcrumbs.

*Kedgeree

The English version of the Indian Kichiri (page 73). Eaten for breakfast in Victorian times.

1½ lb (3 cups) cooked rice
1 lb (2 cups) cooked filleted fish,
   skinned and flaked
salt and pepper to taste

pinch of nutmeg
2 hard-boiled eggs, chopped
2 oz (¼ cup) butter, melted
lemon juice

Preheat oven to 375° (gas mark 5). Combine the rice and fish and mix well. Season to taste with salt and black pepper and add a pinch of nutmeg. Stir in the hard-boiled egg and butter. Place mixture in a dish and heat in oven until hot enough to serve. Sprinkle with lemon juice and serve.

*Pork and rice hash

2 oz (¼ cup) pork fat or cooking oil
1 medium onion, diced
1 teaspoon paprika
1 lb lean pork in 1 inch cubes
1 pt (2½ cups) water

8 oz (1 cup) rice (white or brown)
3 medium green peppers, sliced
4 medium tomatoes, chopped
salt and black pepper to taste

Preheat oven to 375°F (gas mark 5). Heat the fat or oil in a heavy saucepan, add the onion and sauté until just soft. Sprinkle over the paprika and add the pork. Brown on both sides and then pour in a quarter of the water. Reduce heat and simmer gently for 10 minutes. Now stir in the rice, pepper and tomatoes and remaining water, season to taste with salt and black pepper and return to the boil. Transfer to a casserole, cover and bake in oven for 45 minutes to 1 hour or until all the liquid is absorbed and the rice is tender.

*Rice and fried chicken casserole

2 tablespoons flour
2 teaspoons thyme
2 to 3 lb chicken, jointed in eight
   pieces
4 oz (½ cup) butter or oil
2 medium onions, finely chopped
2 cloves garlic, crushed

1 carrot, chopped
salt and black pepper to taste
8 oz (1 cup) rice (white or brown)
1¼ pt (3 cups) chicken stock (prepared
   from chicken giblets)
2 oz (¼ cup) tomato purée
2 bay leaves

Preheat oven to 350°F (gas mark 4). Combine the flour and thyme, and dust the chicken pieces with the mixture. Heat the butter or oil in a heavy frying pan and fry the chicken brown on both sides. Set chicken aside. In the same pan sauté the onions and garlic until golden, add the carrot and sauté a further 2 to 3 minutes. Season with salt and pepper and stir in the rice. Cook and stir over a moderate heat until the rice is lightly coloured. Pour in the stock, stir in the tomato purée and put in the bay leaves. Grease a casserole dish and turn the rice mixture into it. Put the chicken on top, cover and bake in oven for 1 hour. Remove cover and bake for 30 minutes.

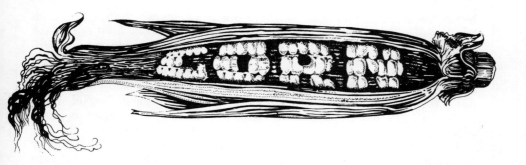

Introduction

Corn grain is not as nutritionally complete as whole rice or whole wheat. However, whole corn kernels or whole corn meal is more nutritious than either white rice or white flour and eaten in combination with other foods, particularly beans, it is an excellent food source. Corn is more generally eaten in its whole form than either rice or wheat and this, coupled with its adaptability to different growing conditions, and its ease of cultivation, makes maize a valuable world food crop. America, where corn is the most valuable annual food crop, is the world's largest producer, but substantial amounts of corn are grown in many other countries.

Wild corn has never been found, nor has any wild predecessor been identified. In the Americas corn has been a staple domestic crop for thousands of years, and during this time the indigenous Indians developed a diversity of types. It now flourishes from as far north as northern Canada to as far south as Argentina. In the Old World corn was unknown until the end of the fifteenth century when Columbus brought some of the grain back from his discovery voyage to America.

The botanical origins of corn will possibly never be discovered, however, the Indians of Ecuador do have a lovely story about its beginnings which I'm sure is much more interesting than the real one would be. Of course this story could be true, and it makes a nice beginning to this chapter.

Many thousands of years ago there was a terrible flood and only two Indian brothers managed to survive. They did so by climbing to the top of the highest mountain in the land. Just as they were about to die of hunger and thirst, two gaily coloured parrots flew to them with food and drink both made from the maize plant. The brothers were revitalized, and one of them quickly captured one of the parrots. It turned into a beautiful woman who gave them maize seeds and taught them how to plant and grow the crop. She became the mother of the first Indian tribe and maize became their basic food.

The history of maize or corn

The various names of corn or maize have created much confusion as to its origins, and to which crop ancient travellers and historians were referring to in their writings. In the USA the crop is known as corn from the English word *corne*, meaning staple grain. Because it was cultivated by the Indians, early settlers in America called it Indian corn. The other name by which the crop is well known, maize, is from the Spanish *maiz*, which was taken from one of the Indian words that sound similar, e.g. *maisi* from the Cuban Indians, or *marisi* from the Indians of Guyana.

The classical name for the plant is *Zea mays*, given to it by the eighteenth-century scholar Linnaeus in his work, *Species Plantarum*, published in 1753. He noted that translations of the Indian words for maize generally meant something similar to 'our life' or 'she who feeds us', and so gave the grain the name *zea*, meaning 'cause of life' in Greek, and *mays* to describe the plant.

There were some theories that corn was introduced into Europe from Asia by the Arabs in the sixteenth century, but it is now generally believed that corn originated from the Americas where it has been grown for 5 to 10 thousand years.

The Indians of the Americas probably migrated there from Asia towards the end of the last ice age, 20,000 years ago. This was before wheat or rice were domesticated crops, and they probably didn't take any seeds of these grains with them. They settled in the highlands of Mexico, but later moved eastwards and settled on the coast lands of the Gulf of Mexico, where the ancient Maya civilization developed. On these fertile lands the Mayan farmers developed many hybrids of corn, some of which are still grown today.

By the time the Americas were discovered by Old World explorers in the late fifteenth century, maize was the chief crop of all North and South America. Columbus after the discovery of Cuba in 1492, took ears of corn back to the court of Spain to show the king. The crop was subsequently cultivated in Spain and later in Portugal. The Portuguese took it to Africa from where it spread to Asia. In less than a century corn spread across the world.

The maize or corn plant

Maize belongs to the grass family *Gramineae* and the more particular category within this family of *Maydae* grasses. This group is composed of eight species, one of which is *Zea mays*, from which all cultivated corns are derived. Five main varieties of corn are grown commercially, they are: dent, flint, flour, sweet and popcorn. Sweet corn or corn on the cob and cornmeal made from dent corn are the types of corn probably best known to the cook. Dent corn can be grown in either yellow or white varieties, but the two are interchangeable for the purpose of cooking.

The plant has long ribbon–like leaves, which allow it to expose a large surface area to the sun. From the leaf bases at the central stalk of the plant the ears of corn start to grow. They are surrounded by a protective layer of leaves, and are tipped with thin silky threads which form part of the female flower of corn. At the top of the central stalk grows a spiked tassel containing the male flowers. During the fertilization stage of the plant's growth pollen from these flowers drops onto the female flowers and fertilizes them. Grains or seeds of corn grow on the developing cob or ear of corn in the tightly packed rows characteristic of corn. The tiny corn seeds fill up with a milky liquid and then harden as the crop ripens.

The hybridization of a corn plant is a simple matter, and it mainly entails dusting the female flower of one type of corn with the pollen from another. In this way corn to suit a variety of conditions has been developed.

For a high-yield crop, the plant needs a well-drained, rich soil with plenty of sun and protection from the frost and cold. Maturing time varies from 2 to 7 months.

Maize and nutrition

Before discussing the nutritional qualities of maize or corn, we should note the difference between dent corn which is grown for use as a cereal grain, sweet corn or corn on the cob which is grown for use as a vegetable, and popcorn. Sweet corn is too soft and too sweet to be dried and ground into a flour. Its protein content is slightly higher than many other vegetables, but it's much lower than that of dent corn, and its nutritional worth should really be compared to that of other fresh vegetables than to other grains. Popcorn is made from a variety of corn with particularly hard endosperms. If the corn is heated rapidly the endosperms burst with a loud bang, hence the name. Popcorn is poor nutritionally and should really only be considered as a fun food.

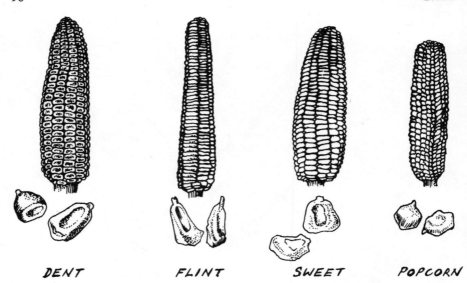

DENT   FLINT   SWEET   POPCORN

Whole dent corn or maize is the most important corn nutritionally. It is slightly less nutritious than whole rice or wheat due to a deficiency in niacin (vitamin B_5), and a slightly lower protein content. However, in its whole form it compares more than favourably with white rice or white flour. It contains substantial amounts of phosphorus and iron and thiamine (vitamin B_1) and smaller quantities of riboflavin (B) and carotene, the precursor to vitamin A. Wholecorn has an average of 9% by weight of protein. Eaten with other foods, particularly beans and vegetables, whole maize or corn is an excellent addition to the diet. See Table 5 on page 57 for a comparison of the nutritional contents of maize, rice and wheat.

Dent corn is the variety from which nearly all commercially available cornmeals or flours are made. It is very rarely eaten in the whole form since milling it into flour increases its digestibility and the variety of ways in which it may be used. Tinned or frozen corn kernels are obtained from sweet corn or dent corn.

The maize grain

The bran which comprises 5% to 6% by weight of the grain is composed of the protective, tough, fibrous outer layer of the grain. Maize flour or meal in which the bran is sifted out is called bolted corn flour. Some valuable roughage and minerals are lost in the process.

The endosperm forms the main part (80% to 85%) of the grain and contains much of the protein and most of the starch. It can be divided into 3 sections. The first is a one cell deep outer layer or aleurose layer, which is rich in protein and fat. The second section underneath the aleurone layer is the horny or tough part of the endosperm. This region is much harder than the corresponding areas of the rice or wheat grain and gives corn meal its characteristic grainy texture. It is, along with the germ, the most nutritionally valuable part of the grain. The third inner section is called the flour endosperm, and is a softer, mainly starchy region.

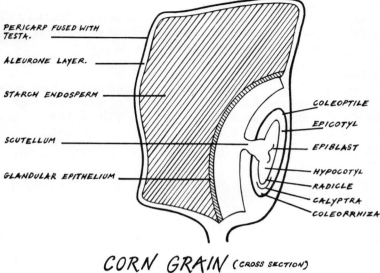

PERICARP FUSED WITH TESTA.

ALEURONE LAYER.

STARCH ENDOSPERM

SCUTELLUM

GLANDULAR EPITHELIUM

COLEOPTILE

EPICOTYL

EPIBLAST

HYPOCOTYL

RADICLE

CALYPTRA

COLEORRHIZA

CORN GRAIN (CROSS SECTION)

The germ of the grain contains the nutrients needed for the development of the grain or seed into a plant. It is much larger than its equivalent in rice or wheat and is rich in fat and protein. Half of the fat is composed of linolin which gives linoleic acid one of the essential unsaturated fatty acids needed but not synthesized by the body.

Types of maize and maize flour

Dent corn is the variety from which nearly all commercially available cornmeals or flours are made. The broad top of the grain has a longitudinal groove or dent from which its name derives. The following definitions refer to dent corn products.

Whole maize
To prepare whole maize the grains are dried on the cob and then removed. However, maize is very rarely eaten in this form since milling it into flour increases its digestibility, and the variety of ways it may be used. Tinned or frozen whole corn kernels are obtained from sweet corn on the cob not dent corn.

Whole maize or cornmeal
The whole grain is ground into flour of 95% to 100% extraction. This meal retains all the goodness of the corn. Stoneground is best if you can obtain it.

Bolted maize or cornmeal
The whole grain is milled and then the coarse bran pieces are sifted out. This is 90% to 95% extraction meal or flour and it contains most of the goodness of the grain. It is better than whole maize meal for preparing breads or other dishes where a smooth texture is desired.

Cornflour (degerminated maize meal)
Made from the whole grain with the bran and germ parts removed. Gives a flour of 85% or less extraction. Not as nutritious as whole maize flour, but excellent for thickening up soups, sauces, etc.

Hominy flour or grits
Hominy, an old American food sometimes called samp, is made by treating kernels of corn with lye, which dissolves the skin. They are then washed several times in water, boiled for several hours and finally dried. Hominy grits are made by coarsely milling dried hominy.

Corn can be cooked in a variety of ways and forms, but the recipe section is concerned primarily with the three most popular methods. The first part of the section is devoted to fresh corn on the cob dishes. In most of the recipes tinned or frozen sweet corn can be substituted when fresh corn is unavailable. The second gives recipes for corn breads, cakes, muffins, etc. Cornmeal does not have the breadmaking qualities of wheat flour that allow risen doughs to be made, but the characteristic granular texture of unleavened cornbreads and cakes is a nice change from lighter more porous wheat products. The final part of the recipe section is concerned with boiled cornmeal dishes, in which cornmeal is boiled in water or milk or other liquids along with oil, spices, cheese, vegetables, etc. Sometimes the boiled cornmeal mixture is chilled, cut into pieces and fried.

To preserve fresh corn

This method is given really for the benefit of American readers, since in Britain fresh corn is normally either too scarce or too expensive to consider preserving it.

Leave the husks on the ears of fresh sweet corn, and bake in a moderate oven for one hour. Remove from the oven, allow to cool, draw back the husks, and remove the silks. Hang the corn by husks in a dry storage area. Cut the corn kernels from the cob as required. As a substitute for fresh whole corn kernels the corn should be soaked overnight before use. For cornmeal, mill the kernels in a hand grinder and soak the meal for about an hour in water to cover before cooking.

Fresh corn and corn on the cob dishes

Boiled corn on the cob

Buy the freshest corn you can, and test for freshness by pressing one of the kernels: if it spurts juice it's fresh. The following recipe gives the simplest and one of the best ways of preparing corn on the cob. Serve the corn with a good size knob of butter.

4 ears of corn	pinch basil (optional)
water	butter
salt	

If the corn hasn't already been stripped, remove the husks and silk. (To remove the silk, hold the ear of corn under a cold running tap and brush with a soft vegetable brush.) Bring a large pan of water to the boil (there should be enough water to just cover all the ears of corn), add a pinch of salt and basil, and then drop in the corn. Return water to the boil and cook corn for 4 to 6 minutes or until tender. Drain and serve with a knob of butter.

Baked corn on the cob

The method following is an excellent way of preparing corn on the cob for out of doors parties or on camping trips when a wood fire or charcoal grill could be used in place of the oven.

4 ears of corn in husks
1 tablespoon vegetable oil

or

melted butter
salt to taste

Preheat oven to 425°F (gas mark 7). Open the ears of corn by gently turning back the husks. Remove the silk and then brush each ear with oil or butter, and sprinkle with salt to taste. Replace the husks and bake until tender, about 15 minutes. To cook on a camp fire, allow the flames to die down and place the corn prepared as above, on the hot embers. Keep turning and bake for 15 to 20 minutes.

Succotash

This is a traditional American Indian dish prepared with fresh corn and vegetables and sometimes meat. You may substitute tinned or frozen corn if fresh corn is unavailable. Serve with rice and noodles, etc., or on its own with crusty French bread.

4 ears of corn, husk and silk removed
or
1 lb (2 cups) tinned sweet corn or
    frozen corn kernels
1 tablespoon oil
2 medium green peppers, diced

12 oz small courgettes (zucchini)
    thinly sliced
salt to taste
2 tablespoons sunflower seeds,
    crushed

Cut the corn kernels off the cob as close to the cob as possible and set aside (or use tinned or frozen corn). Heat the oil in a heavy pan, add the peppers and courgettes (zucchini) and sauté over a moderate heat for 2 to 3 minutes. Add the corn and salt to taste, reduce heat and simmer, stirring, for 10 minutes. Stir in the sunflower seeds and cook for a further 5 minutes. Add a little water if the mixture gets too dry.

Variations
1: Replace courgettes by 12 oz of fresh or tinned string beans, cut into 2 inch lengths.
2: Add 8 oz (1 cup) of cooked beans (haricot, kidney, etc.) to the pan at the same time as you add the corn.
3: Sauté 1 lb minced beef along with the peppers and courgettes and extend cooking time by 5 to 10 minutes.

Spicy corn casserole

2 tablespoons vegetable oil
1 clove garlic, crushed
1 medium onion, diced
3 large ripe tomatoes, chopped
or
8 oz (1 cup) tinned tomatoes
1 small chili pepper, chopped

or
½ teaspoon hot pepper sauce
1 lb (2 cups) of fresh corn, cut from the cobs
or
1 lb (2 cups) tinned or frozen corn
salt and black pepper to taste
8 fl oz (1 cup) milk

Heat the oil in a heavy pan, add the garlic and onion and sauté until golden. Add the tomatoes, chili pepper and corn, mix well, reduce heat and cook, stirring, for 10 minutes. Now season to taste with salt and black pepper, pour in the milk and cover. Reduce heat to low and simmer for 20 to 25 minutes.

Corn baked in green peppers

4 large green peppers
12 oz (1½ cups) fresh corn, cut from the cobs and cooked
or
12 oz (1½ cups) tinned or frozen corn

4 oz (1 cup) dry breadcrumbs
1 teaspoon dried thyme
½ teaspoon black pepper
1 teaspoon salt
8 oz (1 cup) cheese, grated

Preheat oven to 375°F (gas mark 5). Cut the tops off the peppers and deseed. Combine the corn, breadcrumbs, thyme, black pepper, salt and the cheese and mix well. Stuff the peppers with the mixture. Carefully remove the inner stalks from the tops of the peppers and replace the tops on the stuffed peppers. Place the peppers in a casserole and run in hot water to a depth of 1 inch. Cover and bake for 30 minutes or until peppers are tender.

Fresh corn and lentil chowder

This is a delicious thick soup which, if served with slices of wholemeal bread, is as filling as a main meal. Use tinned or frozen corn if fresh is unavailable.

Serves 6

3 ears of corn, husks and silk removed
2 pt (5 cups) water
2 tablespoons vegetable oil
1 medium onion, sliced

2 medium potatoes, diced
3 stalks celery, chopped
4 oz (½ cup) split red lentils
salt and black pepper to taste

Bring the water to the boil in a heavy pan, add the ears of corn and boil for 5 minutes. Remove pan from the heat and allow to stand for 10 minutes. Meanwhile heat the oil in a frying pan and sauté the onion until golden, add the potatoes and celery and sauté, stirring, over a moderate heat for 5 minutes. Remove the corn from the pan leaving the cooking water in the pan. On a cutting board and with a sharp knife, cut the corn kernels off the cob. Return the corn to the pan, add the sautéed vegetables, lentils and season to taste with salt and black pepper. Bring to the boil, cover and gently boil for 30 minutes or until lentils are cooked and vegetables are very tender.

Scalloped (casseroled) corn

A simple dish, quick to prepare and excellent served with a fresh salad. For more elaborate variations see suggestions below.

Serves 4 to 6

1 lb (2 cups) fresh, cooked corn
or
1 lb (2 cups) tinned or frozen corn
8 fl oz (1 cup) milk or water
4 oz (1 cup) dry breadcrumbs

2 oz (¼ cup) melted butter
salt and black pepper to taste
1 medium green pepper, diced
1 small onion, diced
4 oz (½ cup) cheese, grated

Preheat oven to 350°F (gas mark 4). Combine the corn and milk and allow to stand for 10 minutes. Stir the breadcrumbs into the melted butter and season with salt and black pepper. Add the green pepper and onion and mix well. Combine half this breadcrumb and vegetable mixture with the corn and milk and put into a lightly greased casserole. Cover with remaining vegetable mixture and sprinkle cheese over the top. Bake uncovered for 30 minutes.

Variations

1: Add 8 oz (1 cup) tinned tomatoes to the milk and corn.
2: Blend the milk with 4 oz (½ cup) cooked chick-peas before addition to the corn.
3: Omit the cheese topping and top with a mixture of 2 oz (½ cup) breadcrumbs and 1 oz (⅛ cup) butter, melted.
4: Add 6 oz boiled prawns or shrimps to the breadcrumb mixture and serve garnished with slices of hard-boiled egg.

Sweetcorn and apple on toasted bread

This is a Russian treat. Just right for an unusual light supper or afternoon tea.

1 tablespoon vegetable oil
1 medium onion, diced
8 oz (1 cup) tinned sweet corn, drained
2 tablespoons tomato purée

salt and black pepper to taste
2 medium apples, quartered
2 tablespoons water
4 slices hot buttered toast

Heat the oil in a small pan and sauté the onion until just soft. Add the sweet corn, stir in the tomato purée, season to taste with salt and black pepper, and heat through. Cook the apple quarters in the water until just tender, but not mushy. Top the toast with sweetcorn mixture and apple quarters and serve.

Savoury corn pudding

1½ lb (3 cups) fresh corn cut from the cobs
or
1½ lb (3 cups) tinned or frozen corn
1 tablespoon flour
2 teaspoons salt

1 teaspoon black pepper
2 eggs, beaten
1 medium onion, diced
½ pt (1¼ cups) milk
1 oz butter

Preheat oven to 350°F (gas mark 4). Combine the corn with the flour, salt and pepper and mix well. Stir in the beaten egg and onion and finally mix in the milk. Pour the mixture into a lightly greased casserole and dot the top with butter. Bake uncovered for 40 minutes or until set.

Savoury egg and corn cakes

3 ears of corn, boiled tender
or
12 oz (1½ cups) tinned or frozen corn
3 oz (⅔ cup) wholemeal flour or cornmeal

salt and black pepper to taste
3 eggs, separated
3 oz (⅓ cup) vegetable oil or melted
   butter
oil for frying

On a cutting board and with a sharp knife, cut the boiled corn kernels off the cob. Combine the corn with flour or cornmeal and season to taste with salt and black pepper. Beat the egg yolks and stir into the mixture together with the oil or melted butter. Beat the egg whites and fold in. Heat the oil in a heavy frying pan over a high flame and drop in spoonful amounts of the mixture. Brown, turn and brown on the other side. Serve.

Summer vegetable and corn bake

2 tablespoons vegetable oil
2 cloves garlic, crushed
1 medium onion, diced
1 lb courgettes (zucchini) sliced
or
marrow (squash) cubed
1 medium green pepper, diced
3 large ripe tomatoes, chopped
8 oz (1 cup) fresh corn, cut off the cob

or
8 oz (1 cup) tinned or frozen corn
1 tablespoon fresh basil, chopped
or
1 teaspoon dried basil
½ teaspoon cumin powder
½ teaspoon coriander powder
salt and black pepper to taste
2 oz (¼ cup) cheese, grated

Preheat oven to 350°F (gas mark 4). Heat the oil in an ovenproof casserole. Add the garlic and onion and sauté until golden. Stir in the other vegetables and add all the herbs, spices and seasoning. Mix well, cover and bake for 45 minutes. Remove lid, sprinkle with cheese and bake a further 20 minutes. Serve.

Corn and cornmeal dumplings

8 oz (1 cup) tinned sweetcorn
8 oz (1 cup) wholemeal flour

3 tablespoons cornmeal
pinch salt

Mash or blend the corn into a creamy paste. Combine the flour, cornmeal and salt and mix well. Stir into the corn paste and blend well. If the dough is too stiff, add a little water or milk. Drop tablespoonful amounts into boiling soup or stew.

Walnut, corn and potato loaf

Serves 6 to 8

8 oz (1 cup) fresh corn cut off the cob	2 ripe tomatoes, peeled
or	4 oz (1 cup) breadcrumbs
8 oz (1 cup) tinned or frozen corn	2 eggs, beaten
4 oz (½ cup) walnuts, chopped	1 clove garlic, crushed
1 medium onion, finely diced	2 tablespoons fresh parsley, chopped
8 oz (1 cup) boiled, mashed potato	salt and black pepper to taste

Preheat oven to 350°F (gas mark 4). Combine all the ingredients and mix well. Pack into a greased 2 lb bread tin. Bake in oven for 45 minutes to 1 hour. A knife pushed into the centre of the loaf will come out clean when the loaf is cooked.

★Hot beef and corn stew

2 tablespoons lard or oil	*or*
1 lb beef, cut into 1 inch cubes	12 oz (1½ cups) tinned or frozen corn
2 cloves garlic, crushed	8 oz (1 cup) tinned tomatoes
1 medium onion, diced	salt and black pepper to taste
1 chili pepper, shredded	2 tablespoons sunflower seeds,
or	roasted (optional)
½ teaspoon hot chili sauce	
12 oz (1½ cups) fresh corn cut off the cob	

Heat the lard or oil in heavy pan or frying pan, add the beef and brown on all sides. Add the garlic and onion and sauté over a low heat for a further 5 minutes. Add the chili pepper, corn and tomatoes, stir well and season to taste with salt and black pepper. Cover pan and simmer for 20 minutes or until meat is tender. Serve sprinkled with roasted sunflower seeds.

Popcorn

Freshly made popcorn is a treat to eat and bears no resemblance to the cold sweet popcorn eaten in cinemas in Britain or to the slightly warm salted popcorn eaten in cinemas in America.

vegetable oil
popcorn
salt or sugar to taste

Thickly coat the bottom of a heavy saucepan with oil, but do not add so much that the corn floats, otherwise it will fry rather than pop. Heat the oil until a small drop of water splutters if dropped in. Add enough popcorn to cover the bottom of the pan and put the lid on. Carefully shake the corn about and in a minute or two it will start to pop and fill the pan. After a couple of minutes when all the corn has popped, turn the popcorn into a bowl and sprinkle over either salt or sugar to taste. Whilst your guests are finishing off that bowl prepare another.

Corn breads, cakes, muffins, etc.

For all the following recipes be sure to use maize or corn meal that is not deger-minated and which is preferably stone ground. This type of cornmeal should be easy to obtain in America, but it is not that generally available in Britain. Polenta or maize meal bought from health or wholefood stores is normally suitable. British readers should be careful not to confuse cornmeal with cornflour or corn starch which is only suitable as a thickening agent.

Corn bread

This is the basic recipe. You may add to it other ingredients (e.g. soaked dried fruit, cheese, sautéed vegetables, nuts, etc.)

6 oz (1 cup) cornmeal
8 oz (2 cups) wholemeal or strong white flour
1 teaspoon baking powder
¼ teaspoon baking soda

1 teaspoon salt
2 tablespoons melted butter
½ pt (1¼ cups) milk or water
1 egg

Preheat oven to 400°F (gas mark 6). Sift all the dry ingredients together and stir in the melted butter. Mix well. Combine the milk or water and egg and stir into the cornmeal mixture. Pour into a greased 8 inch by 8 inch cake tin or equivalent (a casserole dish will do) and bake for 20 to 25 minutes. If you wish, cut into squares whilst still warm.

Southern corn bread

This is a richer bread with a lighter texture than that made by the corn bread recipe above.

6 oz (1 cup) cornmeal
8 fl oz (1 cup) milk, very hot
4 oz (1 cup) wholemeal or strong white flour

3 tablespoons melted butter or vegetable oil
1 teaspoon salt
2 eggs, separated

Preheat oven to 400°F (gas mark 5). Pour the cornmeal into the hot milk and stir well. Beat in the flour, butter or oil and salt, and set aside. Beat the egg yolks and stir into the cornmeal mixture. Beat the egg whites stiff and fold them into the mixture. Grease an 8 inch by 8 inch cake tin or equivalent and pour the batter in. Bake for 20 to 25 minutes.

Cornmeal and brown rice bread

6 oz (1 cup) cornmeal
½ pt (1¼ cups) boiling water
1 teaspoon salt
8 oz (1 cup) cooked rice

1 tablespoon vegetable oil or melted butter
1 tablespoon wholemeal flour
2 eggs, beaten (optional)
2 tablespoons sesame seeds

Preheat oven to 375°F (gas mark 5). Dry roast the cornmeal in an ungreased frying pan, stirring all the time. Before it starts to burn, transfer it to a mixing bowl and pour over the boiling water in which the salt has been dissolved. Mix and set aside for 5 to 10 minutes to allow the cornmeal to swell. Stir in the rice, oil or butter, flour and, if you are using them, eggs. Grease an 8 inch by 8 inch cake tin or equivalent, and pour the mixture in. Sprinkle the sesame seeds over the top and bake for 40 to 45 minutes.

'Spider' corn bread

This recipe was given to me by Jill, a 'Southern gal', now living in Amsterdam, and initiating the Dutch into the delights of corn bread. It's called spider bread because it's usually baked over hot coals in a frying pan on legs, called a spider. A heavy 12 inch casserole or skillet and oven will do instead.

9 oz (1½ cups) cornmeal
1 tablespoon of sugar
1 teaspoon salt
1 teaspoon baking soda

2 eggs, well beaten
2 cups milk or buttermilk
1½ tablespoons melted butter

Preheat oven to 450°F (gas mark 8), and put in the casserole or skillet to heat. Sift the cornmeal, sugar, salt and baking soda into a bowl. Combine the eggs, milk and butter and stir it into the cornmeal mixture. Beat well to form a smooth batter. Remove the casserole from the oven and pour in the mixture. Return the casserole to the oven and bake for 30 minutes. Serve the corn bread hot with butter.

Variation
Add 4 oz (½ cup) grated cheese to the batter.

Pan cheese and onion corn bread

6 oz (1 cup) cornmeal
1 teaspoon sugar
1 teaspoon salt
4 oz (½ cup) cheese, grated

½ medium onion, finely diced
4 fl oz (½ cup) milk
1 egg, beaten
2 tablespoons vegetable oil

Combine the cornmeal, sugar and salt in a bowl, mix in the cheese and diced onion. Beat the egg and milk together and stir into the cornmeal mixture. Heat the oil in a heavy frying pan and pour in the batter. Cover, reduce heat to low and bake for 10 minutes. Invert the bread onto a plate and then return it to the pan bottom side up. Cover and bake for a further 10 minutes. Cut into portions and serve hot.

Corn spoon bread

1¼ pt (3 cups) water, boiling
12 oz (2 cups) cornmeal
12 fl oz (1½ cups) milk

4 eggs, beaten
2 teaspoons salt
2 tablespoons butter, melted

Preheat oven to 350°F (gas mark 4). Pour boiling water over cornmeal and mix well. Add the remaining ingredients and beat into a smooth batter. Grease a small casserole dish and pour the mixture in. Bake for 45 to 50 minutes. The spoon bread should remain moist inside. Serve hot with butter.

Corn muffins

16 fl oz (2 cups) water
12 oz (2 cups) cornmeal
2 tablespoons vegetable oil

1 teaspoon salt
2 eggs, beaten

Preheat oven to 375° (gas mark 5). Bring the water to the boil in a large saucepan. Add all the cornmeal then remove pan from the heat and stir until the cornmeal swells and starts to come away from the sides of the pan. Beat in the oil, salt and eggs and mix well. Grease a flat baking sheet (if you have muffin tins, grease them and fill to whatever depth you wish since the batter will not rise further) and drop the mixture onto it by tablespoonfuls forming 10 to 12 mounds of batter. Bake for 30 minutes or until muffins are nicely browned.

Variations
1: Add sugar to taste or boiled sultanas or raisins for sweet muffins.
2: For corn cheese muffins add 4 oz (½ cup) grated cheese to the batter.

Corn and rice muffins

8 fl oz (1 cup) water
6 oz (1 cup) cornmeal
2 tablespoons wholewheat or soya
    flour

1 teaspoon salt
8 oz (1 cup) cooked brown rice
2 tablespoons vegetable oil

Preheat oven to 375°F (gas mark 5). Bring the water to the boil in a large saucepan. Add the cornmeal, salt and flour, mix well and set aside to swell up. Mash the rice with the flat side of a wooden spoon and mix in the oil. Combine the corn and rice mixtures in the large saucepan and stir well. Drop the resultant mixture by spoonfuls onto a greased baking sheet to form 10 to 12 mounds of batter. Bake for 30 minutes or until well browned.

Variation
Replace the rice with 8 oz (1 cup) mashed potato.

Whole corn fritters

6 oz (1 cup) cooked sweet corn (fresh
    corn, boiled or tinned or frozen
    corn)
3 tablespoons cornmeal or wholemeal
    flour

1 egg, beaten
4 fl oz (½ cup) milk or water
½ teaspoon sugar
1 teaspoon salt
oil for deep frying

Combine all the ingredients in a mixing bowl and mix well. Heat the oil in a deep pan to 375°F or until it just begins to smoke. Drop tablespoonful amounts of batter into the hot oil and deep fry until fritters are bròwned and crisp. Alternatively, heat 3 tablespoons vegetable oil in a heavy, large frying pan over a moderate heat. Spoon in the batter forming 8 separate mounds. Cover pan and cook for 8 to 10 minutes, turn the fritters over and cook for the same time on the other side. Serve.

Cornmeal and potato fritters

6 oz (1 cup) cornmeal
4 oz (1 cup) wholemeal flour
8 oz (1 cup) cooked, mashed potato
¾ pt (2 cups) boiling water

1 egg, beaten
1 teaspoon salt
½ teaspoon black pepper
oil for deep frying

Combine the cornmeal, flour and mashed potato and mix well. Stir in the boiling water and set aside to swell for 10 minutes. Beat in the egg, salt and black pepper. Heat the oil in a deep pan to 375°F or until it just begins to smoke. Drop the batter from a tablespoon into the hot oil and deep fry until browned and crisp.

Alternatively, fry in a shallow frying pan as described in the Whole corn fritters recipe above.

Cornmeal waffles

This recipe is really for American readers since waffle irons are rare in Britain.

12 oz (2 cups) cornmeal
1 teaspoon salt
1 tablespoon sugar
2 teaspoons baking powder (optional)

2 eggs, separated
½ pt (1¼ cups) milk
2 oz (¼ cup) butter, melted or
   vegetable oil

Mix the dry ingredients. Beat the egg yolks, milk and butter or oil together and blend with the dry ingredients. Beat the egg whites and fold into the mixture. Fry on hot waffle iron until crisp.

Variation
Add 4 oz (½ cup) chopped nuts (walnuts, cashews, peanuts, etc.) to the batter.

Cornmeal pancakes

6 oz (1 cup) cornmeal
½ teaspoon salt
8 fl oz (1 cup) milk
1 egg, beaten

1 tablespoon vegetable oil or melted
   butter
vegetable oil for frying

Combine the cornmeal and salt and mix together the milk, egg and vegetable oil or melted butter. Beat together the 2 mixtures to form a smooth batter. Thicken or thin the batter to your own taste with the addition of either more cornmeal or more milk. Pour ⅛ of the batter into a hot oiled frying pan and fry golden on both sides. Prepares 8 pancakes.

Variations
1: To give the pancakes a nutty taste, dry roast the cornmeal in an ungreased frying pan before addition to the other ingredients.
2: Replace half the milk with sour cream or buttermilk.
3: Add sugar to the batter for sweet pancakes.

Corn dodgers

These are very simple, quick and easy to make corn bread rolls.

6 oz (1 cup) cornmeal
1 teaspoon salt
2 tablespoons melted butter

or
vegetable oil
cold water or milk

Preheat oven to 350° (gas mark 4). Combine cornmeal with salt and mix well. Stir in the melted butter or vegetable oil, and enough cold water or milk to form a firm dough. Form dough into small flat bottomed rolls of about 2 inches in diameter. Place on a greased baking tray and bake for 30 minutes or until nicely browned and well cooked.

Corn griddle cakes

9 oz (1½ cups) cornmeal
4 oz (1 cup) wholemeal flour
1 teaspoon salt
1 teaspoon baking powder
2 eggs, beaten

16 fl oz (2 cups) milk
2 tablespoons melted butter
1 tablespoon finely minced onion
  (optional)

Combine the dry ingredients. Beat the eggs, milk, butter and onion (if used) together. Blend with the dry ingredients. Drop by spoonfuls onto a hot greased griddle or frying pan, forming small cakes. Bake 5 minutes, turn and cook a further 5 minutes on the other side. Makes 12 to 16 small cakes.

Plain Johnny cakes

6 oz (1 cup) cornmeal
1 teaspoon salt
1 tablespoon sugar (optional)
2 tablespoons vegetable oil or melted
  butter

4 fl oz (½ cup) milk
1 egg, beaten
8 fl oz (1 cup) or more of boiling water

Combine the dry ingredients. Mix the oil or melted butter with milk and beaten egg and blend with the dry ingredients. Pour in the boiling water and allow to swell to form a batter that is soft but that which will hold its shape. Drop by spoonfuls onto a hot greased griddle or frying pan, and flatten the mounds into ½ inch thick, and about 3 inch diameter cakes. Fry on both sides until nicely browned.

Johnny cake special

This recipe is excellent for using up sour milk or cream. The Johnny cake is best eaten hot, so serve it as a dessert straight out of the oven, perhaps with cream or custard or just with butter.

6 oz (1 cup) cornmeal
8 oz (2 cups) wholemeal flour
½ teaspoon salt
1 teaspoon baking powder

½ pt (1¼ cups) sour milk or cream
6 oz (⅔ cup) molasses or dark treacle
2 eggs, well beaten

Preheat oven to 400°F (gas mark 6). Combine the dry ingredients in a large bowl and mix well. Beat the other ingredients together and pour into the bowl. Thoroughly mix and then turn the mixture into a greased cake tin. Bake for 30 minutes or until nicely browned on top.

Sweet Indian corn cake

4 oz (½ cup) sugar
or
2 oz (¼ cup) sugar *and*
2 oz (¼ cup) molasses

4 oz (½ cup) butter
9 oz (1½ cups) cornmeal
8 fl oz (1 cup) boiling water or milk
4 eggs, separated

Preheat oven to 350°F (gas mark 4). Beat the sugar and butter into a smooth mixture. Pour the cornmeal into the boiling water or milk and stir well. Now beat in the egg yolks and combine the mixture with the butter and sugar. Beat the egg whites and fold into this mixture. Grease an 8 inch by 8 inch cake tin or equivalent, and pour in the batter. Bake for 25 to 30 minutes or until browned on top and cooked through.

Corn and jam sandwiches

16 fl oz (2 cups) water
2 tablespoons sugar
½ teaspoon salt

6 oz (1 cup) cornmeal
oil for frying
jam, flavour of your own choice

Bring the water to the boil, add the sugar and salt. Reduce the heat and add the cornmeal stirring all the time. Cook until the mixture has well thickened. Grease a baking sheet and layer the mixture ¼ inch thick over the top. Place in refrigerator and allow to cool. Cut the cold batter into 4 inch squares and fry them (in a lightly oiled frying pan), golden brown on both sides. Drain the squares on absorbent paper and spread jam over the tops of half of them. Place the remaining squares over these to form the jam sandwiches.

Cornmeal dishes
Breakfast cornmeal mush

This is a traditional American Deep South breakfast. Serve on its own or with honey and nuts. Any leftovers can be fried and served with a little soy sauce as a snack.

1 teaspoon vegetable oil   1½ pt (3 cups) water
6 oz (1 cup) cornmeal   ½ teaspoon salt

Coat the bottom of a heavy saucepan with the oil and pour in the cornmeal.
Sauté over a moderate heat with constant stirring. The cornmeal will start to
brown and smell slightly nutty, at this point remove the pan from the heat and
allow to cool a little. Now slowly add the water and salt to the pan and mix well.
Bring to the boil, cover, reduce heat to the minimum and leave to simmer for 30
to 35 minutes. Stir and serve.

Variations
Stir 2 tablespoons of butter into the pan just before the cornmeal is to be served.

Fried mush

Ingredients as for Breakfast cornmeal mush (above).
oil for frying
2 tablespoons fine cornmeal or wholemeal flour

Prepare cornmeal mush as above and pour the cooked cereal into a greased
baking dish or tray to form a ½ inch thick layer. Cover and chill in the refrigerator. Cut into slices and dust with cornmeal or flour. Heat the oil in a frying pan
and sauté the slices browning both sides. Serve with honey molasses or sugar.

Mamaliga

This is a Romanian peasant dish, very similar to polenta. Serve hot or chill and
fry in slices as in the recipe for Fried mush.

1 teaspoon salt   1 small onion, diced
1¼ pt (3 cups) boiling water   6 oz (⅔ cup) cheese, grated
6 oz (1 cup) cornmeal   1 teaspoon paprika

Dissolve the salt in the boiling water and slowly stir in the cornmeal. Continue
stirring occasionally and cook over a moderate heat for 10 minutes. Add the
onion, stir, and cook a further 5 minutes. Stir in the cheese and paprika, mix
well and serve.

Corn breakfast crumbles

Use like granola or muesli.

8 fl oz (1 cup) water, boiling   2 oz (¼ cup) vegetable oil
6 oz (1 cup) cornmeal   2 tablespoons roasted sunflower seeds
8 oz (2 cups) wholemeal flour   1 teaspoon salt
4 oz (½ cup) wheat germ

Preheat oven to 300°F (gas mark 2). In a large mixing bowl stir the cornmeal into
the boiling water and mix well. Add the remaining ingredients and thoroughly
mix together. The resultant dough should be just crumbly. Grease a baking sheet
and crumble the mixture lightly over it. Lightly roll flat and even with a rolling
pin. Bake until dry, crispy and brown on top (about 40 to 45 minutes).

Polenta

Polenta is the Italian name for yellow maize or cornmeal. It is a staple food in parts of northern Italy where boiled polenta, cooled and then fried in oil sometimes takes the place of bread.

Simple Polenta

2 pt (5 cups) water
1 teaspoon salt
12 oz (2 cups) cornmeal

6 oz (¾ cup) cheese, grated (parmesan preferably)

Bring the water to the boil in large pan, add the salt and then pour in the cornmeal. Stir constantly until it is one smooth mass. Cover, reduce heat to a minimum, and cook for 20 minutes. Add half the cheese and mix well. Preheat oven to 350°F (gas mark 4). Grease a casserole and turn the mixture into it. Top with remaining cheese and bake for 15 to 20 minutes or until browned on top. Traditionally served with a spicy tomato sauce.

Polenta pie

1 pt (2½ cups) water
1 teaspoon salt
6 oz (1 cup) cornmeal
6 oz (¾ cup) cheese, grated (preferably parmesan)

8 oz (3 cups) mushrooms, sliced, sautéed in a little oil
1 pt (2½ cups) béchamel sauce (see recipe index)

Bring the water to the boil in a large pan, add the salt and then pour in the cornmeal. Stir constantly until it is one smooth mass. Cover, reduce heat to a minimum and cook for 20 minutes. Add half the cheese and mix well. Preheat oven to 350°F (gas mark 4). Grease a wide shallow dish and layer ⅓ of the mixture on the bottom, layer on top half the mushrooms and pour over half the béchamel sauce. Repeat ending with a layer of cornmeal mixture. Sprinkle remaining cheese over the top and bake for 30 minutes. The top should be browned and bubbly.

Farinata (broccoli, cornmeal and haricot beans)

I once took up gardening for a short time, and my most successful plant was broccoli, it just seemed to grow and grow. This dish was an excellent way to use some of it up.

8 oz (1 cup) haricot beans, soaked overnight in water, drained
1 teaspoon ground cumin
1 teaspoon ground coriander
1 lb broccoli, stems removed, chopped

2 pt (5 cups) boiling water
6 oz (1 cup) cornmeal
salt and black pepper to taste
soy sauce to taste
4 oz (½ cup) vegetable oil

Put beans, cumin and coriander in a large saucepan, just cover with cold water and gently boil until tender (about 40 minutes). Cook the broccoli in the boiling water until just tender. Drain the cooking liquid into the bean pot and stir in the cornmeal. Mix thoroughly to prevent lumps forming and season to taste with salt, black pepper and soy sauce. Cover, reduce heat and simmer for 30 minutes. Now stir in the broccoli and oil, heat through and serve. Alternatively spread the mixture thinly in a flat dish, chill, cut into squares and fry.

Hungarian cheese and sour cream cornmeal

This is an unusual summertime dish. Serve on a warm evening with a fresh, crisp salad.

1¼ pt (3 cups) water	8 oz (1 cup) cheese, grated
pinch salt	½ pt (1¼ cups) sour cream
6 oz (1 cup) cornmeal	1 teaspoon paprika

Bring the water to the boil in a heavy saucepan, add the salt and pour in the cornmeal. Stir well and continue cooking and stirring until the corn has absorbed all the water. Reduce the heat, cover pan and leave to simmer, stirring occasionally for 15 minutes. Meanwhile preheat oven to 425°F (gas mark 7) and grease a baking sheet. Spread half of the cornmeal mixture on the baking sheet and sprinkle the grated cheese over the top. Cover with the rest of the cornmeal mixture and spread the sour cream over the top. Bake for 10 to 12 minutes, sprinkle with paprika and serve.

Variations
For a sweet dish replace the cheese with jam and sprinkle sugar over the sour cream rather than paprika.

Bombay corn pudding

1 pt (2¼ cups) milk	oil for frying
pinch salt	lemon juice and sugar
3 tablespoons cornmeal	*or*
2 oz (¼ cup) butter	maple syrup
flour for dusting	

Bring the milk to the boil in a heavy pan, add the salt and sprinkle in the cornmeal. Cook over a moderate heat with frequent stirring until the mixture thickens (10 to 15 minutes). Grease a baking sheet and spread the mixture ½ inch thick over the top. Chill. Cut into triangles and dust with flour. Heat the oil in a frying pan and fry the triangles brown on both sides. Serve hot with lemon juice and sugar or maple syrup.

Egg corn pudding

1 pt (2¼ cups) milk	1 egg, beaten
3 tablespoons cornmeal	pinch salt
3 tablespoons golden syrup or maple syrup	½ teaspoon cinnamon
	½ teaspoon nutmeg

Preheat oven to 350°F (gas mark 4). Heat half the milk to boiling and pour into a mixing bowl. Stir in the cornmeal, mix well and add the remaining milk, the syrup, egg, salt and cinnamon. Beat well together. Grease a 2 pint or thereabouts heatproof bowl and pour in the mixture. Place the bowl in a pan of water and bake for 40 to 45 minutes or until set. Sprinkle with nutmeg and serve.

Hominy recipes

For a description of hominy (steamed whole corn kernels) see page 92.

Boiled hominy

5 oz (1 cup) hominy, soaked overnight
2 teaspoons salt
1¼ pt (3 cups) water

Drain the hominy. Bring the water to the boil in a heavy pan, add the salt and hominy and mix well. Return to the boil, reduce heat to minimum setting, cover and simmer for 1½ to 2 hours. Serve with butter or sugar and cream, or use as a side dish to accompany a main meal of meat, fish or vegetables.

Hominy bread

8 oz (1 cup) boiled hominy, cooled   *or*
8 fl oz (1 cup) milk   4 oz (1 cup) wholemeal flour
2 eggs, beaten   1 teaspoon salt
1 tablespoon butter, melted   1 teaspoon baking powder
4 oz (⅔ cup) cornmeal

Preheat oven to 350°F (gas mark 4). Combine the boiled hominy, milk, eggs and butter and mix well. Combine the dry ingredients and beat into the hominy mixture. Grease an 8 inch × 8 inch cake tin and pour the mixture in. Bake for 30 minutes or until browned and cooked in the middle. A knife pushed into the centre of the bread should come out clean when it is cooked. Serve hot with butter. Reheat by frying squares in butter.

Hominy grits

Hominy grits as a rule can be substituted for cornmeal in the preceding recipes.

Up to the early nineteenth century, oats were the main cereal crop of much of Scotland and northern England and widely used for bread-making. They were, however, considered very much a working class food and Dr Samuel Johnson wrote, 'oats are a grain that is generally given to horses, but which in Scotland support people'. The reply of a wise Scotsman was, 'and that is why in England you have such fine horses and in Scotland we have such fine men'. Although oats are a tasty food and a rich source of protein, vitamins and minerals, they still contribute very little to the overbalanced, meat rich British diet.

The name oat derives from the Old English word *ate*, which is from the Old English verb *etan* to eat. Samples of the common cultivated oat (*Avena satira*) have been found in cave dwellers' sites in Switzerland dated 1000 to 2000 BC. Although there is no real evidence of where or when it was first cultivated, the crop thrives in cool temperate climates, and it possibly originated in North West Europe where two wild grasses, wild red oat and common wild oat are found. These wild grasses are particularly successful at broadcasting their seeds and for thousands of years oats were considered not as a food source but as a weed amongst other cereal crops. Hence the phrase 'sowing wild oats' or as the pocket Oxford dictionary defines the phrase 'indulging in youthful follies'.

The earliest evidence of cultivated oats in Britain has been found in iron age sites in Somerset and Wiltshire where carbonized grains dated to 400 BC have been unearthed. Later evidence shows oats to have been a popular cereal grain all over the British Isles. In the Middle Ages in Scotland and parts of far northern England oatmeal porridge for breakfast and oatbread and cheese for dinner was a basic diet. In the same period in most of north England, the staple diet was said to be bread, ale and stew in that order. Dredgecorn, a mixture of barley and oats was usually the basic ingredient of the stew.

Oats were introduced into America in 1602 by a pioneer called Bartholomew Gosnold. He first planted the crop on one of the Elizabeth Islands off the coast of New England, from where it spread all along the East Coast, and today America grows a large proportion of the world crop. Other important areas of production are in Russia, Canada, Argentina and the countries of northern Europe.

Whole oat grain is generally equal to or richer in protein than either whole wheat or rice. The grain is rarely hulled and it is a good source of B vitamins, particularly inositol, as well as the minerals iron and phosphorous. Other trace minerals and vitamins are also present. Eaten with dairy products oats provide for a well balanced diet. See Table 1 on page 12 for a comparison of the nutrient content of oats with the other major cereal grains.

Oatmeal

Oat grains or groats as they are sometimes called, are usually sold as oatmeal or oatmeal flour. There are three types of oatmeal available. The first type, a large flatter oatmeal, is prepared by rolling the husked oats but not cutting them. They take quite a long time to cook. The second variety is prepared by cutting the oatmeal into flakes before rolling it. This medium size oatmeal cooks more quickly than the first variety. Instant or quick-cooking oatmeal is made by this process, but the oats are heated before rolling. It is possible that some nutritional value is lost during the heating. Steel cut, later known as Scotch oatmeal, is the third variety. The steel–cutting process was pioneered by an American called Ferdinand Schumacher in the nineteenth century. He made his fortune from the process and later became known as the 'Oatmeal King'. His method simply consisted of cutting the oat grain into several pieces (on steel blades). Some nutritionists consider steel cut oatmeal to be the best form of oats.

Oats are also ground into flour available in coarse, medium and fine grades. Which grade is used for a particular recipe is usually a matter of taste.

Oatmeal and oatmeal flour are used principally as breakfast foods (e.g. porridge, mush, muesli, etc.) and for the making of breads, cakes, scones, etc., but they can also be used in the preparation of savoury dishes, soups and stews.

Thick oatmeal and vegetable soup

Oatmeal may of course be added to any soup or stew to thicken it and add flavour. This recipe is very simple and may be used as a basis for more elaborate
soups.

2 tablespoons vegetable oil
2 medium onions, diced
2 medium carrots, grated

3 pt (7½ cups) stock or water
4 oz (1 cup) oatmeal
salt and black pepper to taste

Heat the oil in a heavy saucepan and sauté the onions and carrots until they are
soft and the onions are starting to brown. Add the stock or water, sprinkle in the
oatmeal, stir well and bring to the boil. Reduce heat, cover and simmer. Cook
until the soup is well thickened and the oatmeal is cooked, season to taste with
salt and black pepper. Serve.

Kail and oatmeal soup

Kail (Scots for kale) provided the crofters of Scotland with their only source of
green vegetable in a diet that consisted mainly of oatmeal and cheese. The following recipe is a very simple one, and depends for its flavour on the availability
of a good stock.

2½ pt (6 cups) meat or vegetable stock
2 oz (½ cup) oatmeal

1 lb kail, chopped.
salt and black pepper to taste

Bring the stock to the boil in a heavy pan, add the oatmeal, stir well, reduce the
heat, cover and simmer for 30 minutes. Add the kail, return to the boil, reduce
heat, cover and simmer for a further 30 to 40 minutes. Season to taste with salt
and black pepper and serve. Grated cheese sprinkled over the soup is an excellent
accompaniment.

Variation
Substitute spinach or broccoli for the kail.

Cream of oatmeal soup

1 tablespoon butter or margarine	pinch nutmeg
1 large onion, diced	5 fl oz (½ cup) milk
2 pt (5 cups) vegetable or meat	2 egg yolks
stock or 1 dissolved stock cube	salt and black pepper to taste
2 oz (½ cup) fine oatmeal	1 tablespoon fresh chopped parsley
1 inch cinnamon stick	

Melt the butter in a heavy saucepan, add the onion and sauté until soft. Add the stock, bring to the boil, stir in the oatmeal and add the cinnamon and nutmeg. Reduce heat, cover and simmer for 30 minutes. Beat the milk and egg yolks together. Remove soup from the heat and allow to cool for 5 minutes. Now stir in the egg and milk mixture, season to taste with salt and black pepper and serve garnished with chopped parsley.

Porridge

For such an apparently simple dish the preparation of porridge has had much written about it and probably as many different ways of making it have been recommended, as there are Scotsmen and women. One interesting idea is that porridge should be made by adding pinches of uncooked oatmeal to the pot as the porridge boils, so that when the dish is ready it contains a whole range of textures from the completely cooked to raw oatmeal. A method for you to experiment with if you wish.

There are two main things to remember when making porridge. First of all do not add the salt until the oatmeal is well swollen otherwise the salt hardens the meal and prevents proper swelling. Secondly, use a heavy pot and a long cooking time over a very low heat.

1 pt (2½ cups) water	salt to taste
2½ oz (½ cup) coarse oatmeal	cold milk or cream

Bring the water to the boil in a heavy pot and slowly sprinkle in the oatmeal with one hand whilst stirring briskly with a wooden spoon with the other. Return pot to the boil, reduce heat to a very low simmer and cover. Cook for 20 minutes and then season to taste with salt. Cover again and cook a further 10 minutes. Stir occasionally during cooking. Serve with milk or cream. Traditionally the milk or cream is served in individual bowls and each spoonful of hot porridge is dipped into the cold milk before being eaten.

Variations
Serve with honey or sugar and chopped dried or fresh fruit.

Sweet oatmeal milk pudding

1 pt (2½ cups) milk	pinch cinnamon
2 oz (½ cup) medium oatmeal	1 tablespoon brown sugar or honey
pinch salt	1 oz butter

Preheat oven to 300°F (gas mark 2). Bring milk to the boil in a heavy pot. Slowly stir in the oatmeal and cook over a medium heat for 5 minutes, stirring constantly. Remove from the heat and add salt, cinnamon and sugar or honey. Mix well and pour into suitable pie dish. Dot the top of the pudding with butter and bake for 1½ to 2 hours.

Savoury oatmeal pudding

8 oz (2 cups) medium oatmeal
4 oz (½ cup) vegetable fat or suet, finely chopped
1 medium onion, finely diced

1 teaspoon salt
1 egg, beaten
½ teaspoon black pepper
a little water or stock

Sprinkle the oatmeal on a flat tray and toast in a hot oven for 5 minutes. Combine with the remaining ingredients, adding enough water or stock to form a mixture of slightly soft consistency. Pour the mixture into a greased basin, cover with foil. Place the basin in a heavy pan containing one inch of water and steam for 1½ to 2 hours. Turn the pudding out onto a plate and serve with a sauce of your choice.

Skirlie

Skirlie is oatmeal fried with onions and suet (vegetable fat may be substituted). It's served with hot mashed potato and/or boiled cabbage. Uncooked, the mixture may be used as stuffing for poultry or vegetables.

4 oz (½ cup) suet or dripping or vegetable fat
2 medium onions, finely diced

8 oz (2 cups) medium oatmeal
salt and black pepper to taste

Melt the fat or suet in a heavy frying pan. Put in the onions and fry slowly until lightly browned and soft. Add the oatmeal and fry gently, stirring from time to time until it is well cooked, crisp and just browned. Season to taste and serve very hot.

Skirlie dumplings

Prepare skirlie as in recipe above, allow to cool until its hand hot and then form tablespoonful amounts of the mixture into dumplings. Drop into hot soups or stews.

Baked oatmeal and cheese

2 oz (¼ cup) vegetable oil
1 medium onion, finely chopped
4 oz (⅔ cup) fine or medium oatmeal
6 fl oz (¾ cup) water or stock
4 oz (½ cup) grated cheese

1 teaspoon dried thyme
1 tablespoon soy sauce
1 egg, beaten
salt and black pepper to taste

Preheat oven to 325°F (gas mark 3). Heat the oil in a heavy pot. Put in the onions and sauté until soft. Stir in the oatmeal and mix well. Pour in the water or stock, bring to the boil, reduce heat and simmer for 15 minutes. Add half the cheese and the remaining ingredients and mix well. Turn the mixture into a suitably sized greased dish or casserole and sprinkle the remaining cheese over the top. Bake for 30 minutes.

Oatmeal and potato cakes

6 fl oz (¾ cup) milk
2 oz (½ cup) fine oatmeal
1 teaspoon salt
8 oz (1 cup) mashed potato

1 egg, beaten
1 tablespoon fresh parsley, chopped
oil for frying

Bring the milk to the boil. Place oatmeal in a mixing bowl and pour over the boiling milk. Whisk to prevent lumps forming and leave for 5 minutes. Add the salt, potato, egg and parsley and mix well. Form the mixture into ¾ inch thick cakes. Heat oil in a heavy frying pan, fry the cakes over a moderate heat, and brown on both sides.

Yorkshire old wives' sod

I don't know how the old wives of Yorkshire felt about the name of this dish, but it makes a very simple, nutritious and appetizing meal.

5 eggs
16 fl oz (2 cups) milk
salt and black pepper to taste

2 oz (¼ cup) butter
2 or 3 thin oatcakes (see index)

Preheat oven to 350°F (gas mark 4). Break the eggs into a basin and beat well. Add the milk and salt and black pepper to taste and mix well. Grease a shallow baking dish with half the butter and pour the mixture in. Now toast the prepared oatcakes under a grill until nicely browned, butter them with remaining butter and then break them into small pieces. Sprinkle them over the egg mixture and bake for 20 minutes.

Lyn's savoury slices

2 oz (¼ cup) margarine
1 finely chopped onion
4 oz (1½ cups) mushrooms, chopped
   (optional)
5 oz (1 cup) rolled oats
6 oz (1 cup) finely grated carrot
5 oz (½ cup) grated cheese

1 egg, beaten
1 clove garlic, crushed (optional)
1 tablespoon soy sauce
1 tablespoon tomato sauce or purée
1 teaspoon basil
salt and pepper to taste

Preheat oven to 325°F (gas mark 3). Melt margarine in pan. Gently cook onion and mushrooms for 5 minutes. Transfer them to a mixing bowl and add all the other ingredients. Season to taste with salt and pepper and mix well. Press mixture into a greased backing tin and bake for 25 to 30 minutes. Cut into squares when cool.

Lyn's oat and herb rissoles

16 fl oz (2 cups) water
4 oz (1 cup) rolled oats
1 medium chopped onion
1 teaspoon mixed herbs
1 teaspoon basil
1 tablespoon soy sauce

1 tablespoon tomato purée or sauce
salt and pepper to taste
1 egg, beaten
flour
brown breadcrumbs
vegetable oil for frying

Bring the water to the boil. Stir in the oats and cook for 15 minutes, stirring frequently. Add onion, herbs and sauces. Season to taste with salt and black pepper. Add half the beaten egg and enough breadcrumbs to make a stiff dough. Flour hands and roll mixture into rissole shapes, dip into flour, egg and breadcrumbs and fry golden brown on both sides.

Onion and oat roast

2 oz (¼ cup) vegetable oil
2 medium onions, finely diced
2 oz (½ cup) coarse oatmeal
1 egg, separated
6 oz (⅔ cup) cheese, grated

1 teaspoon miso or yeast extract
½ teaspoon dried thyme
½ teaspoon dried parsley
black pepper to taste

Preheat oven to 325°F (gas mark 3). Heat oil in a heavy frying pan. Add onions and sauté until lightly browned. Add the oats and sauté, stirring, for a further 2 to 3 minutes. Put the onion and oat mixture into a mixing bowl and beat in the egg yolk. Mix in the remaining ingredients, finally folding in the well beaten egg white. Transfer mixture to a suitable greased baking dish or casserole and bake for 30 to 40 minutes or until nicely browned on top.

Oatmeal soufflé

2 oz (¼ cup) butter
1 medium onion, finely diced
4 oz (1 cup) medium oatmeal
8 fl oz (1 cup) milk

6 oz (⅔ cup) cheese, grated
2 eggs, separated
salt and black pepper to taste

Preheat oven to 350°F (gas mark 4). Melt butter in a heavy pan, put in the onion and cook slowly over a low heat for 15 minutes. Stir in the oatmeal, pour in the milk and bring to the boil. Reduce heat and simmer for 30 minutes. Remove from the heat and allow to cool for 10 minutes. Add half the cheese and beat in the egg yolks, season to taste and mix well. Fold in the well beaten egg whites and pour the mixture into a greased baking or soufflé dish. Top with remaining cheese and bake for about 20 minutes or until set.

★Pan or quick haggis

Haggis is traditionally cooked in the stomach bag of a sheep. This recipe allows you to forgo that pleasure and replaces it with a stove top method that makes a delicious and nutritious haggis pudding.

8 oz (1 cup) sheep's liver, coarsely
    chopped
1 medium onion, quartered
1 pt (2½ cups) stock or water

2 oz (¼ cup) suet, grated
4 oz (½ cup) fine oatmeal
salt and black pepper to taste

Put the liver, onion and stock or water in a pan, bring to the boil, reduce heat,
cover and gently cook for 40 minutes. Drain off the liquid and reserve. Meanwhile stir fry the oatmeal in a heavy frying pan until lightly browned. Pass the
liver through a mincer or finely chop by hand. Dice the cooked onion. Combine
the liver, onion, oatmeal, suet and enough cooking liquid to form a mixture of
soft consistency. Season to taste and transfer the mixture to a greased bowl.
Cover the bowl with silver foil and place in a pan of water. Steam for 1½ to 2
hours over a low heat. Serve with mashed turnip and boiled potatoes.

*Scotch collops

2 tablespoons dripping or suet
1 medium onion, diced
1 lb minced beef

2 tablespoons oatmeal
16 fl oz (2 cups) stock
salt and black pepper to taste

Melt the dripping or suet in a heavy pan. Put in the onions and sauté until soft.
Add the minced beeef and brown whilst constantly stirring to prevent lumps
forming. Stir in the oatmeal and add enough stock to just cover the mixture.
Season to taste with salt and black pepper, cover and simmer for 40 to 45 minutes. Serve on toast or with mashed potato.

*Herrings fried in oatmeal

4 fresh herrings, cleaned & filleted
2 oz (¼ cup) oatmeal

salt and black pepper
oil for frying

Season the oatmeal with salt and black pepper and sprinkle liberally over the
herrings. Fry the fish in a heavy frying pan over a medium heat until cooked and
browned, about 10 minutes.

Thin oatcakes

4 oz (½ cup) fine oatmeal
½ teaspoon salt
¼ teaspoon bicarbonate of soda
    (optional)

2 teaspoons melted butter
about 2 fl oz (¼ cup) hot water

Combine the dry ingredients and stir in the melted butter with as much of the
hot water as needed to form a dough of soft consistency. Liberally sprinkle a
board with oatmeal and roll out the dough as thinly as possible. Cut into triangles or other shapes and sprinkle with more oatmeal. Cook cakes in a hot,
ungreased heavy frying pan or on a hot girdle (griddle) for 5 minutes. Remove
the oatcakes and grill the top side brown and crisp before serving.

Thick oatcakes

6 oz (1¼ cups) medium oatmeal
4 oz (1 cup) wholemeal flour
½ teaspoon salt
1 teaspoon baking powder

1 egg, beaten
2 oz (¼ cup) butter, melted
about 2 fl oz (¼ cup) water

Preheat oven to 350°F (gas mark 4). Combine the dry ingredients and mix well. Stir in the beaten egg, butter and enough water to form a dough of firm but not stiff consistency. Sprinkle a board with flour and roll the dough to ¼ inch thickness and cut into rounds. Grease a baking sheet and put the oatcakes on it. Bake 15 minutes and serve. Alternatively, fry the oatcakes on a greased girdle (griddle) or frying pan. Serve with butter and cheese.

Variation
Add 1 tablespoon sugar to the ingredients and serve the oatcakes with jam and cream.

Plain oatmeal biscuits (cookies)

4 oz (1 cup) wholemeal flour
4 oz (½ cup) butter
6 oz (1¼ cups) medium oatmeal
½ teaspoon baking powder

1 teaspoon sugar
1 egg, beaten
water as required

Preheat oven to 350°F (gas mark 4). Rub butter into flour and add the rest of the dry ingredients. Mix well. Stir in the egg and enough water to form a dough of firm but not stiff consistancy. Roll out thinly on a floured board. Cut into squares or rounds and place a little apart on a greased baking sheet. Bake for about 20 minutes.

Rich oatmeal biscuits (cookies)

4 oz (1 cup) wholemeal flour
1 teaspoon baking powder
½ teaspoon salt
8 oz (1½ cups) medium oatmeal
½ teaspoon ground ginger
½ teaspoon cinnamon

1 tablespoon butter
2 tablespoons syrup or treacle
1 egg, beaten
About 4 fl oz (½ cup) milk
2 oz (¼ cup) raisins (optional)

Preheat oven to 375°F (gas mark 5). Combine the first 6 ingredients and mix well. Melt the butter in a saucepan and stir in the syrup or treacle. Beat the egg into the butter and syrup mixture and pour the mixture into the dry ingredients. Add the milk and beat until a smooth stiff batter is formed. Add a little more milk if needed. Stir in the raisins if being used. Drop the batter in teaspoon amounts 1½ inches apart onto a greased baking sheet, and bake for 10 minutes. Alternatively, drop the batter onto a hot oiled girdle (griddle) and cook until browned. Turn and brown the other side.

Nut and fruit oat biscuits (cookies)

6 oz (⅔ cup) butter or margarine
6 oz (⅔ cup) sugar
or
3 oz (⅓ cup) molasses *and*
3 oz (⅓ cup) honey
2 eggs, beaten
½ teaspoon ginger
½ teaspoon allspice

¼ teaspoon ground cloves
pinch salt
4 oz (½ cup) chopped nuts
4 oz (½ cup) sultanas or raisins or
    chopped dates
6 oz (1½ cups rolled oats
about 2 fl oz (¼ cup) milk

Preheat oven to 375°F (gas mark 5). Beat the butter and sugar together to a creamy consistancy. Otherwise melt the butter in a pan and stir in the molasses and honey. Add the remaining ingredients and enough milk to form a batter of smooth stiff consistancy. Drop the mixture by teaspoonful amounts onto a greased baking sheet 1½ inches apart. Bake for 10 minutes or until lightly browned.

Carrot and oat cakes

6 oz (⅔ cup) butter or margarine
6 oz (⅔ cup) sugar
1 medium carrot, grated
1 egg, beaten
peel of 1 lemon, grated

8 oz (2 cups) wholemeal flour
3 oz (¾ cup) rolled oats
½ teaspoon salt
1 teaspoon baking powder

Preheat oven to 375°F (gas mark 5). Cream the butter and sugar together, and beat in the egg and carrot. Add the remaining ingredients and blend well together. Drop teaspoonful amounts onto a greased baking sheet 1½ inches apart and bake for 10 minutes or until lightly browned.

Oatmeal scones

4 oz (1 cup) wholemeal flour
2 oz (¼ cup) butter or margarine
4 oz (⅔ cup) fine oatmeal
2 teaspoons baking powder

1 tablespoon honey or sugar
    (optional)
about 2 fl oz (¼ cup) milk

Preheat oven to 375°F (gas mark 5). Rub the butter into the flour and stir in the oatmeal. Add the remaining ingredients including enough milk to form a fairly stiff dough. Roll out on a floured board and cut into ½ inch thick rounds. Place on a greased baking sheet and bake for 15 minutes or until nicely browned.

Scotch parkins

4 oz (1 cup) wholemeal flour
2 oz (¼ cup) butter or margarine
4 oz (⅔ cup) medium oatmeal
2 oz (¼ cup) brown sugar
2 oz (¼ cup) syrup or treacle

1 teaspoon baking powder
1 teaspoon ground ginger
1 teaspoon ground cinnamon
10 almonds, skinned

Preheat oven to 350°F (gas mark 4). Rub the butter into the flour and add the oatmeal and sugar. Mix well. Add the remaining ingredients except almonds, and mix to a smooth paste. Form the paste into small balls the size of walnuts and top each one with an almond. Place on a greased baking sheet and bake for 15 to 20 minutes in the centre of the oven. Cool on a wire rack. Keep in an airtight tin. Alternatively press the mixture onto the greased baking sheet (about ¾ inch thick) decorate with the almonds and bake for 15 to 20 minutes in the centre of the oven. Cut into squares before completely cooled.

Honey and oatmeal bread

Makes three 1 lb loaves.

2 oz (⅔ cup) rolled oats
8 fl oz (1 cup) boiling water
1 oz (1 cake) fresh yeast
8 fl oz (1 cup) lukewarm water
1 teaspoon sugar

4 oz (¼ cup) honey
1 tablespoon vegetable oil
1 teaspoon salt
about 1½ lb (6 cups) wholemeal flour

Place the oats in a mixing bowl and pour over the boiling water. Leave to stand 20 minutes. Meanwhile dissolve the yeast in the lukewarm water and add 1 teaspoon sugar. Set aside. Add the honey, vegetable oil, salt and yeast mixture to the oats and mix well. Beat the flour into the mixture slowly until you have a firm but not stiff dough. Knead the dough on a floured board for 5 to 10 minutes. Clean the mixing bowl, lightly grease the inside and put in the dough. Cover with a damp cloth and leave to rinse in a warm place for 1 hour or until doubled in size. Preheat the oven to 400°F (gas mark 6) and grease 3 1 lb bread tins or 2 larger ones. Form the dough into 3 or 2 loaves and press into the tins. Cover with a damp cloth and leave to rise in a warm place for 45 minutes or until doubled in size. Bake the loaves for 5 minutes at 400°F, then reduce oven temperature to 350°F (gas mark 4) and bake a further 40 to 45 minutes. To test if the bread is done, remove 1 loaf from a tin and tap the bottom, it should sound hollow when properly baked. If not, return bread to the oven and leave a little longer.

Oatmeal and wholemeal flour bread

See recipe for Wholemeal bread (page 29); substitute 8 to 12 oz of oatmeal flour for the same amount of wholewheat flour, otherwise proceed as directed.

Muesli

Muesli was formulated by Dr Bircher–Benner over seventy years ago. He was a well-known, if slightly offbeat, nutritionist who founded a famous health clinic in Zurich. His recipe for muesli included a mixture of oats, raw fruit, nuts and milk. Although intended as a food for any time of the day, this combination and derivatives have since become regarded as a breakfast cereal. The recipe was devised to provide a food that supplied good amounts of protein, vitamins, minerals and roughage without overloading the body with too much or too rich food. His ideas were well ahead of his time but many of them are now supported by medical opinion and muesli is considered an excellent food combination.

Basic muesli

Ingredients per person:

2 level tablespoons oats
1 apple, grated
1 teaspoon lemon juice
2 level tablespoons yoghurt (optional)

1 level tablespoon chopped nuts
milk or cream to taste
honey or sugar to taste

Grate the apple just before it's needed and then combine with the oats, lemon juice and yoghurt. Sprinkle nuts over the top and add milk and honey to taste.

Variations
1: Use 2 to 3 ounces dried fruit, soaked overnight, in place of the apple.
2: Soak the oats overnight in milk. The muesli is softer in texture and more digestable for some people.
3: Use 4 to 6 ounces of any other fresh fruit in place of the apple.
4: Substitute millet or wheat germ for some of the oats.
5: For a crunchier texture, roast the nuts before chopping.

High-energy oat cereal

This is a breakfast cereal designed to help you start the day full of energy. Make more than you need and store the rest in an airtight tin.

1 lb (5 cups) quick-cooking rolled oats
2 oz (¼ cup) dried apricots
2 oz (¼ cup) dates, chopped

4 oz (½ cup) sunflower seeds
2 oz (¼ cup) raisins
4 oz (½ cup) mixed roasted nuts

Combine all the ingredients and serve portions with milk, honey and chopped banana.

Barley was the chief food crop of the ancient Roman and Greek civilizations. The Roman goddess Ceres is usually represented with ears of barley plaited into her hair or crown, and the same symbol appears on ancient Greek and Roman coins. The Roman naturalist Pliny believed barley to be man's oldest food crop and certainly evidence has been found of its use in Egypt as far back as 5000 B C. Barley is one of the hardiest of all the food grains, it has a wide growing range and nutritional worth comparable with the other major cereals.

The name barley derives from the Old English word *baerlic*, which is connected to *beow*, meaning to grow. An even older name is *bere* and the connections between barley and brewing are remembered in our word for that famous drink, beer!

The origins of the plant are thought to be in either the Ethiopian highlands, where barley is still an important crop, or western Asia in the region of the ancient Sumerian civilization, where barley was sometimes used as currency.

The many varieties of barley are subdivided according to the number of rows of grain there are along the ear of the plant. The most common type in ancient times was six-rowed barley, and this variety is still an important food crop in parts of India, Tibet (where it is the only crop that will grow in very high altitudes) and in Japan where barley is second to rice as a grain staple. Other popular varieties are the four-rowed common barley and the two-rowed coffee barley.

Barley contains very little gluten and consequently cannot be used to make light risen breads. Instead it is used to make flat breads and cakes, porridge, soups and stews.

Barley has also been used in the brewery trade for thousands of years and it was from the yeast obtained as a by-product of malted barley that the first yeasted wheat breads were made.

The widespread cultivation of wheat and rice led to a gradual worldwide decline in the importance of barley and by the sixteenth century in Europe, barley was important only in isolated areas (e.g. in the Isle of Man, barley was a staple food crop up to the nineteenth century). Nowadays barley is principally cultivated for use in the brewery industry and for animal food, although it is well suited to human consumption.

Wholegrain barley contains an average 11% by weight of protein, which compares well with wheat and rice, valuable B vitamin and important minerals. See Table 1 on page 12, which compares the nutrient content of barley with that of the other major cereal grains.

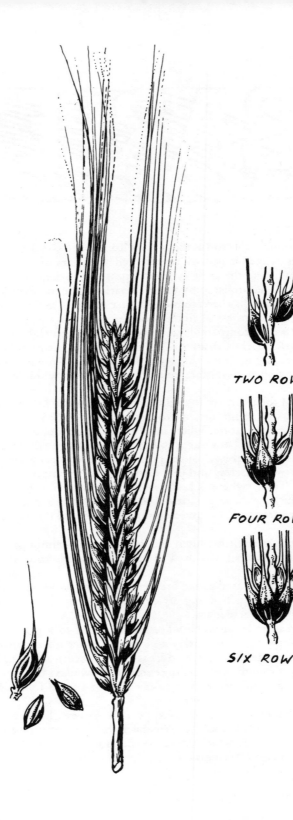

TWO ROW

FOUR ROW

SIX ROW

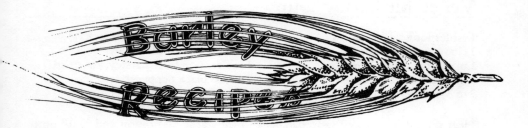

The recipes stipulate whole barley kernels. Where they are unavailable pearl barley may be substituted.

Plain boiled barley

Serves 4

8 oz (1 cup) whole barley
1¼ pt (3 cups) water
salt to taste

Combine the ingredients in a heavy saucepan and bring to the boil. Reduce heat, cover and simmer for 30 to 40 minutes or until barley is cooked. Serve as you might serve rice.

Toasted boiled barley

8 oz (1 cup) whole barley
1¼ pt (3 cups) water
salt to taste

Place the barley in a heavy pot and dry roast over a high heat, stirrring constantly, until the barley darkens to deep brown in colour. Remove from the heat and carefully add the water taking care it does not splutter on you. Salt to taste, bring to the boil, reduce heat, cover and simmer for 30 tor 35 minutes or until barley is cooked.

Barley water

Serve this refreshing drink cold in the summer or hot in the winter months.

2 oz (¼ cup) whole barley, rinsed
2 pt (5 cups) boiling water
2 strips lemon rind
juice of 1 lemon
sugar to taste

Place the barley in the top of a double boiler or a heavy pan. Add the boiling water and lemon rind and juice. Cover and simmer for 2 hours. Strain, sweeten to taste.

Vegetable barley soup

1 tablespoon vegetable oil
1 clove garlic, crushed
1 medium onion, diced
1 medium carrot, grated
2 to 3 sticks celery, chopped

1½ pt (4 cups) vegetable stock
4 oz (½ cup) whole barley
1 tablespoon fresh parsley, chopped
salt and black pepper to taste
juice of 1 lemon

Heat the oil in a heavy saucepan, put in the garlic and onion and sauté until golden. Add the carrot and celery and sauté further until all the vegetables are just soft. Pour in the stock, add the barley, parsley and salt and black pepper to taste. Bring to the boil, reduce heat, cover and simmer for an hour or longer. Just before serving stir in the lemon juice.

Variation
In winter months substitute or add turnip or swede to the ingredients.

★Bacon and sausage barley soup

1 tablespoon oil or fat
4 oz fat bacon, diced
1 medium carrot, grated
2 medium leeks, chopped
1½ pt (4 cups) meat stock

4 oz (½ cup) whole barley
2 medium potatoes, quartered
4 oz garlic sausage or black pudding,
   sliced
1 tablespoon fresh parsley, chopped

Heat the oil or fat in a heavy pan, add the bacon and brown. Put in the vegetables and sauté for 5 minutes, stirring. Pour in the stock, barley and potatoes. Bring to the boil, reduce heat, cover and simmer for 45 minutes. Now add the sausage or black pudding and cook a further 15 minutes. Serve garnished with parsley.

Winter barley casserole

1 tablespoon vegetable oil
1 clove garlic, crushed
† medium onion, diced
2 medium potatoes, sliced
3 sticks celery, chopped
2 medium carrots, sliced
8 oz (1 cup) tinned tomatoes
3 oz (⅓ cup) whole barley

8 oz (1 cup) cooked beans or lentils
   (optional)
1 teaspoon dried basil
2 bay leaves
1 teaspoon salt
½ teaspoon black pepper
16 fl oz (2 cups) water

Heat the oil in an oven-proof casserole, put in the garlic and onion and sauté until soft. Add the potatoes, celery and carrots and sauté, stirring, for 10 minutes. Add the tomatoes, barley, beans, basil, bay leaves, salt and black pepper and mix well. Pour in the water, bring to the boil, reduce heat, cover and simmer for an hour or until everything is cooked. Stir occasionally. Add more water as needed to keep casserole very moist. Serve with oatcakes (page 116).

Mushroom and barley casserole

3 tablespoons butter
8 oz (3 cups) fresh mushrooms, diced
2 medium onions, finely diced
8 oz (1 cup) whole barley

1¼ pt (3 cups) vegetable or meat stock
salt
1 tablespoon fresh parsley, chopped

Preheat oven to 350°F (gas mark 4). Melt the butter in a heavy frying pan, put in the mushrooms and sauté until just soft. Transfer to a casserole dish. Add the onions to the frying pan and fry until golden. Add the barley and stir fry until the kernels turn golden brown. Put the onions, barley and stock in with the mushrooms. Season with salt and black pepper. Cover and bake for 1 hour. Check the casserole occasionally and add more stock if it dries out. Serve garnished with parsley.

Barley kasha

3 tablespoons butter
8 oz (1 cup) whole barley
1½ pt (4 cups) water or vegetable
  stock

1 medium onion, diced
8 oz (3 cups) mushrooms, chopped
salt and black pepper to taste

Melt ⅔ of the butter in a heavy pot over a medium heat. Add the barley and stir fry until it turns a dark brown. Slowly add the stock and then the onion. Cover and simmer for 45 minutes to 1 hour or until the barley has absorbed all the liquid. Stir the pot occasionally and add more liquid if needed (e.g. if it starts to dry up before the barley is cooked). Sauté the mushrooms in the remaining butter and stir into the barley mixture just before serving. Finally, season to taste with salt and pepper.

Rice and barley

Serve in place of rice.

4 oz (½ cup) whole barley
1½ pt (4 cups) water
12 oz (1½ cups) brown rice

Put the barley in a pot, boil half the water and pour it over the barley. Set aside for 30 minutes. Put the rice and remaining water in a heavy pot. Add the soaked barley plus soaking water. Cover, bring to the boil, reduce heat and simmer over a very low heat for 45 minutes.

Lentil and barley kasha

8 oz (1 cup) brown or green
  lentils, soaked overnight
4 oz (½ cup) whole barley
  water
2 tablespoons butter

1 medium onion, diced
1 teaspoon salt
8 oz (1 cup) tinned tomatoes
1 tablespoon sugar
1 clove garlic, crushed

Drain the lentils and combine with barley in a heavy pot. Add water to just cover. Cook for 45 minutes. Add water as necessary to keep the mixture moist. Meanwhile heat the butter in a frying pan, add the onion and sauté until well browned. Stir the onion into the lentil/barley mixture. Add the salt, tomatoes, sugar and garlic and mix well. Simmer uncovered for 15 minutes and serve.

Barley pilaff

4 oz (¼ cup) vegetable oil	1¼ pt (3 cups) vegetable stock
8 oz (3 cups) mushrooms, chopped	1 clove garlic, crushed
1 medium onion, sliced	1 teaspoon dried thyme
1 medium green pepper, sliced	salt and black pepper to taste
8 oz (1 cup) whole barley	

Preheat oven to 350°F (gas mark 4). Heat the oil in a heavy frying pan and sauté the mushrooms until well softened. Transfer the mushrooms to a greased casserole dish. Sauté the onion and green pepper in the frying pan until the onion softens and lightly browns. Transfer to the casserole. Put the barley into the frying pan and stir fry, coating each grain in oil. Add the garlic and pour the stock over the barley. Heat to boiling. Transfer this mixture to the casserole, add the thyme, stir well and season to taste with salt and black pepper. Cover and bake for 30 minutes.

Onion and barley roast

2 tablespoons butter or margarine	4 oz (½ cup) tinned tomatoes
2 medium onions, diced	6 oz (⅔ cup) grated cheese
2 oz (¼ cup) whole barley, soaked overnight, drained	1 teaspoon mixed herbs
1 egg, beaten	1 tablespoon soy sauce or yeast extract
	salt and black pepper to taste

Preheat oven to 350°F (gas mark 4). Melt the butter in a heavy frying pan and sauté the onions until golden. Combine with remaining ingredients keeping back half the cheese. Turn the mixture into a greased casserole. Top with cheese and bake for 35 to 40 minutes. Serve with baked potatoes and green salad.

Peanut butter and barley roast

1 tablespoon vegetable oil	2 oz (¼ cup) wholemeal flour
1 medium onion, diced	2 eggs, beaten
12 oz (1½ cups) whole barley, soaked overnight, drained	1 tablespoon tomato purée
6 oz (1 cup) peanut butter	4 fl oz (½ cup) hot water
4 oz (1 cup) fine breadcrumbs	salt and black pepper to taste

Preheat oven to 375°F (gas mark 5). Sauté the onion in the vegetable oil until nicely browned. Combine with the remaining ingredients and mix well. Turn into a greased baking dish, cover and bake on the middle shelf for 45 minutes to 1 hour or until the barley is cooked. Add more water if the mixture looks too dry.

Barley and cheese pudding

1 pt (2½ cups) milk
4 oz (½ cup) whole barley
1 oz (⅛ cup) butter
2 eggs, separated
4 oz (½ cup) grated cheese

½ teaspoon salt
¼ teaspoon black pepper
pinch cinnamon
pinch nutmeg
¼ teaspoon english mustard powder

Preheat oven to 375°F (gas mark 5). Bring the milk to boiling. Pour it over the barley and set aside for 30 minutes. Now add the butter to the barley and milk and beat in the egg yolks and cheese. Season and then fold in the well beaten egg whites. Transfer the mixture to a greased baking dish and bake for 30 to 40 minutes or until the barley is cooked.

Lentil and barley rissoles

1 lb (2 cups) cooked, drained whole barley
8 oz (1 cup) cooked, drained, split red lentils
4 oz (½ cup) cheese, grated
1 egg, beaten

1 tablespoon tomato purée
1 teaspoon salt
½ teaspoon black pepper
½ teaspoon dried thyme
about 2 oz (¼ cup) wholemeal flour
oil for frying

Combine all the ingredients, adding enough flour to form a mixture of such consistency that it will hold its shape. Form the mixture into 3 inch long oval rissoles. Fry them golden brown in hot oil.

Fried vegetable and barley squares

1 tablespoon vegetable oil
1 medium onion, diced
1 stick celery, diced
2 tablespoons parsley, chopped
4 oz (½ cup) whole barley, soaked overnight, drained
4 fl oz (½ cup) milk

1 teaspoon salt
½ teaspoon black pepper
2 oz (¼ cup) cheese, grated
1 egg, beaten
1 tablespoon milk
oil for frying

Heat the oil in a heavy frying pan. Add the onion, celery, parsley and barley and stir fry until all the vegetables are soft. Add the milk and cook until all the liquid is absorbed by the barley. Add the salt, black pepper and cheese and mix well. Turn the mixture onto a wetted board and press it into a ½ inch thick square. Leave to cool. Cut into 2 inch squares. Beat the egg and one tablespoon of milk together. Dip squares in egg and milk and fry in hot oil browning both sides.

★Scotch broth

1 lb stewing beef
3 pt (7½ cups) water
2 oz (¼ cup) dried peas, soaked over-
    night
1 oz (⅛ cup) whole barley
1 lb mixed diced vegetables (e.g.
    carrot, turnip, leek, cabbage,
    onion)

salt and black pepper to taste
¼ teaspoon nutmeg, grated
1 medium carrot, grated
1 tablespoon fresh parsley, chopped

Put the meat as one piece into a heavy pot and later serve it as a separate course to
the broth or put it into the pot cut into 1 inch cubes and serve the meat as part of
the broth. Add the water, soaked peas, barley and bring to the boil. Remove any
scum that rises to the surface and then add the vegetables. Season to taste with
salt and black pepper and add the nutmeg. Cover and simmer for 2 to 3 hours.
Skim off any excess fat on the surface of the broth and add the grated carrot.
Adjust seasoning. Cook a further 15 minutes and serve garnished with parsley.

★Barley meat loaf

8 oz (1 cup) minced beef
1 lb (2 cups) whole barley, soaked
    overnight, drained
½ medium onion, diced
1 medium leek, finely chopped

1 tablespoon tomato purée
1 tablespoon fresh parsley
1 egg, beaten
1 tablespoon wholemeal flour
salt and black pepper to taste

Preheat oven to 325°F (gas mark 3). Combine all the ingredients and season to
taste with salt and black pepper. If the mixture is a little dry add some water or
stock to make it just moist. Grease a 2 lb bread or paté tin and pack the mixture
in. Stand the tin in 1 inch water in a baking dish and bake for 1 hour or until well
cooked and browned on top.

★Chicken and barley casserole

1 teaspoon dried thyme
2 tablespoons flour
4 chicken joints
3 tablespoon oil
2 oz (¼ cup) whole barley
1 clove garlic
2 medium onions, diced

2 medium carrots, sliced
1 medium green pepper, sliced
1¼ pt (3 cups) chicken stock
or
water and 1 stock cube
salt and black pepper to taste

Combine the thyme and flour and dredge the chicken joints in the mixture.
Heat two tablespoons of oil in a heavy frying pan and fry the chicken joints turning once or twice, for about 5 minutes, or until brown on both sides. Set the
chicken pieces aside and pour half the stock into the frying pan. Put in the barley
and bring to the boil. Lightly boil for 5 minutes. Meanwhile grease a casserole
dish with the remaining oil, put in the garlic and onions and sauté over a
medium heat until they are soft and golden. Add the carrots and green pepper
and sauté a further 5 minutes. Preheat oven to 350°F (gas mark 4). Pour the

barley with stock and remaining stock into the casserole dish and season the mixture with salt and black pepper. Put the chicken pieces in and cover the dish. Bake for 1 hour. Check seasoning and serve.

★Savoury rabbit and barley

This recipe and some of the others on barley have been developed from recipes devised by Browns of Derby, England. They are millers and suppliers of excellent grains.

Serves 6

1 medium rabbit, jointed	1 tablespoon fresh parsley, chopped
1 oz (⅛ cup) lard or fat	salt and black pepper to taste
1 medium onion, diced	2 oz (¼ cup) whole barley
1 tablespoon plain flour	1 pt (2½ cups) water
½ teaspoon dried thyme	2 medium apples, sliced

Preheat oven to 325°F (gas mark 3). Brown the pieces of rabbit in hot fat in a heavy frying pan and then transfer to a greased casserole dish. Put the onion into the pan and fry until golden. Add the flour and stir well over a low heat. Transfer to the casserole dish. Sprinkle in thyme and parsley and season with salt and black pepper. Pour the water into the frying pan and add the barley. Bring to the boil and gently cook for 5 minutes. Arrange the apple slices over the rabbit mixture and pour in the barley and water. Cover the dish and bake for 1½ to 2 hours. The rabbit should be tender but not falling off the bones.

Barley meal scones

8 oz (1 cup) barley meal (coarse barley flour) or flour if meal is unavailable	1½ teaspoons baking powder
	½ teaspoon salt
	1½ oz (⅙ cup) butter
8 oz (2 cups) wholemeal flour	10 fl oz (1¼ cups) milk

Preheat oven to 430°F (gas mark 7). Sift the dry ingredients together and rub in the butter. Add milk to form a soft workable dough. Roll the dough out into two large ½ inch thick circles and divide each into six portions. Or roll the mixture into one ½ inch thick layer and cut out individual scones. Place the scones on a greased baking sheet. Brush with milk and bake for 10 to 12 minutes. Cool on a wire rack.

Barley flour biscuits (cookies)

8 oz (1 cup) barley flour	1 oz (⅛ cup) butter or vegetable oil
½ teaspoon salt	4 fl oz (½ cup) buttermilk or milk
1 teaspoon baking powder	1 egg, beaten

Preheat oven to 375°F (gas mark 5). Combine the flour, salt and baking powder and rub the butter or oil into the mixture. Beat the milk and egg together and combine the 2 mixtures. The dough should be quite soft, but firm enough to almost hold its shape. Grease a baking sheet and drop on to it spoonful amounts of the dough 1½ inches apart. Bake for 10 to 12 minutes.

Barley bread

Barley bread has a flavour distinct from regular wheat flour bread and it makes a nice change. It's particularly good toasted.

2 teaspoons sugar or honey
1¼ pt (3 cups) lukewarm water
1 oz fresh yeast
or
2 teaspoons dry yeast

1 lb (2 cups) barley flour
1 lb (4 cups) wholemeal flour
2 teaspoons salt
2 tablespoons vegetable oil

Dissolve the sugar or honey in the water and stir in the yeast. Set aside for 15 to 20 minutes in a warm place. Sift the flours and salt together. Make a well in the mixture and pour in the oil and yeast mixture. Mix well and knead for 5 minutes or more on a floured board. The dough should be smooth and elastic. Clean out the mixing bowl, lightly oil the inside and place the dough in it. Cover with a damp cloth and leave in a warm place for 45 minutes to 1 hour. Oil two bread tins. Knead the dough again for 2 to 3 minutes. Divide the dough in 2 and press into the bread tins. Cover tins with a damp cloth and set in a warm place for about 40 minutes. Preheat oven to 375°F (gas mark 5). Bake bread for about 40 minutes or until the bottom of bread sounds hollow when knocked. Cool bread on a wire rack.

Barley flour pancakes

Makes 8 pancakes.

8 oz (1 cup) barley flour
½ teaspoon salt
1 teaspoon sugar
1 teaspoon baking powder

1 egg, beaten
8 fl oz (1 cup) buttermilk or milk
oil for frying

Combine the dry ingredients and mix well. Beat the egg and milk together and mix into the dry ingredients to form a smooth batter. Leave to stand for 5 minutes. Grease a frying pan or griddle and heat until the fat just starts to smoke. Pour about ⅛ of the batter into the pan. Brown both sides of the pancake and serve with lemon juice and sugar. Repeat for remaining batter.

Barley milk pudding

2 oz (¼ cup) whole barley
1 pt (2½ cups) milk

pinch of salt
sugar to taste

Preheat oven to 300°F (gas mark 2). Put the barley, milk and sugar in a baking dish. Add sugar to taste and heat the dish on top of the oven. As soon as the contents come to the boil, put the dish in the oven and bake for 1½ to 2 hours.

Variations
1: Add 1 teaspoon cinnamon or few drops of vanilla essence to the ingredients.
2: Add 2 oz (¼ cup) raisins or sultanas.
3: Beat the milk with 1 tablespoon cocoa, before addition to the barley.

Apple and barley crumble

2 oz (¼ cup) whole barley
1 oz (⅛ cup) brown sugar
3 medium cooking apples, peeled,
    cored and sliced
6 fl oz (⅔ cup) water

2 oz (½ cup) flour
3 oz (⅓ cup) sugar
pinch salt
1 oz (⅛ cup) butter

Preheat oven to 350°F (gas mark 4). Mix barley and sugar and put half the mixture into a greased baking dish. Layer the apples on top and finish off with remaining barley and sugar mixture. Pour in the water. Combine the flour, sugar and salt and rub in the butter. Sprinkle the crumble over the barley and bake for 40 minutes or until nicely browned on top.

Millet is said to be the very first cereal grain cultivated by man. Plants of the millet family, to which sorghum also belongs, are prolific growers and they can be grown very successfully even with primitive farming methods. 12,000 years ago, before the introduction of rice, millet was the staple food of China. Today it is still a major food crop in parts of Africa, Asia and India. It is a particularly useful crop in areas likely to suffer drought, since during long periods without rain the plant stops growing but thrives again once there is water available. Millet has a short growing cycle and under suitable conditions 2 crops a year can be sown and harvested.

In the west millet is generally demoted to an animal food, but why this is so is a mystery. Millet compares well nutritionally with other cereals, and the cooked grains and flours are delicious. It contains vitamins of the B complex, important minerals, especially iron, and 9% by weight of protein. Millet grain is always hulled since the outer part is too hard to cook. Fortunately this does not involve a large nutrient loss, and millet grain is almost as nutritious as whole millet flour which includes the milled hull or bran section of the grain. See Table 1, page 12, to compare the nutrient content of millet with other cereals. Many long-lived peoples, including the famous Hunzas of the Himalayas, cultivate millet as a staple crop.

The general name millet derives from the Old English word *mil*, which itself was derived from the Latin name *milium*. Common millet, the most widely grown member of the millet family, is known by a host of other names including French, Indian, white, hog, broom (the branches of this plant are well suited for making brooms) and the old Slavic name *Prosso*. There are two other popularly grown millets: pearl, cat tail or bulrush millet, and fox-tail, Italian or yellow millet. This latter plant is the most widely used millet for human consumption in Britain and the U S A. It is easily identified from other millets by its light yellow, small, spherical kernels.

Sorghum, a member of the millet family, is little known in the West, but it is a cereal grain of major importance in many parts of Africa, and was ranked only behind wheat, rice and corn in world food consumption in a recent United Nations survey. Sorghum originated in Africa many thousands of years ago. In prehistoric times it entered Egypt and from there spread to Asia, reaching India and China where it is still an important crop. The Spaniards introduced sorghum to the New World via Mexico, and nowadays sorghum is cultivated in both North and South America as an animal food.

COMMON   BULRUSH   FOXTAIL

Within the sorghum family there are many varieties of plant but the most important in terms of food for human consumption is great or dourra millet. It has large white seeds, and it is this grain which is the leading cereal in Africa.

Nutritionally sorghum is similar to common millet although on average the protein content of sorghum is a little higher (11% compared to 9% by weight). Sorghum grain is usually eaten unmilled and sorghum flour is made from whole unhulled grain. Both these factors add to sorghum's nutritional worth, particularly in areas where it is a staple food crop.

DETAIL OF
SINGLE EAR

Sorghum grains are generally bigger than millet grains, and thus take longer to cook, but both expand enormously. 1 lb of millet or sorghum will serve more people than 1 lb of rice, wheat or corn.

Methods for preparing both plain boiled millet and sorghum are given below. All the other recipes are for millet alone, but where cooked millet is stipulated cooked sorghum may be substituted. Where uncooked millet is an ingredient parboiled sorghum may be substituted. Both plain cooked millet and sorghum can be used much as you would use rice.

Both whole sorghum and whole millet flour should be kept refrigerated since they contain the germ of the grain and its constituent oil and thus go rancid quite quickly.

Plain millet

Method 1
1¾ pt (4½ cups) water
½ teaspoon salt
8 oz (1 cup) millet

Bring the water to the boil in a heavy pan with a good tight-fitting lid. Add the salt and millet, stir and return to the boil. Cover, reduce heat and simmer for about 20 minutes or until all the water is absorbed.

Method 2
This method requires a little more trouble but brings out the natural flavour of the grain more than the plain boiling method above.

1 teaspoon vegetable oil   1½ pt (4 cups) water
8 oz (1 cup) millet   ½ teaspoon salt

Coat the bottom of a heavy saucepan with the oil and heat over a medium heat. Add the millet and sauté with constant stirring until lightly browned. Allow to cool a little and then stir in the water. Add the salt, bring to the boil, cover, reduce heat and simmer for 20 minutes.

Plain sorghum

8 oz (1 cup) sorghum
1¾ pt (4½ cups) water
½ teaspoon salt

Put the sorghum in a heavy pot, add the water and bring to the boil. Cover, reduce heat and simmer over a very low heat for around 1 hour. The cooked grains remain quite chewy but should be well swollen and separate. Check the water in the pot two-thirds of the way through cooking time and add more if needed. The cooked sorghum should be moist but not sloppy.

Millet porridge

4 oz (½ cup) millet
¾ pt (2 cups) water
½ teaspoon salt
honey and milk to taste

Soak the millet in the water overnight in a heavy pan. Bring to the boil cover, reduce heat and very gently simmer for 20 minutes. Stir in the salt and serve with honey and milk.

Millet and fruit porridge

4 oz (½ cup) millet
16 fl oz (2 cups) milk
½ teaspoon salt
1 apple, grated
4 oz (½ cup) raisins
honey and milk to taste

Put the millet in a heavy saucepan, add the milk, bring to the boil, reduce heat, cover and very gently simmer for 35 to 40 minutes. Stir in the salt, apple and raisins and leave to simmer a further 15 minutes. Serve with honey and milk to taste.

Millet croquettes

1 lb (2 cups) cooked millet
1 medium onion, finely diced
1 small carrot, grated
4 oz (½ cup) cheese, grated (optional)
1 egg, beaten
1 tablespoon soy sauce
about 4 oz (½ cup) wholewheat flour

Combine all the ingredients in a bowl adding enough flour to hold the mixture together. Form the mixture into burger shapes for shallow frying or ball shapes for deep frying. For shallow frying, oil a frying pan and fry the burgers (croquettes) on both sides over a low heat until nicely browned. For deep frying, heat the oil in a deep fryer until it just starts to smoke and deep fry the millet balls a golden brown. Drain on absorbent paper and serve.

Millet cheese and nut rissoles

2 tablespoons vegetable oil
1 medium onion, diced
4 oz (½ cup) millet flakes (grits)
4 oz (½ cup) cheese, grated
4 oz (½ cup) ground or flaked nuts

1 tablespoon fresh parsley, chopped
1 teaspoon salt
½ teaspoon black pepper
1 egg, beaten
oil for deep frying

Heat the oil in a heavy frying pan and sauté the onion until soft. Stir in the millet and sauté a further 3 or 4 minutes with constant stirring. Remove from the heat and transfer the mixture to a mixing bowl. Add the remaining ingredients and mix well. Add a little water if the mixture is very stiff. Form into oval patties (rissoles) and deep fry a golden brown. Drain on absorbent paper and serve.

Alternatively, preheat an oven to 400°F (gas mark 6), grease a baking sheet, place the rissoles on it and bake until brown and crisp (about 20 minutes).

Millet and lentil burgers

8 oz (1 cup) cooked lentils
8 oz (1 cup) cooked millet
1 teaspoon salt
½ teaspoon black pepper

2 eggs, beaten
About 2 oz (¼ cup) wholewheat flour
4 oz (1 cup) breadcrumbs
oil for frying

Combine the lentils, millet, salt, black pepper, half the beaten egg and enough flour to form a mixture that holds its shape. Form the mixture into burger shapes, brush them with the remaining egg and coat with breadcrumbs. Heat the oil in a heavy frying pan and fry the burgers on both sides until nicely browned.

Millet with onions

8 oz (1 cup) millet
2 oz (¼ cup) butter or margarine
2 medium onions, diced
1 teaspoon salt

½ teaspoon black pepper
1¼ pt (3 cups) boiling water
2 tablespoons fresh parsley, chopped

Put the millet in a heavy pot and dry roast with constant stirring over a medium heat until browned. Add the butter or margarine and onions and sauté the mixture for 2 to 3 minutes. Add the salt, black pepper and boiling water, cover the pot, reduce the heat and simmer for 30 minutes. Stir in parsley and serve. Excellent with curried vegetables.

Variation
Just before the millet is cooked, stir in 2 oz (¼ cup) raisins and 4 oz (½ cup) of mixed nuts and sunflower seeds. (Roasted pine nuts or almonds or cashews or a mixture of them are particularly good). Continue cooking and serve when the millet is cooked.

Millet with beans

Ingredients as for Millet with onion, plus 8 oz (1½ cups) cooked beans (red beans, chick-peas, haricot beans, aduki beans, etc.). Proceed as directed in the recipe above and add the cooked beans at the same time as the water. Continue as in recipe above. Some or all of the water may be replaced by the liquid the beans were cooked in.

Millet and vegetables

1 tablespoon vegetable oil
1 medium onion, sliced
6 oz (⅔ cup) millet
1 medium potato, diced
4 oz (1 cup) cabbage, shredded
2 sticks celery, chopped

2 tablespoons fresh parsley, chopped
1¼ pt (3 cups) water
½ teaspoon dried rosemary
salt and black pepper to taste
2 oz (¼ cup) butter

Heat the oil in a casserole dish and sauté the onion until golden. Add the millet and sauté, stirring, until it starts to darken in colour. Put in the vegetables and parsley and 1 pint (2½ cups) water and bring to the boil. Add the rosemary, season to taste with salt and black pepper. Cover the casserole and simmer over a very low heat for 30 minutes or until the vegetables and millet are tender. Add a little more water if the mixture starts to dry out. Serve topped with knobs of butter.

Millet with cheese

8 oz (1 cup) millet
12 fl oz (1½ cups) vegetable or meat
   stock

salt to taste
2 oz (¼ cup) butter
8 oz (1 cup) cheese, grated

Put the millet in a heavy saucepan, add the stock and salt to taste and bring to the boil. Cover, reduce heat and simmer for 30 minutes. Stir in the butter and half the cheese and stir until the cheese melts. Pour into a serving dish, top with remaining cheese and serve.

Millet, cheese and onion pie

8 oz (1 cup) wholemeal flour
4 oz (½cup) millet flakes or flour
6 oz (⅔ cup) butter or margarine
water
2 tablespoons vegetable oil

4 medium onions, sliced
8 oz (1 cup) cheese, grated
oregano
salt and black pepper

Preheat oven to 375°F (gas mark 5). Combine the flour and millet flakes or flour and rub in the butter. Add enough water to form a soft pastry. Divide the pastry into 2 equal portions and use one half to line a pie dish. Heat the oil in a heavy frying pan and sauté the onions until golden. Layer the cooked onion and cheese in the pie dish and sprinkle a little oregano, salt and black pepper over each layer. Cover dish with remaining pastry and press the edges down. Make two small cross cuts in the pastry case and bake for 35 minutes or until nicely browned. Served with baked potato and salad.

Millet casserole

8 oz (1 cup) millet
1¼ pt (3 cups) water
½ teaspoon salt
2 tablespoons vegetable oil
1 clove garlic, crushed
1 medium onion, diced
1 medium carrot, sliced

2 tablespoons tomato purée
1 teaspoon dried basil
1 tablespoon fresh parsley, chopped
1 pt (2¼ cups) béchemal sauce (see index)
4 oz (½ cup) cheese, grated

Put the millet, water and salt in a heavy pot. Bring to the boil, cover, reduce heat and simmer for 30 minutes. Meanwhile heat the vegetable oil in a heavy frying pan and put in the garlic, onion and carrot. Sauté until the vegetables are soft. Stir in the tomato purée, basil and parsley and set aside. Preheat oven to 350°F (gas mark 4). In a casserole dish make alternate layers of the cooked millet and the vegetable mixture. Pour over the béchemal sauce and top with grated cheese. Bake for 30 minutes or until top is nicely browned.

Millet, mushroom and green pepper pudding

1 tablespoon vegetable oil
1 medium green pepper, diced
4 oz (1½ cups) mushrooms, diced
6 fl oz (⅔ cup) milk, hot

3 oz (⅓ cup) millet flakes (grits)
4 oz (½ cup) cheese, grated
salt and black pepper to taste
2 eggs, separated

Preheat oven to 350°F (gas mark 4). Heat vegetable oil in a heavy frying pan and sauté the green pepper for 2 or 3 minutes. Add the mushrooms and sauté a further 2 or 3 minutes. Transfer the mixture to a mixing bowl, add the milk and millet flakes and set aside for 5 minutes. Stir in the cheese, season to taste with salt and black pepper and beat in the egg yolks. Fold in the beaten egg whites and transfer to a greased baking dish. Bake for 35 minutes or until nicely browned on top and cooked in the centre.

Millet soufflé

3 eggs, separated
1 lb (2 cups) cooked millet
4 oz (½ cup) grated cheese

6 fl oz (⅔ cup) milk
½ teaspoon salt
¼ teaspoon black pepper

Preheat oven to 350°F (gas mark 4). Beat the egg yolks lightly and beat the egg whites stiff. Combine the millet, the cheese, the beaten egg yolks milk and salt and pepper and mix well. Fold in the egg whites and transfer the mixture to greased baking or soufflé dish. Bake for 20 minutes or until set.

Millet omelette

8 oz (1 cup) millet flakes (grits)
10 fl oz (1¼ cups) milk, hot
3 eggs, beaten

1 tablespoon fresh parsley, chopped
salt and black pepper to taste
oil for frying

Put the millet flakes into a mixing bowl and pour in the hot milk. Allow to stand for 30 minutes and then beat in the eggs, parsley and season to taste with salt and black pepper. Prepare omelette(s) in a heavy frying pan. Add your favourite omelette filling, e.g. grated cheese, sweetcorn, mushrooms, etc.

Millet stuffed green peppers

4 to 6 medium sized green peppers,
    with the tops cut off and deseeded

Stuffing
1 tablespoon vegetable oil
1 clove garlic, crushed
1 medium onion, diced
1 green or red pepper, chopped
2 oz (½ cup) mushrooms, sliced
8 oz (1 cup) cooked millet *or*
    cooked millet and onion (see p. 136)

1 egg lightly beaten
2 oz (¼ cup) cheese, grated *or*
    cottage cheese
1 ripe tomato, chopped
½ teaspoon salt
¼ teaspoon black pepper
½ teaspoon dried basil
1 tablespoon fresh parsley, chopped

Preheat oven to 375°F (gas mark 5). Submerge green peppers in a pan of boiling water for 3 to 4 minutes. Remove, rinse under cold water and drain. Heat oil in a heavy frying pan and sauté garlic, onion, pepper and mushrooms until the onion is softened. Combine the millet and cooked vegetables with the remaining ingredients and pack the mixture into the green peppers. Cut the cores out of the tops of the green peppers and place the tops back on the stuffed peppers. Put the stuffed peppers in a greased baking dish and run in ½ inch of hot water. Put dish in the preheated oven and bake for 30 minutes.

Variations
Stuff the peppers with the mixtures used to make Millet and lentil burgers, or Millet croquettes or Millet cheese and nut rissoles (see index for page numbers).

Millet stuffed tomatoes

8 large firm tomatoes
4 oz (½ cup) cooked millet *or*
    uncooked millet flakes (grits)

½ medium onion, grated
4 oz (½ cup) grated cheese
1 tablespoon soy sauce

Preheat oven to 325°F (gas mark 3). Cut the tops from the tomatoes and remove the centre pulp. Combine this with the remaining ingredients and stuff the mixture back in the tomatoes. Put the tops on and place on a greased baking dish. Bake for 15 minutes.

★Chicken and millet pilaff

8 oz (1 cup) millet
2 tablespoons oil
4 portions chicken, skinned
2 medium onions, sliced
1 teaspoon paprika

1 medium carrot, quartered
1 teaspoon salt
¼ teaspoon black pepper
2 pt (5 cups) chicken or meat stock
8 fl oz (1 cup) sour cream (optional)

Preheat oven to 350°F (gas mark 4). Put the millet in a heavy casserole and dry roast over a moderate heat with constant stirring until lightly browned. Remove millet, allow casserole to cool a little and add the oil. Put the chicken in and brown for 5 minutes. Remove chicken and add the onions and paprika. Brown the onions. Return chicken and millet to casserole, add the carrot, salt and black pepper and pour in the stock. Cover casserole and bake for 1 to 1½ hours or until chicken is tender. Check occasionally to make sure contents are moist and not dried up. Add stock as required. Serve with sour cream if desired.

Millet and peanut squares

8 oz (1 cup) millet flour or millet flakes
8 oz (2 cups) strong white flour
4 oz (½ cup) flaked peanuts
½ teaspoon salt
1 teaspoon cinnamon

1 tablespoon honey (optional)
water
1 egg, beaten
1 tablespoon poppy seeds (optional)

Preheat oven to 350°F (gas mark 4). Combine all the ingredients except egg and poppy seeds, and enough water to form a firm dough. Roll the dough ¼ inch thick on a greased baking sheet. Cut into squares with a sharp knife, brush the top with beaten egg and sprinkle over poppy seeds. Bake for 20 to 25 minutes.

Sweet millet and milk pudding

4 oz (½ cup) millet flakes (grits)
1 pt (2½ cups) milk
1 egg, beaten
1 teaspoon cinnamon

pinch nutmeg
1 tablespoon honey or sugar
pinch salt

Preheat oven to 350°F (gas mark 4). Combine millet and milk and beat in the egg. Bring the mixture to the boil and stir in remaining ingredients. Pour the mixture into a greased pie dish and bake for 20 to 25 minutes or until set and nicely browned on top.

Rye grass is thought to have originated in an area close to the Caspian Sea. It is closely related to wheat but in ancient times was thought to be just a troublesome weed and was not considered as a food source. Late in the history of the Roman Empire the Romans started to plant rye as a crop and by the Middle Ages rye was a staple grain in much of Europe. In medieval Britain rye and barley bread was as popular as the wheat variety. Rye bread is still common in Scandinavian countries, Germany and parts of Russia. Rye was introduced into the USA by early European settlers. It became popular as both a food and for making rye whisky for which much of present day rye is grown.

Although rye itself doesn't share the distinguished history of wheat grain, ergot, a fungus that grows on rye grain, probably had a considerable influence on the spiritual climate of medieval Europe. Ergot, from which the drug LSD is derived, has the same affect on the central nervous system as this very powerful hallucinogen and under damp conditions it forms as a mould on growing rye grains. Flour made from these grains and eaten will have bizarre affects on the consumer, and historians believe that many of the 'Devil-induced' plagues of the Middle Ages were probably caused by such a phenomona. I wonder how many witches died at the stake for eating rye bread.

Rye flour contains less gluten than wheat flour and consequently rises less in the bread-making process. Rye bread is flatter and more filling than yeasted wheat bread. It has a distinctive taste and texture. Thin slices of dark rye bread are excellent for preparing Danish-style open sandwiches. Combination wheat- and rye-flour breads, which combine some of the qualities of both grains, are also popular.

Dark rye flour is prepared from the whole grain while the lighter coloured rye flour has had some of the bran removed. Wholerye grains or groats may be used in the same ways as wholewheat grains or brown rice (see recipe index) while cracked rye (grits or flakes) cook more quickly and are useful in stews, soups and cake making.

Wholerye grains or flour are an excellent source of the B vitamins, particularly niacin. They contain an average 12% by weight of protein, which compares well with rice, wheat and corn, and a significant amount of important minerals. For a comparison of the nutrient content of rye with other grains see Table 1 on page 12.

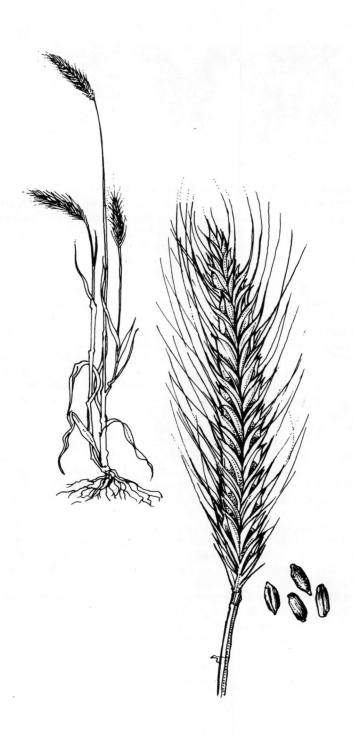

Plain boiled rye grains

8 oz (1 cup) whole rye,
   soaked overnight

1 pt (2½ cups) water
½ teaspoon salt

Drain the rye and put into a heavy saucepan. Add the water and bring to the boil. Stir in the salt, cover and reduce heat to very low. Simmer for one hour.
   Substitute cooked whole rye for brown rice or wholewheat either as a side dish or as an ingredient in savoury dishes such as pilaffs, risottos, etc.

Rye porridge

Serves 2

8 oz (1 cup) rye flakes (grits)
1¼ pt (3 cups) water
½ teaspoon salt

Milk, honey, fresh fruit, etc., to
   accompany porridge

Put the rye and water into a heavy pot and bring to the boil. Add the salt, mix well. Cover, reduce heat to a minimum and simmer for about 30 minutes. Stir occasionally. This makes quite a thick porridge. For a thinner, creamier porridge use more water and a longer cooking time. Serve with honey and milk to taste.

Variation
Prepare the porridge and beat in the yolk of 1 egg and 1 tablespoon of butter. Pour the porridge into a greased dish and allow to cool. Cut into slices and fry brown on both sides. Serve on its own with grated cheese as a snack or substitute for potatoes in a main meal.

Cream of rye and vegetable soup

1 tablespoon vegetable oil
4 oz (½ cup) rye flakes (grits)
1 medium carrot, sliced
2 sticks celery, chopped
1 clove garlic, crushed
1 medium onion, diced

1 tablespoon tomato purée
1¼ pt (3 cups) stock (or water and
  stock cubes)
salt and black pepper to taste
chopped chives *or*
  chopped fresh parsley for garnish

Heat the oil in a heavy pot, put in the rye flakes and sauté, stirring, until browned. Add the remaining ingredients and bring to the boil. Cover, reduce heat and simmer for 40 to 45 minutes. Blend the mixture smooth and serve garnished with chives or parsley.

Rye and winter vegetable stew

2 tablespoons vegetable oil
2 medium leeks, chopped
2 medium beetroots, peeled, chopped
2 medium parsnips, sliced

8 oz (1 cup) cooked whole rye
4 oz (½ cup) cooked beans or lentils
1¼ pt (3 cups) water or stock
salt and black pepper to taste

Heat the oil in a heavy pot and sauté the leeks and beetroot for 5 minutes. Add the parsnips and sauté a further 5 minutes. Add the rye, beans and water. Mix well, season to taste. Bring to the boil, cover, reduce heat and simmer for 45 minutes to 1 hour. The soup is a beautiful hearty red colour.

Nut and rye rissoles

2 oz (¼ cup) rye flakes
8 oz (1 cup) ground nuts
1 medium onion, diced
1 medium carrot, grated
1 teaspoon dried thyme
1 teaspoon salt

½ teaspoon black pepper
1¼ pt (3 cups) hot water or stock,
  approximately
4 oz (1 cup) toasted breadcrumbs
oil for frying

Mix together the rye flakes and ground nuts and stir in the vegetables, thyme and seasoning. Add enough hot water or stock to form a firm, but quite sticky mixture. Wet your hands and form the mixture into rissoles or balls (about ½inch in diameter). Roll the rissoles or balls in breadcrumbs and either shallow or deep fry golden brown.

Variations
1: Add 4 oz (½ cup) grated cheese to the ingredients.
2: Prepare the mixture and pack into a greased bread tin. Bake in a preheated oven at 350°F (gas mark 4) for 30 minutes. Serve in slices hot or cold.

Rye grain soufflé

3 eggs, separated
8 oz (1 cup) cooked rye grains or
  cooked rye flakes (grits)
½ teaspoon salt
½ teaspoon mace

¼ teaspoon black pepper
1 oz (⅛ cup) butter, melted
8 fl oz (1 cup) milk
4 oz (½ cup) grated cheese

Preheat oven to 375°F (gas mark 5). Beat the egg yolks lightly and beat the egg whites stiff. Add the egg yolks to the other ingredients and mix well. Fold in the egg whites and put the mixture in a greased baking dish or soufflé dish. Bake for 25 minutes or until nicely browned and firm.

★Beef and rye casserole

8 oz (1 cup) rye flakes (grits)
2 tablespoons fat or oil
1 lb beef, cubed
1 clove garlic, crushed
2 medium onions, quartered

4 small carrots
½ teaspoon english mustard
½ teaspoon paprika
salt and black pepper to taste
1¼ pt (3 cups) water or stock

Preheat oven to 375°F (gas mark 5). Dry roast the rye flakes in a heavy frying pan until nicely browned all over. Set aside. In a heavy pot melt the fat and brown the beef. Add the garlic and onion and sauté until the onion is soft. Layer the base of a casserole dish with toasted rye flakes and put in the meat and onions and the carrots. Combine the seasoning with the water and pour into the casserole. Cover and bake for 1 hour or until the beef is tender.

Simple rye bread

In this recipe rye flour is used undiluted with wheat flour. It makes a very tasty but heavy bread. Cut it in thin slices and use for open-topped sandwiches.

It's best to prepare the dough early evening on one day and then allow it to rise overnight. The second rising will take the whole of the next day and the bread can be baked the following evening.

½ oz (1 cake) fresh yeast
1 teaspoon sugar
10 fl oz (1¼ cups) warm water

½ teaspoon salt
12 oz (3 cups) dark rye flour

Add the yeast and sugar to the water, mix well and set aside in a warm place for about 10 minutes. Put the salt in the rye flour and stir it with a wooden spoon. Pour in the yeast mixture, stirring all the time. Turn the dough onto a floured board and knead for 5 to 10 minutes. Put the dough into a clean, greased mixing bowl, cover with a damp cloth and set in a warm place. Leave for 12 to 15 hours. Knead the dough again for 2 to 3 minutes, and then press it into a greased bread tin. Cover again and set aside in a warm place for 6 to 8 hours. Preheat oven to 375°F (gas mark 5) and bake bread on the middle shelf for 1 hour.

Light rye bread

1 lb (4 cups) light rye flour
2 lb (8 cups) wholewheat flour
2 tablespoons caraway seeds
1 tablespoon salt

1 oz (1½ cakes) yeast
1½ pt (4 cups) warm water
1 tablespoon honey or sugar
1 oz (⅛ cup) butter, oil or margarine

Combine the rye flour, wheat flour, caraway seeds and salt in a large mixing bowl and set aside in a warm place. Add the yeast to the warm water, stir in the sugar and melted butter or oil. Whisk well together and set aside in a warm place for 5 to 10 minutes. Pour the yeast mixture into the flours and beat to form a smooth dough. Add a little flour if the dough is too soft. Turn the dough onto a floured board and knead for about 5 minutes. Clean the mixing bowl and lightly grease. Put the dough inside and cover. Leave to rise in a warm place for 1 to 1½ hours. Grease 4 bread tins and pack the dough in. Cover again and set aside in a warm place for 30 to 40 minutes or until dough has doubled in size. Preheat oven to 375°F (gas mark 5). Bake for 45 minutes or until the loaves sound hollow when tapped on the bottom.

Rye rolls

Prepare half the quantity of dough as above. Pinch off pieces of dough after the first rising and knead into balls. Place them on a greased baking sheet and leave to rise until doubled in size (about 30 minutes). Bake in a preheated oven at 350°F (gas mark 4) for 30 minutes.

Rye and buckwheat bread

Substitute 8 oz (2 cups) buckwheat flour for the same weight of wholewheat flour in the Light rye bread recipe and proceed as directed in that recipe.

Rye rusks

Rusks are pieces of re-baked thinly sliced bread. They are dry, crisp and very light and excellent for children or people with upset stomachs.

1 oz (1½ cake) fresh yeast
4 fl oz (½ cup) warm water
1 teaspoon sugar or honey
1 pt (2½ cups) milk
1 teaspoon salt

12 oz (3 cups) rye flour
12 oz (3 cups) wholemeal flour
4 oz (½ cup) melted butter
2 teaspoons caraway seeds

Add yeast to warm water and sugar, whisk well and set aside in a warm place to bubble (about 10 minutes). Add the milk and salt and stir. Combine the flours and stir in the yeast mixture, melted butter and caraway seeds. Knead the dough on a floured board for 5 minutes and then pinch pieces off and form into 4 inch diameter ¾ inch thick rounds. Place on greased baking sheet and set aside in a warm place to rise until doubled in size. Preheat oven to 400°F (gas mark 6) and bake for 30 minutes or until well browned. Remove from the oven and allow to cool. Split the rounds in 2 horizontally with a sharp knife. Return the halves to a low oven and bake until crisp and dry. Store in an airtight tin.

Rye crackers

4 oz (1 cup) rye flour
6 oz (1½ cups) wholewheat flour
1 teaspoon caraway seeds
1 teaspoon powdered fennel
2 teaspoons orange rind, grated
½ teaspoon salt

1 tablespoon honey
4 fl oz (½ cup) warm milk or water
2 oz (¼ cup) butter, melted or
 vegetable oil
1 egg white, lightly beaten

Preheat oven to 425°F (gas mark 7). Combine the first 6 ingredients and mix well. Whisk the honey, milk and butter together. Pour into the flour mixture and beat into a firm dough. Roll out into a thin sheet less than a ¼ inch thick and cut into squares, triangles or rounds. Brush the tops with beaten egg white. Place the shapes onto a greased baking sheet and bake on the top shelf of the oven for 15 minutes. Cool and store in an airtight container.

Nut and rye crunch

6 oz (⅔ cup) rye flakes (grits)
4 oz (½ cup) wholewheat flour
½ teaspoon salt
4 oz (½ cup) butter or margarine

4 oz (½ cup) brown sugar
1 tablespoon molasses or syrup
2 tablespoons water
2 oz (¼ cup) mixed chopped nuts

Preheat oven to 325°F (gas mark 3). Combine rye, flour and salt. Melt butter in a saucepan and stir in the sugar, molasses and water. Add the rye and flour mixture and mix well. Grease a shallow baking dish or tray and press the mixture into the base. Sprinkle mixed nuts over the top and bake for 1 hour or until nicely browned.

Rye and cottage cheese cakes

2 oz (½ cup) rye flour
½ teaspoon salt *and* (for savoury
 cakes)
½ teaspoon black pepper

or
1 teaspoon sugar (for sweet cakes)
2 eggs, beaten
8 oz (1 cup) cottage cheese
oil for frying

Combine all the ingredients and mix well. Add a little milk if the mixture is very thick. Drop tablespoonful amounts into a hot greased frying pan or griddle and lightly fry on both sides until set. Serve with chopped chives if savoury, or honey and cream if sweet.

Date and almond rye biscuits (cookies)

4 oz (½ cup) chopped dates
2 fl oz (¼ cup) hot water
4 oz (½ cup) butter or margarine
4 oz (½ cup) brown sugar

2 tablespoons ground almonds
8 oz (1 cup) rye flakes (grits)
12 blanched almonds

Preheat oven to 350°F (gas mark 4). Put the dates in the hot water and leave to soften. Melt the butter in a heavy saucepan and dissolve the sugar in it. Combine the ground almonds and rye flakes and stir into the saucepan. Add the soaked dates and water and mix well. Grease a 6 inch cake tin and press the mixture in, decorate the top with the blanched almonds. Bake for 20 minutes or until firm and nicely browned. Cut into portions and leave to cool.

Rye and cornmeal muffins

4 oz (1 cup) rye flour
2 oz (½ cup) cornmeal
½ teaspoon salt
1 teaspoon baking powder

2 oz (¼ cup) dried fruit
1 egg, beaten
8 fl oz (1 cup) milk
2 tablespoons honey

Preheat oven to 350°F (gas mark 4). Combine the rye flour, cornmeal, salt, baking powder and dried fruit and mix well. Whisk together the egg, milk and honey and stir into the flour mixture. Grease the muffin tins and pour the dough in. Fill the tins no more than ⅔ full. Bake for about 20 minutes.

BUCKWHEAT

Although buckwheat is commonly regarded as a grain, it is in fact the seed of a herbacious plant called *brank buckwheat* which is native to Central Asia. It was brought to Europe from Russia by the Tartars and was first cultivated here in Germany in the fifteenth century. It was from the German *buchweizen* or beech-wheat that the name was derived since the seeds of the plant resemble those of the seeds of the beechnut tree. In Italy buckwheat is called *faggina* while the name of the beech tree is *faggio*. Saracen wheat is another name for the seed which refers to the belief that the Crusaders introduced the plant into Europe.

Buckwheat grows to a height of about 2 feet, it has heart-shaped leaves and beautiful pink flowers and is sometimes grown as a garden flower. In areas of Russia where the plant grows wild, buckwheat honey is a great favourite. It is a tough, hardy plant that will grow in the harshest conditions without requiring much attention. The seed is expensive however, since the outer husk is difficult to remove and the grower must either invest in expensive equipment or time-consuming methods to process his crop.

The hulled grain is normally roasted before use and this roasted seed or kasha as it is called, is popular in parts of northern Europe as well as being part of the national cuisine of Russia. Kasha has an interesting nutty flavour and it makes a pleasant change from the regular grains. It is served both as a side dish in the way that potatoes or rice may be and as an ingredient in savoury dishes. The crushed seeds called groats cook more quickly than kasha. They are used in the same way or in sweet dishes and breakfast cereals to add crunchiness to the texture. Roasted groats are readily ground into flour if you have a hand grinder at home.

Buckwheat flour is used to make pancakes, muffins, cakes, etc. The flour is rather heavy and expensive and is usually mixed with lighter, cheaper flours such as wheat.

Buckwheat contains valuable amounts of all the B vitamins as well as quantities of minerals, particularly iron and, on average, 11% by weight of protein.

Plain buckwheat or kasha

8 oz (1 cup) buckwheat
16 fl oz (2 cups) boiling water
½ teaspoon salt

½ teaspoon salt
2 oz (¼ cup) melted butter

Toast the buckwheat in a heavy dry saucepan over a medium heat until it turns a deep colour and starts to smell nutty. Stir constantly to prevent it from burning. Pour over the boiling water, add the salt and cover. Reduce heat and simmer for 15 to 20 minutes or until all the water has been absorbed.

Middle Eastern kasha

8 oz (1 cup) buckwheat
1 egg, beaten
16 fl oz (2 cups) boiling water

Toast the buckwheat in a heavy dry saucepan over a medium heat and vigorously stir in the beaten egg. Continue heating and stirring until each grain is darkened in colour and separate. Pour in the water, add the salt and cover. Reduce heat and simmer for 15 to 20 minutes or until all the liquid is absorbed. Stir in the melted butter and serve.

Macrobiotic kasha

1 teaspoon sesame oil
8 oz (1 cup) buckwheat

16 fl oz (2 cups) boiling water
pinch salt

Heat the oil in a heavy frying pan over a medium heat. Put in the buckwheat and stir fry for about 5 minutes. Pour in boiling water, add salt and cover. Reduce heat and simmer for 15 minutes. Allow to stand for 5 minutes and serve.

Buckwheat cream

2 tablespoons vegetable oil
2 oz (¼ cup) buckwheat flour
16 fl oz (2 cups) water
1 medium onion, diced

soy sauce to taste
1 tablespoon chopped spring onions
  or scallions

Heat a heavy frying pan over a moderate flame and pour in half the oil. Add the buckwheat flour and sauté with constant stirring for a few minutes. Pour in the water and stir constantly over a low heat until the cream thickens (about 10 minutes). Sauté the onions in the remaining oil until soft and golden. Stir the onions into the buckwheat cream, season to taste with soy sauce and serve garnished with chopped spring onions or scallions. Serve on its own as a side dish or as a sauce with vegetables or other cooked grains.

Kasha loaf

1 lb (2 cups) cooked buckwheat
8 oz (1 cup) cooked brown rice
1 medium onion, diced
2 tablespoons fresh parsley, chopped

1 tablespoon fresh sage, chopped
4 oz (1 cup) cabbage, finely shredded
1 teaspoon salt
16 fl oz (2 cups) boiling water

Preheat oven to 350°F (gas mark 4). Combine the ingredients and mix well. Pack into a greased baking dish, cover and bake for 45 minutes. Remove the cover and brown the top. Serve with vegetables or a spicy sauce. To reheat, slice and toast or fry.

Kasha croquettes

1 lb (2 cups) cooked buckwheat
2 oz (½ cup) wholewheat flour
1 onion, diced
4 oz (1 cup) cooked vegetables or
   beans

1 tablespoon soy sauce
water
oil for frying

Combine the ingredients and mix in enough water (if needed) to form a moist mixture that will hold its shape. Form dough into balls of about 2 inches diameter or into burger shapes. Deep fry the balls in hot oil until golden brown or shallow fry the burger shapes in a little oil in a heavy frying pan. Brown both sides.

Buckwheat stuffed cabbage rolls (with apple sauce)

1 small white or chinese cabbage
8 oz (1 cup) cooked buckwheat
1 tablespoon sesame seeds, toasted
pinch of salt
1 tablespoon vegetable oil
1 medium onion, finely sliced
½ pt (1¼ cups) soup stock *or*
   water *and* 1 tablespoon miso

Apple sauce
2 lb apples
4 fl oz (½ cup) water
1 tablespoon fresh mint leaves,
   chopped
½ teaspoon salt

Preheat oven to 300°F (gas mark 2). Cut off the stem of the cabbage and separate the leaves. Soften them by steaming or dipping them into boiling water briefly. Mix the buckwheat, sesame seeds and pinch of salt. Place two or three tablespoons of mixture on each leaf and roll up. Lay the rolls seam side down in the bottom of an oiled casserole. Cover with onion rings and pour over the soup stock or water and miso. Cover and bake for 30 minutes. Meanwhile, prepare the apple sauce. Core and cut the apples into eighths. Place them in a heavy pan, add the water, mint and salt, cover and cook over a moderate heat for 20 minutes. Pass through a sieve if you wish to remove skins and serve with cabbage rolls.

Potato and kasha

8 oz (1 cup) buckwheat	1 teaspoon salt
2 tablespoons vegetable oil	½ teaspoon black pepper
2 medium potatoes, diced	1½ pt (4 cups) water
1 medium onion, sliced	8 oz (1 cup) grated cheese

In a heavy pan, dry roast the buckwheat over a medium heat until darkened in colour. Transfer the buckwheat to another container. Coat the pan with the oil and put in the potatoes and onion. Sauté, stirring, for about 5 minutes. Add the buckwheat, salt, pepper and water and bring to the boil. Reduce heat and simmer for 20 to 30 minutes or until all the liquid is absorbed. Serve topped with grated cheese.

Variation
Add other winter vegetables to the pot such as cabbage, swede, parsnip, etc.

Buckwheat stuffing

Use this stuffing for stuffed vegetables or poultry.

1 tablespoon vegetable oil	4 oz (½ cup) mixed nuts (lightly fried pine nuts are excellent)
1 clove garlic, crushed	
1 medium onion, diced	1 teaspoon salt
1 green pepper, diced	½ teaspoon black pepper
8 oz (1 cup) cooked buckwheat	1 teaspoon cinnamon

Heat the oil in a heavy frying pan. Put in the garlic and onion and sauté until soft and golden. Add the salt and pepper and sauté a further 3 or 4 minutes. Combine the cooked vegetables with the remaining ingredients and mix well together.

Buckwheat noodles

Buckwheat noodles are tastier and chewier than the wheat flour variety. They are most popular in Japan where buckwheat noodles (called soba) are a particular favourite at New Year when they are thought to bring happiness and a lucky year ahead.

Buckwheat flour noodles

1 lb (4 cups) buckwheat flour	1 egg, beaten
1 teaspoon salt	4 fl oz (½ cup) water, approximately

Place the flour and salt in a large mixing bowl, thoroughly mix and then beat in the egg. Gradually add water to form a firm dough. Roll out, shape and cook the noodles as described for wheat flour noodles page 36.

Fried buckwheat noodles with spinach

2 tablespoons oil
4 cloves garlic, crushed
1 lb fresh spinach, washed, coarsely
  chopped and drained

12 oz (1½ cups) buckwheat noodles,
  cooked
salt and black pepper to taste

Heat the oil in a heavy pan. Add the garlic and sauté until light brown (about 3 minutes). Drop in the spinach, cover pan and lower heat. Stir occasionally. Simmer until spinach is completely wilted. Now stir in noodles, season with salt and black pepper and heat through. Serve.

Fried buckwheat noodles with eggs

3 tablespoons vegetable oil
4 eggs, beaten
pinch of salt and black pepper
6 oz (1½ cups) chinese cabbage,
  chopped
1 medium onion, thinly sliced
3 tablespoons soy sauce

or
2 tablespoons miso (creamed with a
  little water)
12 oz (1½ cups) buckwheat noodles,
  cooked and drained

Coat a heavy pan or frying pan with a tablespoon oil, heat and pour in the eggs. Season with salt and black pepper and scramble until well cooked. Remove eggs from pan and reserve. Add remaining oil to pan and lightly sauté cabbage and onion for about 3 minutes. Stir in the soy sauce or miso, mix well. Add noodles and egg and heat through.

Buckwheat pancakes

Buckwheat pancakes have a more definite flavour than their wheat flour cousins and make excellent savoury as well as sweet pancakes.

4 oz (1 cup) buckwheat flour
1 oz (⅛ cup) wholewheat flour
pinch of salt
1 teaspoon baking powder (optional)
12 fl oz (1½ cups) water

or
half milk/half water
1 egg, beaten
oil for frying

Combine all the ingredients and mix well. Heat a greased heavy frying pan or griddle and when it is hot ladle in a thin layer of batter. Turn and brown both sides. To prepare stuffed savoury pancakes stuff the pancakes with cooked vegetables or meat, place in a greased dish, cover them with a béchemal sauce or cheese sauce and bake in a medium oven. For sweet pancakes serve with sugar or honey and lemon juice, apple sauce or other stewed fruit, etc.

Japanese buckwheat omelette (okonomi-yaki)

This recipe prepares two omelettes.

3 oz (¾ cup) buckwheat flour
3 fl oz (⅜ cup) water
3 eggs, lightly beaten
1 teaspoon soy sauce

½ medium onion, diced
2 oz (½ cup) mushrooms, sliced
½ medium pepper diced
2 tablespoons vegetable oil

Combine the flour, water, eggs and soy sauce and mix into a smooth batter. Stir the vegetables into the batter. Heat half the oil in a heavy frying pan and ladle in half the batter mixture. Cook on both sides over a low heat, until nicely browned. Repeat for remaining batter mixture. The vegetables remain slightly uncooked and the omelette has a nice crunchy texture.

Variation
Add cooked meat, fish or shellfish to the batter mixture.

Sweet buckwheat cake

5 oz (1½ cups) buckwheat flour
2 oz (½ cup) plain flour
¼ teaspoon salt
½ teaspoon cinnamon
¼ teaspoon ginger

2 oz (¼ cup) currants
4 fl oz (½ cup) honey
2 oz (¼ cup) brown sugar
8 fl oz (1 cup) vegetable oil
water

Preheat oven to 375°F (gas mark 5). Combine the dry ingredients and mix well together. Blend or whisk together the honey, sugar and oil and beat the mixture into the dry ingredients. Add enough water just to moisten the mixture and then press it into a greased cake or bread tin. Bake for 30 minutes or until nicely browned on top.

Variation
For a crunchier cake use 4 oz (½ cup) toasted buckwheat groats and 4 oz (1 cup) plain flour, the other ingredients remain the same.

Sesame buckwheat cakes

8 oz (2 cups) buckwheat flour
1 teaspoon salt
2 tablespoons sesame oil

16 fl oz (2 cups) boiling water
1 egg, beaten
2 tablespoons toasted sesame seeds

Preheat oven to 350°F (gas mark 4). Combine flour and salt and rub oil into the mixture. Slowly pour the boiling water over the mixture while beating vigorously with a fork. Knead the dough for a few minutes and then roll into a sheet ½ inch thick. Cut out rounds and brush the top of each with beaten egg. Sprinkle sesame seeds over them and place on a greased baking sheet. Bake for 20 to 25 minutes or until nicely browned.

Buckwheat biscuits (cookies)

4 oz (1 cup) buckwheat flour
½ teaspoon salt
½ teaspoon cinnamon
1 tablespoon brown sugar

1 oz (⅛ cup) butter
water
2 oz (¼ cup) flaked peanuts

Preheat oven to 350°F (gas mark 4). Combine the flour, salt, cinnamon and sugar. Rub in the butter and add enough water to form a soft batter. Mix well. Drop spoonful amounts onto a greased baking sheet and top each with flaked peanuts. Bake for 20 minutes or until nicely browned.

Buckwheat onion biscuits (cookies)

4 oz (1 cup) buckwheat flour
4 oz (1 cup) toasted buckwheat groats
½ teaspoon salt

1 medium onion, diced, sautéed in 1
    tablespoon vegetable oil
water

Preheat oven to 375°F (gas mark 5). Combine all the ingredients adding enough water to form a firm but moist dough. Roll into a sheet ⅓ inch thick and cut into rounds. Put the rounds onto a greased baking sheet and bake for 20 minutes or until nicely browned. They should be crisp and crunchy. Serve with cheese and salad.

Buckwheat and apple muffins

6 oz (1½ cups) buckwheat flour
2 oz (½ cup) wholewheat flour
1 teaspoon salt
1 teaspoon cinnamon
1 egg, beaten

1 large apple, diced
16 fl oz (2 cups) milk *or* milk and water
2 tablespoons honey

Preheat oven to 425°F (gas mark 7). Combine all the dry ingredients and mix well. Beat the egg, milk, apple and honey together and stir into the dry mixture. Grease muffin tins and pour in the mixture. Bake for 30 minutes.

Introduction

The title of the book is something of a misnomer since in this section on beans I am also dealing with peas and lentils. I took this step to avoid confusion since in Britain this group of foods are known as pulses, and in America only as legumes although I suspect that many people in either country would not recognize either name. The solution was to call them beans, which everyone recognizes even if the name tends to stand for the baked variety in tomato sauce, as 'Beanz meanz Heinz.'

Beans, peas and lentils are the seeds of plants which belong to the family of plants called legumes. Legumes, together with cereal grains, were the earliest food crops cultivated by man. They grow in a wide range of climates and provide an excellent protein and carbohydrate source as well as some vital vitamins and minerals. Eaten in combination with cereal grains legumes can provide all the essential amino acids needed by the body. In spite of these important considerations and although many famous regional dishes contain legumes as a principal ingredient, e.g. cassoulet, chili con carne, cholent, etc., beans, peas and lentils have normally been considered a poor man's meat. This is regardless of the fact that they are a very versatile, nutritious, tasty and economical food source in their own right and a comparison with meat is unnecessary. Leguminous plants return valuble nitrates to the soil, their seeds (the part we eat) store well and in a world short of agricultural land and an expanding population it may well be that they will become an even more important particularly as meat and dairy products become too expensive for most people to afford.

This part of the book devoted solely to legumes is divided into four sections. The first deals briefly with the history, botany and nutrient content of legumes in general. The second describe in detail each of the common beans, peas and lentils and the third outlines the basic preparation and cooking of each of these. The fourth and largest is the recipe section. This is divided into soups, dips and spreads, salads and main dishes. Within these separate categories individual legumes are grouped together.

History and botany of beans

The Leguminosae or bean family is a huge one. It contains over 14,000 species and it is the second largest family of seed plants. These leguminous (meaning pod-bearing) plants have the valuable property of fixing atmospheric nitrogen in nodules in the roots of the plant and converting it into nitrates which enrich the soil in which the plant grows. They are thus of double value as both food source and fertilizer and are particularly important in areas of the world where fertilizer is not available or too expensive for farmers to buy. The edible seeds of the leguminous plants are the parts we eat. The dried seeds which are what we are generally talking about when discussing pulses or legumes are seeds left on the plant to ripen in the sun and become fully mature. Fully ripe seeds have a tough outer skin which is why they store so well and also why they need soaking before being cooked. Of the enormous Leguminosae family only about twenty species are cultivated in appreciable quantities and of these we will only be talking about those legumes generally available and eaten in western countries.

The English word pulse is derived from the Latin *puls* or *pultis* meaning pottage or porridge. It was first used by the French and was introduced into the English language after the Norman French invasion of the eleventh century. It became the most commonly used word to describe beans and peas although scholars writing in the seventeenth and eighteenth century preferred the term legumes. Pulse never gained popular usage in America.

The cultivation of legumes has a long history in human civilization and an ancestory as distinguished as that of the cereal grains. Remains of field beans and lentils radiocarbon dated to 6000 or 7000 B C have been found at neolithic sites in the Near East. In the New World remains of beans more than 5000 years old have been discovered at sites in Mexico. These finds even pre-date the earliest remains of domesticated maize. Lentils were well liked by the Ancient Egyptians and extensively cultivated. Apart from providing food, lentils also served the unusual role of packing material when the infamous Roman Emperor Caligula shipped an obelisk from Egypt to Rome. The obelisk is still standing to this day (perhaps with a few very old lentils tucked away in secret cracks). The Egyptians, however, were not fond of other beans (particularly broad beans!) and the priests forbade their use believing that each one contained the soul of a dead man! Pythagorus who introduced many Egyptian ideas into his religious theories believed the same. Legend has it that he was killed by soldiers of Dionysus who had ransacked Pythagorus' home town and who were in hot pursuit of him and his followers when suddenly they stopped trying to escape rather than cross a bean field. Other Greeks felt differently towards beans, and Plato, a vegetarian, regarded them as a vital requirement for a long and healthy life. The Greeks even had a God of Beans called Kyanites to whom they dedicated a temple. The Romans had mixed views. Funerals were followed by a bean feast but generally beans were thought to be fit only for peasants. Broad beans were used as counters in voting matters. White ones signified a vote for, and black ones a vote against, and during election times candidates for office generally distributed beans (probably only white ones) to their followers.

The Bible also contains many references to beans and lentils and the first chapter of the Book of Daniel contains probably the earliest record of the long standing controversy over the relative merits of beans and meat.

Nebuchadnezzar, King of Babylon, had captured Jerusalem and ordered that certain of the children of the captured Israelites including young Daniel should be brought up in his palace and given a daily provision of the King's meat and wine. Daniel, a proud young man, decided he was not going to humiliate himself to that extent and insisted that all he wanted was a simple diet of beans and water. The Prince of the Eunuchs entrusted with the task of caring for the children was upset by Daniel's suggestion and said, that he feared what the king might do to him if Daniel and his friends after a diet of beans and water started to look ill by comparison to the children fed on meat and wine. Anyway he put it to the test for a trial period of ten days. At the end of this period much to the Eunoch's relief 'the children appeared fairer and fitter in flesh than all the children which did eat a portion of the king's meats.'

Well it was only for ten days but Daniel did stay fit and healthy. In chapter 4 of the book of Ezekiel The Lord is quoted as saying that Ezekiel could eat a small quantity of bread during a period of fasting, but that besides wheat and barley it should also contain beans and lentils. Excellent advice from a nutrition point of view!

In the Americas before colonization, kidney beans were an important staple diet of the indigenous Indians. Columbus took samples back to Spain and they were considered a delicacy by the Court of Ferdinand and Isabella. Their introduction into Europe and subsequent cultivation created an increase in the popularity and use of beans. They became very popular as a ship's food and their long storage qualities made them a provision well suited to the long sea voyages of the times. Later they became part of the staple diet of many parts of Europe before falling in popularity with the advent of the industrial revolution.

In India, beans and lentils have always been an important food for all castes and religions and particularly for Hindus who are vegetarians. In China, Japan and much of South East Asia, soya-bean products have made a major contribution to food requirements for thousands of years and continue to do so.

Beans and nutrition

Beans, peas or lentils in their dried forms contain as many calories per weight as grains and in general twice as much protein. The protein content of most legumes varies between 15% to 25% and is as high as 38% for soya beans. Surprisingly these figures are slightly higher than for meat, fish or eggs, although the quality of protein is not as high. See Table 6 (p.162). Further, legumes if properly soaked and cooked are well digested by the human body. Although the amino acids (which are essentially the proteins) of legumes are rich in lysine they are low in sulphur-containing amino acids and this means all the proteins present are not available to the body. However, cereal grains are lacking in lysine but rich in sulphur-containing aminos, just the reverse of legumes, and if the two are eaten in combination they provide a full complement of all the essential amino acids. This is illustrated by Table 7 (p. 162) which shows the biological value of particular foods. As you can see, the biological value of legumes is improved by combination with 40% by weight of wholewheat rice or maize.

In all these figures soya beans are the exception since they contain an exceedingly high proportion of good quality protein.

Legumes in general contain little fat, 1 to 2% for the majority of beans, rising to 4% for chick-peas. The figure is much higher for soya beans (18%) and peanuts (also called ground nuts) (43%), both of which are used as sources of vegetable oil. Although low in content the fats present in legumes are usually rich in essential fatty acids.

NUTRIENTS IN LEGUMES COMPARED TO OTHER FOODS.

	CALORIES PER 100g.	PROTEIN	FAT
SOYA BEAN	335	38%	18%
KIDNEY BEAN	341	22%	17%
LENTIL	346	24%	18%
RICE (WHITE)	360	7%	1·7%
BEEF (LEAN)	198	19%	13%
FISH (WHITE, SEA)	75	16%	0·5%
EGGS	163	12%	11·5%

Table 6

BIOLOGICAL VALUE OF LEGUMES COMPARED WITH OTHER FOODS.

IDEAL PROTEIN	100
EGGS	96
LEGUMES 60% WITH 40% OF WHOLEWHEAT RICE OR MAIZE	80
MEAT	80
SOYA BEANS	75
RICE	70
MAIZE	55
LEGUMES IN GENERAL	40-50

Table 7

Legumes are a good source of the B vitamins thiamine and niacin, and the minerals calcium and iron. Cooked, dried legumes do not contain vitamin C but sprouted beans are an excellent source (see page 198 for methods of sprouting beans).

Individual beans, peas and lentils

Aduki bean

Alternative names – adzuki, azuki and feijao
Botanical name – *Phaseolus angularis*

The aduki plant is small and bushy and there are many varieties. The seed or bean is small, shiny and red and it is most popular in the far eastern countries of Japan, Korea and China. It has a sweet taste and apart from its use in savoury dishes, the cooked mashed beans are used as a sweet filling in cakes and buns. In Japan aduki beans are thought to have curative properties particularly for kidney complaints. These beliefs have recently been supported by medical evidence. Aduki beans are also rich in protein and are known as King of the Beans by the Japanese.

Black beans

Alternative names – turtle soup beans, *frijoles negros*; a smaller variety are called Chinese black beans
Botanical name – member of *Phaseolus vulgaris* group
A black shiny bean popular in South America and the Caribbean. They are slightly sweet and particularly good in soups and casseroles. In the Caribbean they are traditionally flavoured with cumin, garlic and a spicy tomato sauce. The smaller variety popular in China are normally fermented with salt and served in small quantities with fish or chicken. Black bean sauce is also a popular Chinese accompaniment to main dishes (it is sometimes made from soya beans).

Black-eyed beans

Alternative names – cowpea, blackeye pea
Botanical name – *Vigna unguiculata*
White or creamy bean with a black or dark yellow eye. The plant is native to Africa but now widely cultivated in India, China and the Americas. Spanish explorers took the beans to the West Indies in the sixteenth century, from where it spread to the Americas. The yard-long bean or asparagus bean which grows pods 3 feet long and the field pea are members of the same family. Black-eyed beans were given as food to the slaves carried from Africa to America, and they are still traditionally served with rice in black communities in the USA on New Year's Eve to ensure a lucky year ahead. In Africa the young pea pods are eaten as a vegetable and the leafy shoots eaten like spinach. Black-eyed beans, pork and sweet potato are said to be a splendid combination.

Black bean

Black eyed bean

Broad beans

Alternative names – fava, wox, Windsor and Horne
Botanical name – *Vicia faba*
Either a creamy white or brown variety available. Broad beans have been grown since ancient times and remains have been found on the bronze age sites of lake-side dwellings in Switzerland. They were very popular in Britain in the Middle Ages and important enough to warrant the death sentence for their theft from open fields! They were mainly dried and saved for use in the winter months, hence the proverb: 'Hunger makes hard beans sweet.'

Immature pods can be eaten as vegetables as can the young green beans. The mature dried beans need a good soaking and long cooking before use. They are popular in casseroles, salads, puréed or in pies.

Lentils

Alternative names – red dhal, split pea
Botanical name – *Lens esculenta*
One of man's oldest food plants, they originated in South East Asia, but by early times were being cultivated in Egypt and Greece. They are grown as a cold-season crop throughout the tropics and are particularly popular in India and South America. Lentils are available in a variety of sizes and colours, although the red, green and brown types are those most easily found in the West. Red lentils are often sold split for easier cooking. Chinese varieties are generally smaller than Indian lentils. Lentils cook quickly and need little or no soaking although some people believe soaking increases their digestibility. They have a higher protein content than most other legumes and a high carbohydrate content. They provide good food for cold days or labour-intensive work.

Lentils are used in India for the preparation of dhal and other curries. They are an excellent accompaniment to vegetables or meat or in a soup. One word of warning – lentils are often packed with lots of small stones or grit and need careful picking over before use.

Lentil

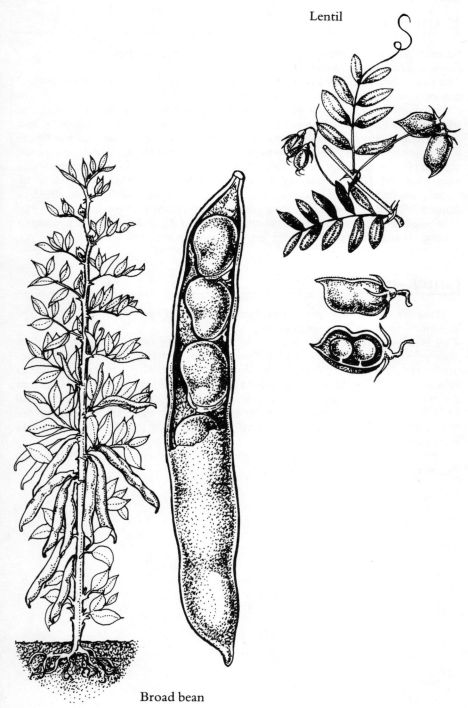

Broad bean

Butter beans

Alternative names – lima bean, sieva bean, curry bean and pole bean
Botanical name – *Phaseolus lunatus*
The butter bean is really a type of lima bean but since the lima is better known as butter bean I have included it here under that heading.

Phaseolus lunatus is a native of tropical America but it is now cultivated in tropical areas all over the world. The species is divided into two groups, the small-seeded, dwarf, climbing variety which give sieva beans and the large-seeded butter-bean types with which we are more familiar. The large-seeded varieties grow in a range of colours from white to brown. They all contain toxic substances which are removed after long soaking and cooking. The white variety are less toxic than the brown and it is this type which is sold dried or canned as butter beans. They are a good accompaniment to pork or poultry or combined with sweetcorn to make the traditional American dish succotash, or in soups, casseroles, puréed or served with sour cream in salads.

Chick-peas

Alternative names – Garbanzo pea, Bengal grain and ceci
Botanical name – *Cicer arientinum*
This is my favourite bean. It is native to the Mediterranean region but now grows throughout the sub-tropics. The peas are normally yellow but are sometimes creamy white or brown with a dimpled surface. They are most famous as an ingredient of hummus (or houmous or hummous) in which the cooked peas are ground to a paste mixed with sesame-seed paste (tahini), garlic, lemon, oil and salt and served with pita bread. Or as falafel in which ground chick-peas are flavoured with onion, parsley, cumin, coriander then rolled into walnut size balls and deep fried.

The peas are most nutritious and nutritionists are encouraging their cultivation in India as protein supplement.

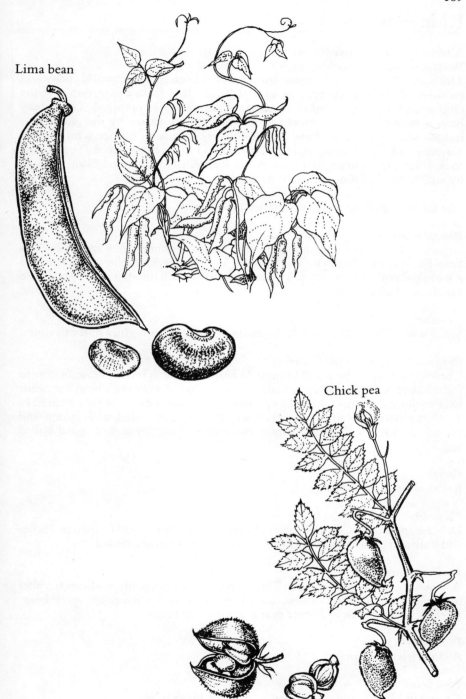

Lima bean

Chick pea

Kidney beans

Alternative names – see list below
Botanical name – *Phaseolus vulgaris*
This species of bean is the most commonly cultivated in the world today and
includes all the various type of haricot beans. It is from this group that the
famous and ubiquitous baked beans in tomato sauce are prepared. The kidney
bean is native to the Americas and they have been grown by the indigenous
Indians since prehistoric times. Columbus took back to Europe a number of
varieties and they quickly became popular and widely cultivated. The French
took a liking to them and chauvinistically christened them French beans, a name
by which they are sometimes still known.

The following all belong to the kidney bean family:

Barlotti beans
Grown in Kenya and Italy and popular in Italian cooking. They are available in
brown and white. The main ingredient in Venetian bean soup in which barlottis
are cooked with ham bones and spices and served with noodles and topped with
parmesan cheese.

Canellini
Small white haricot beans from Argentina. They have a slightly nutty flavour.

Egyptian kidney beans (ful medames)
These are similar to hyacinth bean, field bean and Dutch brown bean. Native to
India but very popular in Egypt and the Near East. A very tasty bean but needs
long soaking and cooking. In Egypt they are a national dish and they even have
ful (Egyptian for bean) cafés. Traditionally they are boiled with cumin and
served seasoned with garlic, lemon, oil, chopped parsley and chopped boiled
egg.

Fagioli
Italian white haricot bean.

Flageolets
Delicate, pale green, young haricot beans with a subtle taste. Grown in France
and Italy and usually only available outside these countries tinned.

Haricot beans
A smallish, tender, white bean. The main ingredient in many traditional dishes
including cassoulet and *cholent*. Similar or same as the American navy bean,
Great Northern bean and other beans called white beans.

Pearl bean
A small haricot bean.

Pink beans
Grown in Mexico and often eaten refried (see Pinto bean).

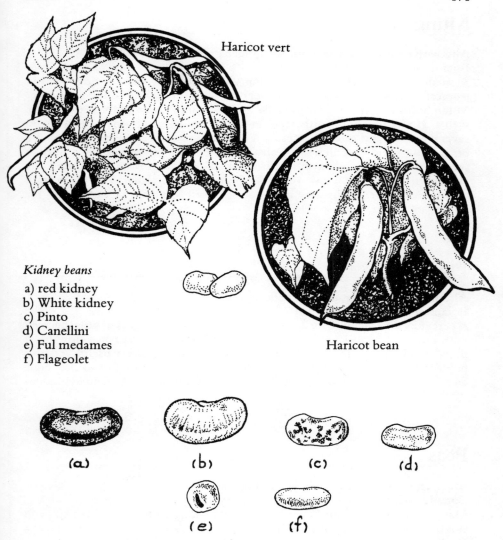

Haricot vert

Haricot bean

Kidney beans

a) red kidney
b) White kidney
c) Pinto
d) Canellini
e) Ful medames
f) Flageolet

(a)   (b)   (c)   (d)

(e)   (f)

Pinto bean
Speckled brown beans from Mexico. Used in chili dishes instead of red kidney beans. Cooked in large quantities and then refried for later use. Known as refried or re-awakened beans (*Frijoles refritos* in Mexican).

Red kidney beans
Also known as Mexican or chili beans. Very popular in chili con carne, soups and salads, and in Spain and Japan served with white rice.

Mung bean

Alternative names – green gram and golden gram
Botanical name – *Phaseolus aureus*
A small olive-green bean, rounded but with flattened curves, it originated in tropical Asia and it is still most widely grown in India and South East Asia. Mung beans contain an exceptionally high vitamin A content for a legumes as well as B vitamins and a little vitamin C. The mung plant grows quickly and several crops a year can be harvested. For this reason it is excellent for growing bean sprouts and in China the beans are used solely for sprouting. The bean sprouts most commonly available commercially in both Britain and the USA are grown from mung beans. The mung bean is closely related to the black gram or urd bean which is grown throughout the East, both for sprouting and for milling into flour.

Pigeon peas

Alternative names – gunga and yellow dhal
Botanical name – *Cajanus cajan*
A perennial vine yielding for 2 to 3 years. It gives small, round, flat peas speckled with brown marks. The plant originated in South East Asia but is now most popular in India where its drought-resisting properties are very useful. It is also popular in the Caribbean where together with rice it forms part of the staple diet. The young seeds can be eaten fresh as a vegetable or dried and used like lentils.

Peas

Alternative names – common pea and garden pea
Botanical name – *Pisum sativum*
Many varieties of this annual vine are available, ranging from dwarf to tall, and smooth skinned to wrinkled. The plant originated in the area between the Euphrates and Tigris rivers known as The Garden of Eden. It is now grown in temperate regions throughout the world.

The pea plant has a long and illustrious history and remains have been found in the ruins of ancient Greece and Egypt. The word pea is derived from the Sanskrit *pis* meaning piece or 'piece of pod'. In Latin this became *pisum* and finally in early English *pease* (e.g. pease pudding). Throughout Europe in the Middle Ages peas were grown and dried for use as a winter food. They were generally preferred to either beans or lentils. Strangely, it wasn't until the seventeenth century that fresh peas in the pod became popular. Suddenly at the court of Louis XIV young peas or *petits pois* became all the fashion and nowadays of course fresh, frozen or tinned peas are much more common than the dried variety, although split peas are still popular.

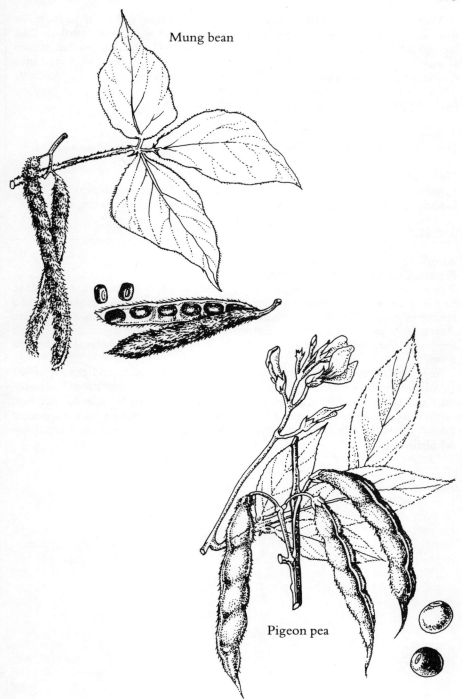

Mung bean

Pigeon pea

There are two main types of common pea. The first and most popular for human consumption is the garden pea with which we are all familiar. The second is the field pea, considered inferior in taste to the garden pea and grown as animal food. Garden peas available commercially have been separated into size and shape and are sold according to their sweetness and starch content. Thus we have sugar peas, snow peas, *petits pois* and marrowfat peas ranging from the sweet to the starchy marrow fats.

Yellow split peas
Used in soups, casseroles and in India like lentils for preparing dhal and rissoles.

Green split peas
Famous in pea and ham soup and in the northern England dish pease pudding. Good in soups, stews and casseroles or as an accompaniment to fish and chips.

Peanuts

Alternative names – ground nut and monkey-nut
Botanical name – *Arachides hypogaea*
The peanut is strictly speaking, a legume, and not a nut. It's best known to us in its salted and roasted form as a snack food, although it's grown principally as a source of vegetable oil. The plant originated in the tropical forests of South America. It was taken back to Europe and Africa by Portugese and Spanish explorers and reached North America via slave ships which carried peanuts as food.

Peanuts contain a high proportion of essential fatty acids and peanut butter should be a nutritious food. Unfortunately to increase the shelf life of their product manufacturers hydrogenate the butter and thus turn its essential oils into fats good only for providing calories. It's worthwhile making your own peanut butter, a simple process (page 202), or being sure to buy it from a reputable wholefood store.

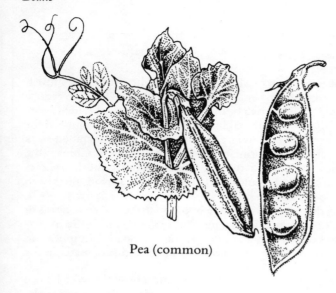

Pea (common)

Peanut (groundnut)

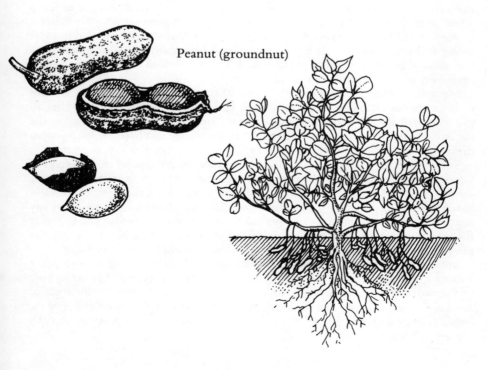

Soya beans

Alternative names – soybean and soya
Botanical name – *Glycine max*

Soya beans are the most nutritious of all the legumes. They contain as much high-quality protein as steak and further contain unsaturated fats that can reduce cholesteral levels in the blood. The soya bean is the first legume of which written records are available and its nutritional importance has been recognized for thousands of years. Emperor Shen Nung of China in 2800 B C included soya beans in his description of the five principal and sacred crops of China, (the others being rice, wheat, barley and millet). His advisors published exact accounts of how the crop should be cultivated and the plant spread quickly to Japan and other areas of South East Asia.

In the last twenty years there has been a huge boom in the use of soya beans in the west. This largely followed the financial measures taken by the US government to encourage farmers to grow more of the crop and the parallel application of advanced technology to convert it into food products and raw material for manufacturing processes.

Much of the extra crop is converted into simulated meat products which taste awful to me, and I can see no reason why manufacturers should try and make food that tastes or looks like meat. It's quite possible to make excellent natural foods from soya beans that have their own tastes and textures, and the Chinese and Japanese have done it for thousands of years.

The three main soya bean products they make are bean curd (*tofu* in Japan), miso (bean paste in China) and soy sauce (*shoya* in Japan). Bean curd or tofu is a fermented soya bean product, it is white and has the consistency of a delicate custard. Fried bean curd develops a tougher outer coat and can be used in casseroles and soups without disintegrating. Fresh bean curd is used in salads, as a side dish or in ways we may use cheese. It is a rich source of protein and minerals, contains no fat and is an aid to digestion.

Miso is a fermented soya bean paste that keeps indefinitely, its flavour even improves with age. Combined with rice or other grains miso supplies all the essential amino acids and also contains enzymes that are helpful to the digestion process. It is a versatile ingredient and is used as a base for soups, salad dressings and sauces, as a marinade for fish, meat or vegetables or as a spread.

Soy sauce is the best-known soya bean product. Its appearance on the tables of Chinese restaurants has probably misled many people about the true taste of soy sauce. The stuff on the tables is normally an artificially flavoured, chemically based liquid that has only a passing association with real soya beans. Real soy sauce is made from a mixture of soya beans, wheat and salt, fermented together for up to two years, then mashed and filtered. It is available but it is more expensive than the chemical stuff. Tamari is a brand name for real soy sauce.

In the east soya beans are not usually soaked and boiled whole as with other legumes, but then there is no great tradition for casserole type dishes in this part of the world and whole dried soya beans lend themselves best to this style of cooking. Long soaking and cooking times are essential if the true flavour of the beans is to be appreciated and if the dish is to be completely digestible. Recipes are given later.

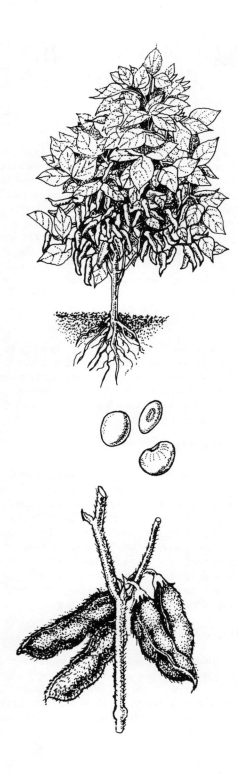

PREPARATION AND COOKING OF BEANS, PEAS AND LENTILS

Buying beans

Buy your beans from a reputable and busy health or wholefood store (that's if you have the choice, of course) since, although beans can be stored for very long periods, if they get really old they take longer to cook and taste tough. Also some sacks of beans and particularly lentils contain more small stones and grit than others, and these are to be avoided if you want to escape the tedious task of picking over the beans before cooking them. You may avoid the problem altogether by buying pre-packed beans from a supermarket, but you will probably pay more for them than for the loose variety and also have your choice strictly limited. Store the beans in airtight containers in a dry coolish place. They come in many fascinating shapes and colours so, if you have the space, store them in glass containers on open shelves in the kitchen.

Soaking beans

Nearly all beans and peas must be soaked before cooking to ensure they are digestible. This long soaking does require you to remember to do it in advance of the meal. The usual soaking times are twelve to twenty-four hours although there is a quicker soaking method which is discussed below. Strictly speaking lentils and split peas do not require soaking but if you do soak them it doesn't do any harm and speeds up the cooking time.

Long-soaking method

Weigh out the beans you require (8 oz/1 cup serves about 4 people) and pick over to remove any grit or stones or odd looking beans. Cover the beans in water (2 pints/5 cups water per 8 oz/1 cup beans). Leave according to the recommended soaking times given in the chart (p. 180). If the beans are cooked in the water they were soaked in, volume as directed above, by the end of the cooking time the water is almost completely absorbed and the beans do not need to be drained. This method reserves any vitamins lost in the water. Of course more water may be added during cooking as necessary. If you forget or need to leave the beans longer than the recommended soaking time then they should be drained and covered with fresh water before cooking.

Quick-soaking method

In a heavy saucepan weigh out the beans and cover with water as directed in tne long soaking method. Cover the pot and bring to the boil, reduce heat and simmer for 5 minutes. Now remove the pot from the heat and leave the beans to soak for the quick-method time given in the chart (p. 180). Then bring the beans to the boil in the same water and cook until tender. Cooking times are the same as for the long-soaking method.

Cooking times

There are two schools of thought on whether beans should be cooked for a long time without pressure or for a short time under pressure in a pressure cooker. The pressure cooker faction claim their method saves on fuel, time and labour and also increases the digestibility of the beans. The long-cooking lobby claim fast-cooking results in beans crumbly on the outside and hard inside. Further, they claim that it is very difficult to gauge exactly how long a particular type of bean will take to cook and that it is impractical to keep cooling down the pressure cooker to check. Also it's not possible to add ingredients during the cooking process, and not possible to remove any scum that forms.

My preference is for the long-cooking method. Once the beans are on, cooking, they can be forgotten about except for the occasional look. Seasoning and herbs can be adjusted as you feel necessary and the tastes of other ingredients have much longer to mingle and merge together with that of the beans. From my experience long soaking and slow cooking produces the tastiest bean dishes and those least likely to give problems with flatulence later.

Cooking tips

1: Do not add salt to the beans until near the end of the cooking time otherwise they harden and take longer to cook.
2: Other seasoning should be added later as well since cooking beans seems to absorb and neutralize flavours. Lentils and split peas are the exception to this rule and can be seasoned at the start of cooking.
3: If a bean dish is to be reheated the following day check the seasoning and add more if necessary before serving.
4: Do not add bicarbonate of soda to the cooking water. It's not needed and destroys vitamins.
5: Do not discard any water in which beans have been cooked as it makes excellent stock.
6: Chick-peas and red beans tend to foam when first cooked; remove the scum after 20 or 30 minutes and again later if any more forms.
7: Cook twice as many beans as you need and store the extra in the fridge until needed. I find they keep best if only lightly covered. They will keep for four to five days. Use for making soups, salads, spreads, dips, mashed for rissoles, combined with cooked grains or as an accompaniment to a main meal.
8: One volume of dried beans gives 2 to 2½ volumes of cooked beans. One weight of dried beans gives 2 to 2½ weights of cooked beans. Thus: 8 oz/1 cup beans gives 1 lb to 1¼ lb cooked beans *or* 2 to 2½ cups cooked beans.

SOAKING AND COOKING LEGUMES

Type of legume	Soaking times		Cooking times	
	long method	*short method*	*without pressure*	*with pressure*
Aduki beans	2 to 3 hours	1 hour	1–1½ hours	8–10 minutes
Black beans	overnight★	3 hours	1½–2 hours	10–15 minutes
Black–eyed beans	overnight★	2 hours	1–1½ hours	8–10 minutes
Broad beans	overnight★	4 hours	1½–2 hours	10–15 minutes
Lima/butter beans	overnight★	4 hours	1½–2 hours	10–15 minutes
Chick–peas	overnight★	3 hours	1½–2 hours	10–15 minutes
Kidney beans including:				
Barlotti	overnight★	2–3 hours	1–1½ hours	10–15 minutes
Canellini	overnight★	2–3 hours	1–1½ hours	10–15 minutes
Dutch brown bean	overnight★	2–3 hours	1½–2 hours	10–15 minutes
Egyptian brown bean (ful medames)	overnight★	2–3 hours	1½–2 hours	10–15 minutes
Fagioli	overnight★	2–3 hours	1–1½ hours	10–15 minutes
Field bean	overnight★	2–3 hours	1–1½ hours	10–15 minutes
Flageolets	overnight★	2–3 hours	1–1½ hours	10–15 minutes
Great northern bean	overnight★	2–3 hours	1½–2 hours	10–15 minutes
Haricot beans	overnight★	2–3 hours	1½–2 hours	10–15 minutes
Navy bean	overnight★	2–3 hours	1–1½ hours	10–15 minutes
Pink bean	overnight★	2–3 hours	1–1½ hours	10–15 minutes
Pinto bean	overnight★	2–3 hours	1–1½ hours	10–15 minutes
Pearl bean	overnight★	2–3 hours	1–1½ hours	10–15 minutes
Red kidney beans	overnight★	2–3 hours	1–1½ hours	10–15 minutes
White bean	overnight★	2–3 hours	1–1½ hours	10–15 minutes
Lentils	no soaking needed		small lentils 20–30 minutes	6–10 minutes
			large lentils 35–40 minutes	6–10 minutes
Mung beans	overnight★	45–60 minutes	45 minutes	10 minutes
Pigeon peas	overnight★	2 hours	1 hour	10 minutes
Peas	overnight★	2 hours	1 hour	10 minutes
Split peas	no soaking needed		20–30 minutes	6–10 minutes
Soya beans	24 hours	do not use this method	3–4 hours	30 minutes

★ 'Overnight' means 8 to 12 hours
†These times are for a 13 lb pressure cooker. Double them for a 10 lb cooker

Soups

The recipes are listed in the alphabetical order of the main bean used in the soup. All the recipes are for 4 to 6 servings.

Black-eyed pea soup with croûtons

This is a simple but very tasty soup and with the addition of croûtons it makes a hearty beginning to a meal.

1 tablespoon vegetable oil
3 cloves garlic, crushed
8 oz (1 cup) black-eyed peas, soaked
   overnight and drained
1½ pt (4 cups) water or stock
1 tablespoon fresh parsley, chopped

1 tablespoon fresh mint, chopped
salt and black pepper to taste

Croûtons
2 rounds of wholewheat bread
1 tablespoon vegetable oil

Put the oil into a heavy saucepan, add the garlic and sauté until golden over a moderate heat. Add the peas and water or stock and bring to the boil. Cover, reduce heat and simmer until the peas are tender (about 45 minutes). 5 minutes before the end of cooking time, stir in the parsley and mint, season to taste with salt and black pepper and adjust the thickness with more water or stock as needed. Meanwhile cut the bread into ½ inch squares and fry golden brown in the oil in a heavy frying pan. Serve the soup with the croûtons in a separate bowl.

Black bean soup

These shiny black beans are popular in the whole Caribbean area and particularly in Cuba and Puerto Rica. They make excellent soups. This recipe uses cumin seeds and lemon juice to spike the taste of the beans.

8 oz (1 cup) black beans, soaked
   overnight and drained
1½ pt (4 cups) water or stock
2 tablespoons vegetable oil
1 medium onion, diced

3 cloves garlic, crushed
½ teaspoon ground cumin
½ teaspoon dried oregano
salt and black pepper to taste
4 to 6 slices lemon

Put the beans in a heavy saucepan and add the water or stock. Bring to the boil, cover and set to simmer. Heat the oil in a heavy frying pan, add the onion and garlic and sauté until the onion is soft and golden brown. Stir in the cumin and oregano and sauté a further 2 or 3 minutes. Pour the mixture into the bean pot when the beans have been simmering for 30 minutes and continue simmering until the beans are soft (about another 30 minutes). Season to taste with salt and black pepper, adjust the thickness with water or stock if needed, and if you wish, blend in an electric blender, otherwise serve immediately with a slice of lemon per person.

★Bacon and black bean soup

8 oz (1 cup) black beans, soaked overnight, drained
2 pt (5 cups) water or ham stock
2 tablespoons oil (olive oil is best)
2 cloves garlic, crushed
1 medium onion, diced
8 oz lean bacon or ham, cubed

8 oz tin tomatoes, chopped
½ teaspoon dried oregano
¼ teaspoon nutmeg
¼ teaspoon chili powder *or* hot pepper sauce
salt and black pepper to taste
2 fl oz (¼ cup) sherry, optional

Put the beans in a heavy saucepan and add water or stock. Bring to the boil, cover and set to simmer. Heat the oil in a heavy frying pan and add the garlic, onion and bacon. Sauté the bacon light brown on both sides and then stir in the tomatoes, oregano, nutmeg and chili powder. Sauté a further 2 or 3 minutes. Pour mixture into the bean pot after the beans have simmered 30 minutes. Stir well and simmer a further 30 minutes or until the beans are soft and tender. Season to taste with salt and black pepper, stir in sherry and adjust the thickness of the soup with water or stock as needed. Blend if you wish or serve immediately.

Chick-pea soup Italian style

This soup served with plenty of garlic bread and fresh salad makes for a substantial meal. If you wish you may add 8 oz sliced salami 10 minutes before the end of cooking time.

2 tablespoons vegetable oil
1 medium onion, diced
2 cloves garlic, crushed
1 medium green pepper, sliced
2 medium courgettes (zucchini), sliced
1 bay leaf

1½ pt (4 cups) water or stock
8 oz (1 cup) chick-peas, soaked overnight, drained
4 oz (1 cup) macaroni or broken spaghetti
salt and black pepper to taste
parmesan cheese

Heat the oil in a heavy saucepan and add the onion and garlic. Sauté until the onion is just soft and then add the green pepper and courgettes. Sauté a further 3 or 4 minutes, add the bay leaf, water or stock and chick-peas. Bring to the boil, reduce heat, cover and simmer for 1 hour. Now add the macaroni and simmer a further 30 minutes or until the chick-peas are very soft and tender. Season to taste with salt and black pepper. Serve immediately with parmesan cheese or blend part of the soup if you desire a thicker consistency.

*Middle eastern meat ball and chick-pea soup

8 oz (1 cup) chick-peas, soaked overnight, drained
1½ pt (4 cups) water or stock
1 tablespoon fresh parsley, chopped
salt and black pepper to taste
1 teaspoon dried mint
½ teaspoon cinnamon

Meat Balls
2 slices, white bread, crusts removed
8 oz finely minced beef
1 egg, beaten
¼ teaspoon cinnamon
¼ teaspoon black pepper
½ teaspoon salt
1 tablespoon parsley, chopped
1 small onion, finely diced

To prepare meat balls cover the bread with water and set aside for 15 minutes. Drain and squeeze the bread dry. Break it into small pieces and combine with the minced beef. Add the other ingredients and pound the mixture to a paste with a wooden spoon or blend it in an electric blender a portion at a time. Roll this mixture into walnut size balls and set aside. Put the beans and water into a heavy saucepan and bring to the boil. Reduce heat and simmer for 30 minutes. Add the meat balls and parsley and season to taste with salt and black pepper. Simmer a further 45 minutes or until chick-peas are soft and tender. Rub the dried mint into a powder and sprinkle into the soup along with the cinnamon. Adjust the seasoning and serve.

Variations
Substitute 1 lb lean lamb, cubed and lightly browned in butter for the meat balls.

Haricot bean and leek soup

White beans, great northern beans or navy beans may be substituted for haricot beans.

2 oz (¼ cup) butter or vegetable oil
2 leeks, cleaned and chopped
12 oz (1½ cup) haricot beans, soaked
   overnight, drained

2 pt (5 cups) water or stock
salt and black pepper to taste
juice of 1 lemon
2 tablespoons fresh parsley, chopped

Heat the butter or oil in a heavy saucepan and add the leeks. Sauté until soft and then add the beans and water or stock. Bring to the boil, cover, reduce heat and simmer for 1 to 1½ hours or until the beans are very soft. Season to taste with salt and black pepper and add the lemon juice. Blend or pass through a sieve or cook until the beans start to disintegrate. Adjust seasoning and, if needed, the thickness by adding more water or stock. Serve very hot, garnished with chopped parsley.

Variation
Replace the leeks by 1 medium onion, 2 sticks of celery and 2 crushed cloves of garlic.

Creamy haricot bean soup

8 oz (1 cup) haricot beans, soaked
  overnight, drained
2 pt (5 cups) water
2 cloves garlic, crushed
1 bay leaf
½ teaspoon dried thyme

1 medium onion, studded with 2
  cloves
1 medium carrot, sliced in two
  lengthwise
4 fl oz (½ cup) single cream
salt and black pepper to taste

Put the beans and water into a heavy saucepan. Add the garlic, bay leaf, thyme, onion and cloves and carrot. Bring to the boil, cover, reduce heat and simmer for 1 to 1½ hours, or until beans are very soft. Remove onion and carrot and discard. Stir the mixture well and with a slotted spoon remove half the beans to a blender. Blend this and return the purée to the pot. Stir in the cream, season to taste with salt and black pepper and return soup almost to the boil. Remove from the heat and serve. Croûtons (see index) go well with this soup.

Tuscan haricot bean soup

2 tablespoons vegetable oil
2 cloves garlic, crushed
1 medium onion, sliced
1 carrot, chopped
2 stalks celery and leaves, chopped
8 oz (1 cup) tinned plum tomatoes
1 teaspoon rosemary, finely chopped

¼ teaspoon chili powder *or*
  hot pepper sauce
1 ham hock or bone (optional)
8 oz (1 cup) haricot beans, soaked
  overnight, drained
2 pt (5 cups) water
salt and black pepper to taste
parmesan cheese

Heat the oil in a heavy saucepan and sauté the garlic and onion until just softened. Add the carrot and celery and sauté until the onion is browned. Stir in the tomatoes, rosemary and chili powder. Add the ham hock (if used), haricot beans and water and bring to the boil. Reduce heat, cover and simmer for 1½ to 2 hours. With a slotted spoon remove half the beans and blend. Return this purée to the pot, season to taste with salt and pepper, and return to the boil. Serve garnished with parmesan cheese.

Variations
After puréeing half the beans, add 1 oz spaghetti, broken into 1 inch pieces, to the pot. Bring to the boil and cook until the spaghetti is *al dente* (about 6 minutes). Serve.

Lentil soup

2 tablespoons vegetable oil
1 medium onion, chopped
1 green pepper, chopped
2 medium carrots, chopped

8 oz (1 cup) green or brown lentils,
  washed and picked over
2 pt (5 cups) water
salt and black pepper to taste

Heat the oil in a heavy saucepan and sauté the onion, green pepper and carrots until the onion is lightly browned. Add the lentils and water and bring to the boil. Reduce heat, cover and simmer until the lentils are well cooked but still firm (about 1 hour). Season to taste with salt and black pepper 15 minutes before the end of the cooking time.

Variations
1: For a more substantial dish add 4 oz (½ cup) cooked rice or wholewheat to the soup and heat through before serving.
2: For Curried lentil soup add 1 teaspoon curry powder, ¼ teaspoon chili powder and 1 clove garlic, crushed, to the pot at the same time as you add the lentils.
3: For Ham and lentil soup use ham stock instead of water or add 1 ham hock to the pot along with the lentils and water.

Lentil and potato soup

8 oz (1 cup) brown or green lentils, washed and picked over
2 pt (5 cups) water
salt and black pepper to taste
½ teaspoon cumin powder
1 large onion, diced
2 medium potatoes, coarsely chopped
1 tablespoon vegetable oil
1 medium onion, finely sliced

Put the lentils and water in a heavy saucepan and bring to the boil. Reduce heat, cover and simmer for 20 minutes. Season to taste with salt and black pepper and add the cumin powder, diced onion and potatoes. Return mixture to the boil, reduce heat, cover and simmer until the lentils and vegetables are cooked (about 30 minutes). Meanwhile fry the onion rings in the oil until nicely browned. Serve the soup garnished with the onion rings.

*Lentil, chick-pea and lamb soup

This is a beautiful soup (it's really substantial enough for a main meal) which combines 3 ingredients, very popular in Middle Eastern cooking.

1 tablespoon butter
8 oz lean lamb, cubed
1 medium onion, diced
1 stalk celery and leaves, chopped
1 medium tomato, chopped
½ teaspoon powdered coriander
½ teaspoon paprika
½ teaspoon turmeric
4 oz (½ cup) chick-peas, soaked overnight, drained
4 oz (½ cup) lentils, washed, picked over
2 pt (5 cups) water
salt and black pepper to taste
1 egg (optional)
juice 1 lemon (optional)

Melt the butter in a heavy saucepan and fry the lamb brown on all sides. Add the onion and celery and fry a further 3 minutes. Add the tomato, coriander, paprika, turmeric, chick-peas, lentils and water and bring to the boil. Cover, reduce heat and simmer for 1 to 1½ hours or until the chick-peas and lentils are tender. Season to taste with salt and black pepper and serve. Alternatively, beat the egg and lemon juice together and stir into the soup. Remove from the heat and serve immediately.

Mixed bean soup

This is an excellent soup to prepare if you have small amounts of a variety of cooked beans left over from the preparation of another meal. If you wish to start from the beginning and prepare beans especially for this soup then black beans, chick-peas and lentils make a good combination of colours, shapes and flavours as do red beans, whole dried peas and butter or lima beans.

1 tablespoon vegetable oil
1 clove garlic, crushed
1 medium onion, sliced
2 medium carrots, sliced
2 sticks celery, sliced
8 oz (1 cup) tinned tomatoes

4 oz (½ cup) brown or green lentils
2 pt (5 cups) water or stock
1 lb (2 cups) cooked mixed beans
½ teaspoon cumin powder
½ teaspoon coriander powder
salt and black pepper to taste

Put the oil in a heavy saucepan and sauté the garlic and onion for 2 or 3 minutes. Add the carrots and celery and sauté until the onion is lightly browned. Put in the tomatoes, lentils and water or stock and bring to the boil. Reduce heat, cover and simmer for 15 minutes. Add the cooked beans, cumin and coriander and season to taste with salt and black pepper. Return to the boil, cover, reduce heat and simmer for 30 to 50 minutes. The longer you leave the soup cooking the thicker it gets as the beans start to disintegrate.

Variations
For a special garnish for the soup, melt 1 tablespoon butter in a heavy frying pan and lightly fry 1 medium onion, sliced. Add 1 teaspoon of dried mint, stir well and fry for another minute. Put the soup in a tureen and decorate with the mint and onion slices.

Winter pea soup

8 oz (1 cup) split peas (green or
   yellow)
or
8 oz (1 cup) dried peas, soaked
   overnight, drained
2 pt (5 cups) water or stock
2 tablespoons vegetable oil

1 medium onion, sliced
1 medium carrot, diced
2 medium potatoes, coarsely diced
1 bay leaf
½ teaspoon dried thyme
½ teaspoon dried marjoram
salt and black pepper to taste

Put the split peas and water in a heavy saucepan and bring to the boil. Reduce heat and simmer for about 1 hour or until the peas are quite mushy. Meanwhile heat the oil in a heavy frying pan and sauté the onion, carrot and potatoes until soft. Add these cooked vegetables, thyme and marjoram to the cooked peas and season to taste with salt and black pepper. Return soup to the boil, reduce heat and simmer for 15 minutes. Now dilute and/or blend the soup to the desired thickness and serve.

Summer pea soup

8 oz (1 cup) split peas (green or
   yellow) washed
or
8 oz (1 cup) dried peas, soaked
   overnight, drained
2 pt (5 cups) water

1 tablespoon butter
1 large onion, sliced
2 tablespoons fresh parsley, chopped
4 to 6 leaves fresh mint, chopped
salt and black pepper to taste
2 tablespoons white wine (optional)

Put the peas and water in a heavy pot and bring to the boil. Reduce heat and simmer for 1 hour or until peas are soft and mushy. Lightly brown the onion in the butter and add to the cooked peas. Add the parsley and mint and season to taste with salt and black pepper. Heat the soup through and stir in the wine (if used). Serve.

Fresh pea soup

2 oz (¼ cup) butter
1 medium onion, diced
2 sticks celery, chopped
2 small potatoes, diced
1 lb (3 cups) fresh peas, shelled
1½ pt (4 cups) water or stock

½ teaspoon english mustard
pinch ground cloves
1 teaspoon dried basil
salt and black pepper to taste
parmesan cheese

Melt the butter in a heavy saucepan and sauté the onion for 2 or 3 minutes. Add the celery and potatoes and sauté a further 2 minutes. Add the peas, water or stock, mustard, cloves and basil, stir well. Season to taste with salt and black pepper and bring to the boil. Reduce heat and simmer until the peas and other vegetables are soft and tender (10 to 15 minutes). The soup may be served immediately or blended and reheated before serving. Serve garnished with parmesan cheese.

Variation
Substitute 4 oz (½ cup) natural yoghurt for the parmesan cheese. Beat the yoghurt smooth and stir into the soup just before serving.

Iranian rice, lemon and pea soup

2 tablespoons vegetable oil or butter
2 medium onions, diced
4 oz (½ cup) split peas (yellow or
   green) washed *or* dried peas, soaked
   overnight, drained *or* green lentils,
   washed
4 oz (½ cup) brown *or* white rice

2 pt (5 cups) water
salt and black pepper to taste
1 lb spinach, chopped
½ teaspoon coriander powder
1 tablespoon fresh parsley, chopped
1 teaspoon dried mint
juice of 2 lemons

Heat the oil in a heavy saucepan and fry the onions until well browned. Add the peas, rice and water and bring to the boil. Reduce heat, cover and simmer for one hour. Season to taste with salt and black pepper, add the spinach, coriander, parsley and mint and cook for a further 30 minutes. Stir in the lemon juice and thin the soup down to desired thickness by the addition of boiling water. Stir well and serve.

Red bean soup

2 tablespoons vegetable oil
1 clove garlic, crushed
1 medium onion, sliced
1 green pepper, deseeded, sliced
2 large tomatoes, chopped
or
8 oz (1 cup) tinned tomatoes

8 oz (1 cup) red kidney beans (or pinto or pink beans) soaked overnight, drained
2 pt (5 cups) water
½ teaspoon hot pepper sauce *or* chili powder
salt and black pepper to taste

Heat the oil in a heavy saucepan and add the garlic, onion and green pepper. Sauté until the onion is golden. Add the tomatoes, beans, water and hot pepper sauce. Stir well and season to taste with salt and black pepper. Bring to the boil, reduce heat, cover and simmer until the beans are soft and tender (about 1 hour). Remove half the beans with a slotted spoon and purée in a blender or crush with the back of a wooden spoon. Return to the soup, heat through and serve.

Variation
To convert the soup into a substantial meal place in each soup bowl before serving the soup a piece of sliced, toasted French bread liberally sprinkled with parmesan or other grated cheese.

★Jamaican pork and red bean soup

8 oz (1 cup) red beans (or pinto or pink beans) soaked overnight, drained
2 pt (5 cups) water
¼ lb salted pork, diced
1 large onion, diced
1 hot red pepper, chopped

or
1 teaspoon hot pepper sauce
1 tablespoon fresh parsley, chopped
½ teaspoon dried thyme
2 stalks celery (including leaves) chopped
salt and black pepper to taste

Put the beans, water, pork, onion and hot pepper into a heavy saucepan. Bring to the boil, reduce heat, cover and simmer for about 2 hours. Now add the parsley, thyme and celery, season to taste with salt and black pepper and continue cooking for a further 30 minutes or until the beans are very soft and on the point of disintegrating. Lightly blend half the soup and then return it to the pot. Heat the soup through stirring well, adjust the seasoning and serve.

Soya bean soup

4 oz (½ cup) cooked soya beans
2 pt (5 cups) water or stock
1 medium onion, finely diced
1 leek, washed, chopped
1 medium potato, diced

4 oz (1 cup) cabbage, shredded
2 tablespoons soy sauce
salt and black pepper to taste
2 tablespoons fresh parsley, chopped

Put the soya beans, water or stock, onion, leek, carrot and potato into a heavy saucepan and bring to the boil. Reduce heat, cover and simmer until all the vegetables are soft and tender. Add the cabbage and soy sauce and cook a further 5 minutes. Season to taste with salt and black pepper and serve garnished with chopped parsley.

Savoury bean cakes and breads

The following recipes require cooked lentils or beans which may be prepared by one of the methods for cooking pulses given at the beginning of the section. You may of course use the recipes to make use of any cooked lentils or beans left over from the preparation of another dish. The breads and cakes may be eaten for snacks or used as part of a light meal or as accompaniments to main meals.

Lentil loaf

1 lb (2 cups) cooked lentils
4 oz (1½ cups) breadcrumbs
or
8 oz (1 cup) cooked rice
1 medium onion, finely diced
1 clove garlic, crushed

4 fl oz (½ cup) stock or water
1 tablespoon tomato purée
½ teaspoon thyme
1 tablespoon fresh parsley, chopped
1 teaspoon salt
1 egg, lightly beaten

Preheat oven to 375°F (gas mark 5). Combine the ingredients and pack into a greased bread tin. Bake for 45 to 55 minutes or until set.

Lentil and millet patties

12 oz (1½ cups) cooked lentils
8 oz (1 cup) cooked millet
1 medium onion, finely diced
¼ teaspoon ground cloves
½ teaspoon cinnamon

¼ teaspoon nutmeg
salt and black pepper to taste
2 eggs, lightly beaten
breadcrumbs
oil for frying

Combine the lentils, millet, onion, cloves, cinnamon and nutmeg and mix well. Season to taste with salt and black pepper and form the mixture into oval patties. Dip them into the beaten egg and then roll them in breadcrumbs. Fry patties light brown on both sides in shallow oil.

Lentil and bulgar wheat cakes

2 oz (¼ cup) whole lentils, soaked for
   4 hours, drained
1 pt (2½ cups) water
4 oz (½ cup) bulgar wheat
2 tablespoons vegetable oil
2 small onions, finely diced

1 clove garlic, crushed
1 teaspoon cumin powder
½ teaspoon coriander powder
1 teaspoon paprika
salt to taste

Put the lentils and water in a heavy pot and bring to the boil. Cover, reduce heat and simmer until the lentils are cooked (about 40 minutes). Add the bulgar wheat to the pot, mix well and set aside for 1 hour. During this time all the water in the pot should be absorbed. Meanwhile heat the oil in a heavy frying pan and sauté the onion and garlic until golden. Stir in the cumin, coriander and paprika and cook a further minute. Put the lentil and bulgar wheat mixture into a bowl and stir in the onion and spices mixture. Mix well and form into small circular cakes. Serve them uncooked on a bed of lettuce with, if you wish, a spicy tomato dipping sauce.

Lentil and cheese roast

2 tablespoons vegetable oil
1 large onion, diced
1 lb (2 cups) cooked lentils
1 teaspoon mixed herbs

1 teaspoon cayenne pepper
8 oz (1 cup) grated cheese
½ teaspoon salt

Preheat oven to 350°F (gas mark 4). Sauté onion in oil until softened. Combine with remaining ingredients. Place mixture in a greased casserole. Cover and bake for 30 minutes. Uncover and bake a further 15 minutes. Serve hot or cold.

Lentil burgers

1 lb (2 cups) cooked lentils
4 oz (1 cup) wholewheat
   breadcrumbs
1 small onion, finely diced

salt and black pepper to taste
wheatgerm or wholewheat flour
oil for frying

Combine the lentils, breadcrumbs and onion and mix well. Season to taste with salt and black pepper and form into 8 circular patties or burgers. If the mixture is too dry to stick to itself add some stock (the cooking liquid from the lentils) or water. Coat the burgers in wheatgerm or wholewheat flour and fry on both sides until nicely browned in a lightly oiled heavy frying pan.

Variations
1: Add lightly sautéed vegetables to the mixture.
2: Add 1 tablespoon tomato purée and 2 cloves crushed garlic to the mixture.
3: Add 8 oz (1 cup) grated cheese to the mixture.

Chick-pea and wholewheat bread

1 lb (2 cups) cooked chick-peas
8 oz (1 cup) cooked wholewheat
2 stalks celery, finely chopped
2 tablespoons tomato purée

4 oz (½ cup) chopped nuts
2 eggs, lightly beaten
1 teaspoon sage
salt and black pepper to taste

Preheat oven to 375°F (gas mark 5). Mash or blend the chick-peas with 8 fl oz (1 cup) of the liquid they were cooked in or water and combine them with the remaining ingredients. Pack into a greased bread tin and bake for 30 minutes or until the mixture is well set. Serve hot or cold.

Chick-peas and potato patties

8 oz (1 cup) cooked chick-peas
1 large potato, peeled and boiled
2 oz (¼ cup) butter

2 tablespoons chopped parsley
salt and black pepper to taste
oil for frying

Combine the chick-peas, potatoes and butter and purée together in a blender. Add liquid (potato or chick-pea cooking liquid) as needed. Alternatively, pass them through a fine food grinder. Add the parsley and salt and black pepper to taste and mix well. Form the mixture into small patties and fry on both sides until nicely browned.

Variations
Soya beans or other beans may be substituted for chick-peas

Falafel

Falafel are a favourite snack food in the Middle East, and they are sold from kiosks on the pavements of many towns in many countries. They are normally sold packed inside an envelope of pita bread with a variety of sauces (including tahini and mint sauce), pickles and salads available to put over them.

8 oz (1 cup) chick-peas
2 cloves garlic, chopped
1 large onion, finely diced
1 egg, lightly beaten
1 teaspoon cumin powder

½ teaspoon coriander powder
pinch cayenne powder
1 tablespoon fresh parsley, chopped
salt and black pepper to taste
oil for deep frying

Put the chick-peas in a bowl and cover well with water. Leave to soak overnight and then drain, reserving the water. Divide the chick-peas into 2 equal portions and blend each half with half of the remaining ingredients. By this method your blender will not get overloaded. If the mixtures are too thick for the machine to handle add reserved soaking water as needed. Now combine the two portions and proceed. Alternatively, pass the chick-peas through a food grinder or mincer and mix the mashed peas with the remaining ingredients by hand.

The falafel mixture made by whichever method is now shaped into balls ¾ inch in diameter. The balls are deep fried in very hot oil until deep brown and then served.

Haricot bean patties

1 lb (2 cups) cooked haricot beans
1 clove garlic, crushed
¼ teaspoon cayenne
1 tablespoon fresh parsley, chopped

salt and black pepper to taste
wholewheat flour
oil for deep frying

Purée the beans in an electric blender or pass through a food grinder. Combine with the remaining ingredients, except for wholewheat flour, and mix well. Chill the mixture and then form into small circular patties. Dust them with flour and deep fry in hot oil until golden brown.

Haricot bean rissoles

1 lb (2 cups) haricot beans, cooked
2 tablespoon vegetable oil
1 medium onion, finely diced
2 medium green peppers, finely diced
1 medium carrot, grated
1 clove garlic, crushed

1 teaspoon mixed herbs
salt and black pepper to taste
2 eggs
breadcrumbs
oil for frying

Purée the beans in an electric blender or pass through a food grinder. Sauté the vegetables and garlic in the oil until well softened. Combine the puréed beans, cooked vegetables, mixed herbs and one egg. Mix well and season to taste with salt and black pepper. Shape the mixture into small rissoles. Beat the remaining egg, dip in it each rissole and then roll in breadcrumbs before frying on both sides in shallow oil until nicely browned.

Lima or butter bean loaf

12 oz (1½ cups) cooked lima or butter
   beans
4 oz (1 cup) breadcrumbs
1 egg, lightly beaten
2 oz (¼ cup) grated or cottage cheese
1 small onion, finely chopped

1 medium green pepper, diced
2 tablespoons fresh parsley, chopped
2 oz (¼ cup) chopped nuts
salt and black pepper to taste
1 oz (2 tablespoons) butter

Preheat oven to 350°F (gas mark 4). Slightly mash the beans with some cooking liquid, then combine with the remaining ingredients except the butter. Mix well and add more cooking liquid if mixture seems too dry. Grease a bread tin and pack the mixture in. Dot the top with butter and bake for 35 to 40 minutes.

Lima or butter bean cakes

1 lb (2 cups) cooked lima or butter
   beans
1 small onion, finely diced
2 tablespoons vegetable oil

4 tablespoons fresh parsley, chopped
¼ teaspoon dried dill seeds
salt and black pepper to taste
oil for frying

Purée the beans with some cooking liquid in a blender or pass them through a fine grinder. Combine with the remaining ingredients and form the mixture into small circular cakes. This task is somewhat easier if the mixture is chilled first. Fry the cakes in shallow oil until nicely browned on both sides.

Soya bean patties

8 oz (1 cup) cooked soya beans
1 medium onion, diced
2 cloves garlic, crushed
1 tablespoon miso
2 oz (¼ cup) chopped nuts
1 tablespoon tahini

1 teaspoon cumin powder
salt and pepper to taste
breadcrumbs or wheatgerm
2 tablespoons sesame seeds, toasted
oil for frying

Mash half the soya beans. Combine them with the whole beans and add the remaining ingredients except for breadcrumbs, sesame seeds and oil. Add breadcrumbs or wheat germ to the mixture until it's firm enough to roll into patties. Roll the patties in sesame seeds and fry on both sides in 1 to 2 inches oil until nicely browned.

Variation
Add 4 oz (½ cup) cottage or grated cheese to the mixture.

Toasted soya beans

This method may be used for most types of beans.

1 lb (2 cups) soy beans
2½ pt (3 cups) water
2 oz (¼ cup) butter

Put the beans in a bowl and cover with the water. Leave to soak overnight. Drain and spread the beans on a flat baking tray. Leave to dry in a warm place for 6 hours. Preheat oven to 350°F (gas mark 4). Dot the beans with the butter and put them on the tray into the oven. Bake for 40 minutes, stirring occasionally. Allow to cool and store in an airtight container. Use as you might use roasted peanuts.

Soya bean surprise loaf

1 lb (2 cups) cooked soya beans,
  reserve cooking liquid
1 egg, lightly beaten
4 oz (1 cup) wholewheat
  breadcrumbs
1 tablespoon sesame seeds
2 oz (½ cup) chopped nuts
1 teaspoon paprika

1 teaspoon cumin powder
1 teaspoon basil
salt and black pepper to taste
2 tablespoons vegetable oil
1 medium onion, finely chopped
4 oz (1½ cups) mushrooms, sliced
1 tablespoon butter

Slightly mash the soya beans and combine with the next 8 ingredients. Mix well and add reserved cooking liquid to give a moist consistency. Preheat oven to 350°F (gas mark 4). Heat oil in a heavy frying pan and sauté the onion until golden. Add the mushrooms and cook until softened. Combine the cooked vegetables with the soya bean mixture and pack the whole into a greased bread tin. Dot the top with butter and bake for 30 minutes.

Bean salads, dips and spreads

Bean salads, dips and spreads are most useful dishes. They can be used as starters to a meal or as side dishes. Hot bean salads can also be served as a vegetable dish. The spreads and dips with bread or toast make a delicious and substantial snack.

For a light but delicious and nutritious meal rich in taste, colour and texture serve a fresh green salad with a bean salad, a bean dip dressed with lemon juice and olive oil and a basket of newly baked bread.

Simple bean salad

This is a basic bean salad that may be tried with any type of bean.

8 oz (1 cup) beans, soaked overnight, drained
1¼ pt (3 cups) water
3 tablespoon vegetable oil (olive oil is probably the best to use)
juice of 1 lemon

or
1 tablespoon vinegar
1 small onion, diced
and/or
1 small green pepper, diced
salt and black pepper to taste

Put the beans in a heavy pot, add the water and bring to the boil. Cover, reduce heat and simmer until the beans are cooked. Allow to cool and do not strain the mixture. Add the oil, lemon juice, onion and/or green pepper and mix well. Season to taste with salt and black pepper and serve.

Mixed bean salad

The varieties of mixed bean salad you can make are limited only by the ingredients you have avaiable and your imagination. I have outlined only the general method of preparing a mixed bean (or single bean) salad.

Prepare 8 oz (1 cup) of a cooked mixture of your favourite beans. Add chopped fresh vegetables. Toss in french dressing, yoghurt or sour cream etc. Season to taste with salt and black pepper, garnish with fresh chopped parsley or chives or spring onions or mint, etc., and serve on a bed of lettuce or chopped spinach.

Fresh broad bean salad

1 lb (2 cups) shelled broad beans (about 2 lb before shelling)
water
salt to taste
3 tablespoons vegetable oil

2 cloves garlic, crushed
juice of 1 lemon
black pepper to taste
1 tablespoon fresh parsley, chopped

Put the beans in a pan just covered with water, salt and bring to the boil. Cover, reduce heat and simmer until just tender. Drain and chill the beans. Meanwhile combine the oil, garlic and lemon juice and season to taste with salt and black pepper. Toss the beans in this dressing and serve garnished with parsley.

Butter beans (lima beans) with apple

2 tablespoons vegetable oil
1 large onion, chopped
¼ teaspoon turmeric
½ teaspoon cinnamon

1 medium cooking apple, peeled, cored and chopped
8 oz (1 cup) butter beans, cooked and drained, reserve cooking liquid
salt and black pepper to taste

Heat the oil in a heavy pan and put in the onion. Sauté until golden brown then stir in the turmeric and cinnamon. Add the apple and simmer over a low light until the apple is cooked. Stir in the beans and enough cooking liquid to moisten the contents of the pan. Season to taste with salt and black pepper. Serve hot or cold.

Chick-pea and wheat salad

2 tablespoons vegetable oil
1 small onion, diced
8 oz (1 cup) chick-peas, cooked and drained

4 oz (½ cup) cracked wheat
4 oz (½ cup) tomato purée
8 fl oz (1 cup) boiling water
salt and black pepper to taste

Put the oil in a heavy pan, add the onion and sauté until golden. Add the chick-peas, cracked wheat and tomato purée. Mix well and pour in the boiling water. Season to taste with salt and black pepper and set to simmer for 20 minutes or until all the water is absorbed and the wheat is cooked. Serve hot or cold.

Chick-peas in yoghurt and french dressing

4 tablespoons vegetable oil
2 tablespoons vinegar or lemon juice
1 clove garlic, crushed
salt to taste
4 fl oz (½ cup) yoghurt

8 oz (1 cup) chick-peas, cooked and drained
3 to 4 leaves of fresh mint, chopped (optional)

Combine the oil, vinegar and garlic and mix well. Season to taste with salt and beat in the yoghurt. Stir in the chick-peas and garnish with fresh mint. Chill the salad before serving.

Variations
Add diced green pepper and/or celery to the salad they will give it a pleasant crunchy texture.

Egyptian ful bean salad

8 oz (1 cup) ful beans, cooked and drained
2 cloves garlic, crushed
½ teaspoon salt
juice of 1 lemon

1 small onion, diced
1 tablespoon fresh parsley, chopped
4 leaves mint, chopped
2 fl oz (¼ cup) olive oil

Put the beans in a bowl. Crush the garlic with the salt and stir into the beans. Add the lemon juice and diced onion and mix well. Garnish the top with parsley and mint and pour over the olive oil. Serve.

Lentil salad

8 oz (1 cup) green or brown lentils, cooked
1 small onion, finely diced
2 tablespoons vegetable oil
2 tablespoon vinegar or lemon juice

1 tablespoon prepared horseradish sauce
½ teaspoon ground cumin
½ teaspoon ground coriander
salt and black pepper to taste

Combine the lentils with the other ingredients and mix well. Put the mixture in a salad bowl and refrigerate. Leave to chill and marinate for 1 to 2 hours before serving.

Variations
1: Add other chopped vegetables to the salad, e.g. green pepper, celery, tomatoes, apple, bean sprouts, etc.
2: Replace the horseradish sauce by 1 teaspoon of mild mustard or ½ teaspoon of hot mustard.

Fresh pea salad

8 oz (1 cup) shelled young peas (1 lb before shelling)
¼ medium cucumber, thinly sliced
2 to 3 spring onions or scallions, chopped

4 tablespoons vegetable oil
2 tablespoons vinegar
salt to taste
4 radishes, halved
2 tablespoons fresh mint, chopped

Combine the peas, cucumber and spring onions in a salad bowl. Whisk the oil and vinegar together and season to taste with salt. Toss the salad in this dressing. Decorate the top with radish halves and garnish with chopped mint.

Red beans, tomato and onion salad

8 oz (1 cup) red beans, cooked and drained (reserve the cooking water)
2 tablespoons vegetable oil
1 large onion, finely diced

2 cloves garlic, crushed
3 medium tomatoes, quartered
salt and pepper to taste
1 tablespoon fresh parsley, chopped

Combine the beans with 8 fl oz (1 cup) of the water they were cooked in and set aside. Heat the oil in a heavy pan and sauté the onions and garlic until golden brown. Add the tomatoes and sauté a further 2 or 3 minutes. Pour in the beans and cooking water, stir well and season to taste with salt and black pepper. Bring the mixture to the boil, cover, reduce heat and simmer for 5 minutes. Leave to cool, chill in the refrigerator and then serve garnished with chopped parsley.

Variation
This salad may be prepared with other beans or mixtures of beans. Haricot beans, chick-peas and red beans combined are a particularly effective mixture in terms of colour and taste.

Spicy red bean salad

8 oz (1 cup) red beans, cooked and
    drained
1 teaspoon chili sauce
1 tablespoon vegetable oil
1 tablespoon vinegar
1 clove garlic, crushed

½ teaspoon oregano
1 medium green pepper, diced
1 medium onion, diced
2 oz (¾ cup) mushrooms, sliced
salt to taste

Combine all the ingredients, mix well and set aside to marinate for 2 to 4 hours.
Serve chilled on a bed of lettuce leaves.

Variation
Combine the salad with 2 tablespoons mayonnaise before serving.

White bean and vegetable salad

Any type of white beans may be used for this salad. If you use soya beans
increase the initial cooking time to 3 hours.

8 oz (1 cup) white beans, soaked
    overnight, drained
1¼ pt (3 cups) water
1 medium potato, peeled and diced
1 medium carrot, thinly sliced
1 medium onion, sliced

2 cloves garlic, crushed
2 medium tomatoes, sliced
1 tablespoon tomato purée
3 tablespoons vegetable oil
salt and black pepper to taste

Put the beans in a heavy pot and add the water. Bring to the boil, cover, reduce
heat and simmer for 1 hour. Add the other ingredients, stir well and return the
mixture to the boil, cover, reduce heat and simmer until all the vegetables are
well cooked (about 30 minutes). Cool and chill. Serve on a bed of lettuce
garnished with slices of lemon.

Turkish white bean salad

8 oz (1 cup) white beans, cooked
1 medium onion, thinly sliced
1 hard-boiled egg, shelled and sliced
2 medium tomatoes, sliced

12 black olives, stoned and halved
juice of 1 lemon
1 tablespoon olive oil
1 tablespoon fresh parsley, chopped

Put the beans in the bottom of a salad bowl and cover with the sliced onion, egg
and tomatoes. Decorate this layer with the olives and pour over lemon juice and
olive oil. Garnish with parsley and serve.

White bean and beetroot salad

Any type of white bean, including butter beans (lima beans) and broad beans
may be used to make this salad. Red beans and other coloured beans are also suitable but the colour contrast with the beetroot is not so vivid and the salad
doesn't look as exciting.

2 medium cooked beetroot, diced
1 tablespoon butter
1 teaspoon vinegar
1 teaspoon honey

8 oz (1 cup) white beans, cooked and drained
salt to taste
2 tablespoons sour cream, optional

Put the beetroot in a pan with the butter and gently heat. Stir the beetroot in the melted butter and add the vinegar and honey. Continue heating and stirring until the honey has melted and homogenised with the butter and vinegar. Combine this mixture with the beans and salt to taste. Chill and serve dressed in sour cream.

Bean sprout salads

Bean sprouts are a rich source of vitamins particularly vitamin C. They are cheap, quick to grow and available all the year round. All that is needed to grow them is a dark, relatively warm place (e.g. an airing cupboard), a jar and some beans. Most beans (and grains) as long as they are not too old to germinate can be sprouted, although the most popular commercially are mung beans. Other favourites are chick-peas, kidney beans, soya beans and lentils. The length of time before the sprouts are ready depends on the bean used and upon the stage at which you decide to harvest them. An average time is from 3 to 5 days. After this time mung bean sprouts will be about 2 inches long while chick-peas, lentils, kidney beans and soya beans will be ½ inch to 1 inch long. Bean sprouts may be used fresh in salads or sandwiches, cooked in soups, omelettes, etc., or in quick fried dishes in the Chinese manner.

To sprout beans, grains and seeds

Place 2 oz (¼ cup) of beans, grains or seeds in the bottom of a large jar and fill it half full of water. The sprouts will be 6 to 8 times as bulky as the unsprouted beans, so make sure the jar is large enough. Leave them to soak overnight and then drain the water away. Rinse the beans and drain again. A piece of cheese cloth placed over the mouth of the jar makes this job easy. Now place the jar in a warm dark place (about 70°F). Repeat the rinse and drain procedure 3 times a day for 3 to 5 days. Now spread the drained bean sprouts on a tray and leave in the daylight (indoors) for 2 to 3 hours. They can now be used as required. Store unused bean sprouts in a covered container in the refrigerator. They can be used fresh for up to 3 days or cooked for up to 5 days after harvesting. If you have 2 jars available for bean sprouting you will have a constantly available source of fresh bean sprouts.

Bean sprout salads

Almost any salad will be enhanced by the addition of bean sprouts. Opposite are two recipes to stimulate your own ideas.

Bean sprout and bean salad

8 oz (1 cup) cooked beans, drained
8 oz (1 cup) cooked green beans,
  drained
4 oz (1 cup) bean sprouts
4 oz (1 cup) chopped peanuts
2 sticks celery, chopped

½ medium green pepper, diced
juice of 1 lemon
4 tablespoons vegetable oil
1 clove garlic, crushed
salt and black pepper to taste

Combine the beans, sprouts, peanuts, celery and green pepper and carefully mix together. Add the lemon juice to the oil and garlic, beat together and season to taste with salt and black pepper. Pour the dressing over the salad and serve immediately.

Bean sprout, beetroot and apple salad

4 oz (1 cup) bean sprouts
1 medium beetroot, sliced
1 medium apple, sliced
2 oz (½ cup) chopped nuts, optional

juice of 1 lemon
1 tablespoon honey
1 tablespoon vegetable oil
pinch salt

Layer the bean sprouts, beetroot and apple slices in a salad bowl. Top with chopped nuts. Beat the lemon juice, honey, vegetable oil and salt together and pour over the salad. Serve immediately.

Spreads and dips

Aduki bean spread

8 oz (1 cup) aduki beans, well cooked
1 tablespoon sesame seeds
1 tablespoon vegetable oil (sesame oil
  if possible)

½ medium onion, finely diced
1 clove garlic, crushed
salt and black pepper to taste

Pound or crush the beans to a paste with the back of a wooden spoon, or a pestle and mortar or in an electric blender. Dry roast the sesame seeds in a frying pan or small saucepan until they are lightly browned and start to pop, and combine them with the aduki bean paste. Heat the oil in a heavy pan and sauté the onion and garlic until golden. Stir in the aduki paste and simmer, stirring, over a low heat for 5 minutes. If the mixture is too thick add a little bean cooking water or oil or both. Transfer to a bowl and allow to cool. Serve on fresh bread, toast or in sandwiches.

Variation
Add 1 tablespoon wine vinegar to the spread; it gives it a little extra tang.

Aduki bean and chestnut spread

4 oz (½ cup) aduki beans, well cooked   salt or sugar to taste
4 oz (½ cup) chestnut purée (available
    tinned)

Blend or crush the ingredients together adding salt for a savoury dip or sugar for
a sweet one. Add some of the water the beans were cooked in if the consistency
of the spread is too thick.

Bean jam

8 oz (1 cup) aduki beans, red kidney   10 fl oz (1¼ cups) water
    beans or haricot beans, soaked   8 oz (1 cup) sugar
    overnight, drained

Put the beans in a heavy pan and add the water. Bring to the boil and gently boil
until the beans are well cooked and starting to crumble. Stir in the salt and sugar
and mash to a paste with a wooden spoon. Alternatively purée in an electric
blender. Store the jam in jars and use as ordinary jam. Bean jam is particularly
good filling for cakes and buns.

Broad bean and peanut butter spread

8 oz (1 cup) cooked butter beans   juice of 1 lemon
2 tablespoons peanut butter   salt to taste
2 tablespoons vegetable oil

Blend or mash the broad beans, add the other ingredients and mix well. Add a
little bean cooking water or more oil or both to get the consistency of spread
desired.

Butter bean and tomato spread

4 oz (½ cup) butter beans, well cooked   1 clove garlic, crushed
1 tablespoon tomato purée   1 tablespoon wine or cider vinegar
2 tablespoons vegetable oil   salt to taste
½ medium onion, finely diced

Blend or mash the beans and mix well with the tomato purée. Heat the oil in a
heavy pan and sauté the onion and garlic until golden. Combine them with the
bean and tomato purée and mix in the vinegar. Season to taste with salt and
allow to cool before serving.

Bean mayonnaise

8 oz (1 cup) haricot (or other white   1 small onion, very finely diced
    beans) well cooked   ½ teaspoon english mustard powder
6 tablespoons vegetable oil (olive oil is   2 tablespoons wine or cider vinegar
    best)   salt to taste

Rub the beans through a sieve or purée them in an electric blender. Beat in the oil a tablespoon at a time and then add the onion, mustard powder and vinegar. Season to taste with salt and beat the mixture to a fluffy consistency.

Variation
Replace the vinegar with juice of 1 lemon and the grated rind of ½ a lemon.

Chick-peas with tahini (hummus bi tahini)

Hummus is widely appreciated throughout the Middle East where it is usually served as a dip with pita bread. There are many different recipes for preparing it but they are mostly very similar differing only in the relative quantities of tahini, garlic and lemon juice used. The best hummus I ever had was from a small snack bar in the old market of Jerusalem. The proprietor was an old man and he was helped by his son and grandson. All they sold was hummus and soft drinks (including very sweet, hot and delicious mint tea). The hummus was made by hand and it was served laced with olive oil and liberally sprinkled with paprika.

8 oz (1 cup) chick-peas, soaked
   overnight, drained
2 pt (5 cups) water
juice of 2 lemons
5 fl oz (1 cup) tahini
3 cloves garlic, crushed
salt to taste

Garnish
Olive oil
Paprika
Chopped parsley

Put the chick-peas in a heavy pot with the water and bring to the boil. Remove any foam that forms and gently boil the peas for 1 to 1½ hours or until the beans are very soft. Drain and reserve any cooking liquid.

Electric blender method
Put the peas, oil, lemon juice and tahini into the blender and enough cooking water or plain water to allow the mixture to purée satisfactorily. Add salt to taste and more lemon juice or tahini as you may need after the first tasting. Blend for a final time and it's ready to be served.

Hand method
Press the cooked peas through a sieve or the fine blade of a mouli or crush in a pestle and mortar. Crush the garlic with some salt and add to the chick-pea paste. Stir in the tahini, lemon juice and enough cooking water or plain water to form a creamy smooth paste. Add salt to taste and adjust the quantities of lemon juice and tahini as required.

Pour the hummus onto a serving dish, sprinkle paprika and chopped parsley over the top and pour over 1 or 2 tablespoons of olive oil. Serve with pita bread, olives and a fresh salad.

Chick-peas and yoghurt dip

8 oz (1 cup) chick-peas, well cooked   *or*
4 fl oz (½ cup) yoghurt   1 teaspoon dried mint
juice of 1 lemon   salt and black pepper to taste
1 tablespoon fresh mint, chopped   rind of half a lemon, grated

Blend the chick-peas, yoghurt and lemon juice together in an electric blender, or crush the chick-peas by hand and mix with the yoghurt and lemon juice. Stir the mint into the dip and season to taste with salt and black pepper. Pour the mixture into a serving bowl and decorate with grated lemon peel.

Haricot bean purée

8 oz (1 cup) cooked haricot beans   *or*
1 clove garlic, crushed   2 to 4 leaves fresh sage, chopped
3 tablespoons olive oil   1 small onion, diced
1 tablespoon vinegar   salt and black pepper to taste
½ teaspoon dried sage

Purée the ingredients in an electric blender or pass the beans through a fine sieve and then mix with the other ingredients. To thin the purée stir in a little water or some of the liquid the beans were cooked in. Serve chilled with pita bread.

Peanut butter

peanuts
vegetable oil
salt

Put the desired quantity of peanuts into an electric blender and add a little oil to facilitate the blending process. Add salt to taste and switch on the machine. If the mixture proves too thick for the machine to deal with add a little more oil. The more oil you add the creamier the butter will be.

Peanut butter and yeast spread

A nutritious and tasty topping for sandwiches or toast.

4 oz (½ cup) peanut butter
1 tablespoon of yeast extract
   (marmite)

Combine the peanut butter and yeast extract and mix well.

Peanut butter and banana spread

A particular favourite with children. It's filling and full of energy.

4 oz (½ cup) peanut butter
1 or 2 ripe bananas

Mash the bananas and combine with the peanut butter.

Red bean and lemon dip

4 oz (½ cup) cooked red beans
3 tablespoons tahini

juice of 2 lemons
salt to taste

Purée all the ingredients together in an electric blender or press the beans through a fine sieve and then mix in the other ingredients. To spike the dip add half a teaspoon of hot pepper sauce.

Soya bean and olive spread

8 oz (1 cup) cooked soya beans
2 oz (¼ cup) olives, stoned
½ green pepper, diced

2 tablespoons mayonnaise
salt to taste

Mash the soya beans with a wooden spoon or pass them through a fine sieve. Add the other ingredients and mix well. Alternatively put all the ingredients into an electric blender and purée.

Soya bean and tomato spread

8 oz (1 cup) cooked soya beans
4 tablespoons olive oil
2 tablespoons tomato purée
juice of 1 lemon

1 small onion, finely diced
½ teaspoon cayenne pepper
salt to taste

Mash the soya beans with a wooden spoon or pass them through a fine sieve. Add the other ingredients and mix well. Alternatively put all the ingredients into an electric blender and purée.

MAIN DISHES CONTAINING BEANS, PEAS AND LENTILS

Aduki beans

Refried aduki beans with miso

2 tablespoons vegetable oil
2 medium onions, sliced
2 cloves garlic, crushed
1 lb (2 cups) cooked aduki beans,
    drained

4 tomatoes, sliced
1 tablespoon miso
¼ teaspoon chili powder
½ teaspoon cumin powder
salt to taste

Heat the oil in a heavy frying pan. Add the onion and garlic and fry until golden. Add the remaining ingredients and sauté until thick and heated right through. Serve with tortillas (see index) and/or brown rice.

Rich aduki bean hotpot

12 oz (2 cups) aduki beans
2 pt (5 cups) water
2 oz (¼ cup) carrots, chopped
2 medium onions, chopped
4 sticks celery, chopped

2 tablespoons oil
2 apples, cut into thin slices
3 oz (½ cup) oats, pre-soaked
2 bay leaves
salt and pepper to taste

Soak the beans in the water for 2 to 3 hours and then gently boil in the same water for 1 hour. Sauté the onions, carrots and celery in the oil until just soft. Add the vegetables, apple, bay leaves and seasoning to the beans and cooking water. Bring to the boil and simmer for 30 minutes. Drain the oats and add to the pot, simmer for a further 10 minutes.

Black-eyed peas

*Hopping john

Black-eyed peas and rice are popular in the southern USA, where it is sometimes known as 'soul food'.

1 tablespoon vegetable oil
4 oz lean salt pork, minced
or
4 oz bacon, chopped
1 medium onion, finely diced
1 clove garlic, crushed

8 oz (1 cup) black-eyed peas, soaked
  overnight and drained
8 oz (1 cup) brown rice, washed
1½ pt (4 cups) water or stock
salt and black pepper to taste

Put the vegetable oil into a heavy saucepan and add the pork or bacon, onion and garlic and sauté until golden brown. Add the peas, rice and water and bring to the boil. Reduce heat, cover and simmer for 1 hour or until the beans are tender. Season to taste with salt and black pepper and serve.

Virginia black-eyed peas

1 lb (2 cups) black-eyed peas, soaked
  overnight and drained
1 medium onion, quartered
½ teaspoon thyme
1 bay leaf

2 whole cloves
¼ teaspoon black pepper
water
salt to taste

Put the peas, onion, thyme, bay leaf, cloves and black pepper into a heavy saucepan. Just cover with water and bring to the boil. Cover, reduce heat and simmer for 1 to 1½ hours or until peas are very tender. Season to taste with salt and serve. During the cooking time, check occasionally and add water as required.

Black beans

Guatemalan black beans

8 oz (1 cup) black beans, soaked
  overnight, drained
1 pt (2½ cups) water
2 cloves garlic, crushed
1 bay leaf
¼ teaspoon hot pepper sauce
2 tablespoons vegetable oil

2 medium onions, sliced
2 stalks celery with tops, chopped
juice of 1 lemon
salt to taste
grated rind of 1 lemon
2 hard boiled eggs, shelled and sliced

Put the beans, water, garlic, bay leaf and hot pepper sauce in a heavy saucepan and bring to the boil. Cover, reduce heat and simmer for 1½ hours or until the beans are tender. Sauté the onions and celery in the oil until soft. Add them to the cooked beans along with the lemon juice and salt to taste. Serve garnished with lemon rind and slices of hard boiled egg.

Korean black beans

8 oz (1 cup) black beans, soaked
  overnight, drained
1 pt (2½ cups) water
2 tablespoons soy sauce
½ teaspoon ground ginger

or
1 teaspoon fresh ginger, peeled and
  grated
1 tablespoon vegetable oil
1 teaspoon sugar
½ teaspoon hot pepper sauce
1 tablespoon sesame seeds, toasted

Put the beans and water in a heavy saucepan and bring to the boil. Cover, reduce heat and simmer for 30 minutes. Add the remaining ingredients and continue gently simmering until the beans are cooked, about 45 minutes. Serve with rice, chutney and plain unsweetened yoghurt.

Broad beans

★Broad beans with garlic sausage

1 lb (2 cups) broad beans, soaked
  overnight, drained
2 pt (3 cups) water or stock
¼ lb fatty bacon, diced
2 medium onions, sliced
2 cloves garlic, crushed

¼ lb garlic sausage, sliced
1 bay leaf
½ teaspoon ground coriander
salt and black pepper to taste
2 tablespoons fresh parsley, chopped

Put the beans and water into a heavy saucepan and bring to the boil. Cover, reduce heat and simmer for 1 hour. Meanwhile, fry the bacon in a heavy frying pan and as the fat runs, add the onions and garlic. Fry until the bacon is crisp and the onion is soft and golden. Put this mixture and the garlic sausage, bay leaf and coriander into the pot with beans and continue simmering until the beans are soft and tender, about 30 minutes. Season to taste with salt and black pepper and serve garnished with parsley. A fresh lettuce and tomato salad goes well with this dish.

Chick-peas

Chick-peas Spanish style

1 lb (2 cups) chick-peas,
  soaked overnight, drained
2 pt (5 cups) water
3 tablespoons vegetable oil (olive oil if
  possible)
3 cloves garlic, crushed
1 medium onion, diced

1 medium green pepper, chopped
1 lb (2 cups) fresh or tinned tomatoes,
  chopped
½ small chili pepper, chopped
1 tablespoon fresh parsley, chopped
salt to taste

Put the chick-peas, water and 1 tablespoon oil in a heavy saucepan and bring to the boil, reduce heat and simmer for about 10 minutes. Meanwhile sauté the onion and garlic until golden in the remaining oil in a heavy frying pan. Add the green pepper and cook until soft. Add the remaining ingredients to the frying pan and gently simmer the sauce for 20 to 30 minutes. As the chick-peas approach tenderness add this tomato sauce to them and cook until completely tender. Serve.

Spiced chick-pea and potato dish

2 tablespoons vegetable oil or butter
2 medium onions, diced
½ teaspoon cumin powder
½ teaspoon coriander powder
¼ teaspoon ground ginger
1 teaspoon turmeric
¼ teaspoon chili powder

juice of 1 lemon
1½ lb (3 cups) cooked chick-peas
2 medium tomatoes, quartered
3 medium potatoes, peeled, diced
8 fl oz (1 cup) water or stock
salt to taste
2 tablespoons fresh parsley, chopped

Heat the vegetable oil in a heavy saucepan, add the onions and sauté until golden. Sprinkle in the cumin, coriander, ginger, turmeric and chili powder and gently fry for 1 to 2 minutes. Add the lemon juice, chick-peas, tomatoes, potatoes and water or stock. Bring to the boil and season to taste with salt. Reduce heat, cover and simmer for 15 minutes or until the potatoes are cooked. Serve garnished with parsley.

Chick-peas with aubergines (eggplant)

2 medium aubergines (eggplant),
  cubed
2 medium onions, sliced
4 fl oz (½ cup) olive oil
1 lb (2 cups) cooked chick-peas,
  drained

8 oz (1 cup) tinned tomatoes
1 tablespoon tomato purée
2 oz (¼ cup) pine nuts (optional)
1 teaspoon dried mint
salt and black pepper to taste

Generously salt the aubergine cubes and set in a colander to drain for 30 minutes. Now wash them under running water to remove excess salt and pat dry on paper towels. Put the aubergines, onion and olive oil in a heavy frying pan and fry until the onion and aubergine are lightly browned. Add the remaining ingredients and cook over a low heat, uncovered for 30 minutes. Serve hot or cold with brown rice and salad.

*Chick-pea, bulgar wheat and meat pilau

4 tablespoons vegetable oil
1 medium onion, diced
4 oz minced beef or lamb
1½ pt (4 cups) water or stock
4 oz (½ cup) chick-peas, soaked overnight, drained

8 oz (1 cup) bulgar wheat
1 teaspoon dried mint
salt and black pepper to taste
8 oz (1 cup) yoghurt (optional)
½ teaspoon paprika (optional)

Put the oil in a heavy saucepan and add the onion. Lightly brown and then add the minced meat. Cook, stirring, for 5 minutes. Pour in the water or stock, add the chick-peas and bring to the boil. Reduce heat and simmer for 45 minutes. Add the bulgar wheat, mint and season to taste with salt and black pepper. Return to the boil, reduce heat, cover and simmer until the peas and wheat are cooked and the mixture is just dry, about 35 to 40 minutes. Serve with yoghurt poured over the top and sprinkled with paprika.

Variation
Add cooked dried apricots to the yoghurt before pouring it over the chick-pea mixture.

*Lamb and chick-pea stew with lentils

2 tablespoons oil
8 oz lean lamb, cubed (½ inch)
2 medium onions, diced
8 oz (1 cup) tinned tomatoes, chopped
1 tablespoon fresh parsley, chopped
½ teaspoon coriander powder
1 teaspoon ground ginger
1 teaspoon cinnamon
1 teaspoon turmeric

4 oz (½ cup) chick-peas, soaked overnight, drained
2 pt (5 cups) water
4 oz (½ cup) lentils, washed and drained
salt and black pepper to taste
2 eggs, beaten
juice of 1 lemon

Heat the oil in a heavy saucepan and brown the lamb on all sides. Add the onion and lightly sauté. Add the tomatoes, parsley, coriander, ginger, cinnamon and turmeric, stir well and cook for 1 to 2 minutes. Stir in the chick-peas, add the water and lentils and bring to the boil. Cover, reduce heat and simmer for 1 hour or until all the ingredients are tender. Stir the lemon juice into the beaten egg and beat the mixture into the stew. Remove the pan from the heat and serve.

Ful beans

Ful medames

This dish is made from ful or foul beans, although brown beans can also be used. It is almost the national dish of Egypt and can be bought in that country in thousands of small cafés and restaurants. The beans are traditionally served with tahini, lemon juice and pita bread which is used as an eating scoop.

To serve 6

1 lb (2 cups) ful beans, soaked over-
    night and drained
2½ pt (6¼ cups) water
6 eggs
4 cloves garlic, crushed
3 tablespoons olive oil
1 tablespoon ground cumin

salt to taste
2 lemons, quartered
tahini
2 tablespoons fresh parsley, chopped
1 teaspoon turmeric
1 teaspoon paprika
olive oil

Put the beans in a heavy saucepan with the water, eggs, garlic, olive oil and cumin. Bring to the boil, cover, reduce heat and simmer on a very low light for 6 hours or more. Remove the eggs and shell them. Serve the beans sprinkled with paprika along with the eggs sprinkled with turmeric, a bowl of tahini garnished with parsley and quartered lemons. Each guest may crumble an egg over his or her beans, squeeze on lemon juice and add olive oil as desired.

Haricot bean

Apart from the regular haricot bean, the great northern bean, navy bean and white bean may be used in these recipes.

Italian beans

1 lb (2 cups) haricot beans, soaked
    overnight, drained
1 clove garlic, crushed
1 small onion, thinly sliced
1 medium green pepper, thinly sliced
2 tablespoons tomato purée

8 fl oz (1 cup) water
2 tablespoons olive oil
2 tablespoons fresh parsley, chopped
8 green olives, stoned and chopped
salt to taste
4 oz (½ cup) parmesan cheese, grated

Preheat oven to 325°F (gas mark 3). Combine beans with all the ingredients except the cheese and salt and place in a heavy casserole dish. Cover and bring to the boil. Transfer to the oven and bake for 2 hours. Salt to taste and sprinkle cheese over the top. Bake uncovered for a further 30 minutes or until cheese melts and browns.

Haricot bean plaki

This is a Middle Eastern dish, served either hot or chilled, in which the beans are cooked in a tomato sauce.

To serve 6

4 fl oz (½ cup) olive oil
2 cloves garlic, crushed
2 medium onions, finely sliced
1 medium carrot, diced
2 stalks celery with leaves, chopped
2 tablespoons fresh parsley, chopped
1 bay leaf, crumbled

½ teaspoon oregano
6 tomatoes, peeled and diced
or
1 lb (2 cups) tinned tomatoes
1 lb (2 cups) haricot beans soaked
    overnight, drained
salt to taste

Heat the oil in a heavy saucepan, add the garlic, onion, carrot and celery and sauté until soft but not browned. Stir in the parsley, bay leaf, oregano and tomatoes, stir well and simmer until well blended. Add the beans, enough water to cover and bring to the boil. Cover, reduce heat and simmer for 1 to 1½ hours or until the beans are tender. Salt to taste and serve. To serve cold, chill the cooked dish, stir in 1 tablespoon each of vinegar and olive oil and garnish with olives and chopped parsley.

Haricot bean goulash

4 tablespoons vegetable oil
1 clove garlic, crushed
2 medium onions, thinly sliced
8 oz (3 cups) mushrooms, sliced
1 tablespoon tomato purée
1 lb haricot beans, soaked overnight,
    drained
16 fl oz (2 cups) water or stock, boiling

1 tablespoon paprika
½ teaspoon dry mustard
pinch cayenne
1 teaspoon caraway seeds
¼ teaspoon black pepper
1 bay leaf
salt to taste

Preheat oven to 325°F (gas mark 3). Heat the oil in a heavy casserole dish, add the garlic and onions and sauté until golden. Add the remaining ingredients, except for the salt, and mix well. Cover, bring to the boil and transfer to the oven. Bake for 2 to 3 hours or until beans are tender. Salt to taste and serve with hot noodles or a simple salad.

*Hungarian sausage and beans

Ingredients as for Haricot bean goulash (above) plus

1 lb garlic sausage cut into ½ inch
    slices

4 fl oz (½ cup) sour cream
½ teaspoon cayenne

Follow Haricot bean goulash as in the recipe above. After the beans have been baking 1 hour stir in the sausage and return the casserole dish, covered, to the oven. When the beans are tender, stir in the sour cream and cayenne and serve.

Creamy haricot beans

To serve 6

4oz fatty bacon, cut in small pieces *or*
  2 tablespoons vegetable oil
1 medium onion, diced
1 medium green pepper, sliced
1 lb (2 cups) haricot beans, soaked
  overnight, drained

2 medium tomatoes, halved
1 pt (2½ cups) stock or water
2 tablespoons tomato purée
¼ pt (⅝ cup) sour cream
salt and black pepper to taste
2 tablespoons fresh parsley, chopped

Put the bacon in a fireproof casserole dish and fry until the fat starts to melt, or use vegetable oil. Add the onion and green pepper and fry until the onion is golden and the green pepper is softened. Add the beans, tomatoes, stock or water and tomato purée and mix well. Cover the dish and bake at 325°F (gas mark 3) for 3 to 4 hours or until the beans are tender. Stir in the sour cream, season to taste with salt and black pepper and serve garnished with parsley.

★Boston baked beans

To serve 6

1 lb (2 cups) haricot beans, soaked
  overnight, drained
¼ lb salt pork, cut in 2 pieces
1 medium onion, sliced

½ teaspoon dry mustard
2 tablespoons molasses
1 tablespoon brown sugar
salt to taste

Put one piece of salt pork and the onion in the bottom of a casserole dish and pour over the beans. Combine the mustard, molasses and sugar and pour the mixture into the dish. Add enough water to cover the top of the beans by ½ inch and place the remaining piece of salt pork on top of the beans rind side up. Cover the dish and bake at 300°F (gas mark 2) for about 6 hours. Uncover the dish for the last 30 minutes, salt to taste toward the end of cooking time.

★Haricot beans with tuna fish

To serve 6

2 tablespoons vegetable oil (olive oil if
  possible)
2 cloves garlic, crushed
1 small onion, diced
12 oz (1½ cups) haricot beans, soaked
  overnight, drained
1½ pt (4 cups) water

8 oz (1 cup) fresh or tinned tomatoes,
  chopped
8 oz tin tuna fish, drained and cut in
  chunks
½ teaspoon dried oregano
salt and black pepper to taste

Heat the oil in a heavy saucepan and sauté the garlic and onion until golden. Add the beans and water, bring to the boil, cover, reduce heat and simmer for 1½ hours or until the beans are just tender. Add the remaining ingredients, mix well and simmer a further 15 to 20 minutes. Serve.

★Meera's cholent with Knaidel (dumpling)

This delicious traditional Jewish recipe was given to me by a lady in Israel after treating a friend and I to a splendid meal she had cooked, in which cholent was the main dish. To achieve the very slow cooking time required in the recipe Meera used a small marble slab placed over a gas ring and a very heavy casserole dish.

To serve 6 to 8 people

1 lb (2 cups) haricot beans, soaked overnight, drained	*Knaidel (dumplings)*
2 lb stewing beef, cubed	4 eggs, beaten
3 medium onions, halved	4 teaspoons sugar
4 medium potatoes, peeled and halved	4 fl oz (½ cup) oil
boiling water	salt to taste
salt and black pepper to taste	4 fl oz (½ cup) water
	12 oz (1½ cups) matzo meal or flour

Cover the beans with fresh water and bring to the boil. Boil for a few minutes and then drain. In a heavy casserole dish melt the sugar over a low heat. Add the meat and onions and brown them in the syrup. Add the beans, potatoes and boiling water to cover. Mix well and season to taste with salt and black pepper. Set to simmer and prepare the dumplings. Combine the eggs, sugar and oil and mix well. Add the water and enough matzo meal or flour to form a firm dough. Wet your hands and form the mixture into small sausage shape dumplings. Put the dumplings in the casserole dish and bring the whole to the boil. Cover and cook in a very low oven at 275°F (gas mark 1) for over 12 hours and up to 24 hours. For quicker cooking time bake at 325°F (gas mark 3) for 6 hours.

Variation
Place 6 to 8 eggs in their shells in the pot at the beginning of the baking time. They gradually turn light brown and acquire a distinctive flavour.

Kidney beans

The recipes below are generally prepared with red kidney beans although any of the other members of the kidney bean family (see page 170) may be tried. Pink and pinto beans are particularly suitable substitutes.

Sweet and sour kidney beans

This dish makes a fine accompaniment to a main meal or to use it as a main dish add a variety of cooked vegetables to the casserole before baking.

12 oz (1⅔ cups) kidney beans, soaked overnight, drained	juice of 1 lemon
2 pt (5 cups) water	grated rind of 1 lemon
2 oz (¼ cup) butter	2 tablespoons sugar or honey
2 oz (¼ cup) flour	salt to taste
	2 tablespoons fresh parsley, chopped

Cook the kidney beans in the water until just tender, about 90 minutes. Drain and reserve the liquid. Melt the butter in a small heavy pan and stir in the flour. Stir and heat to form a smooth browned paste. Add some of the reserved liquid and beat to form a smooth, moderately thick sauce. Add the lemon juice, lemon rind, sugar or honey and season to taste with salt. Preheat oven to 375°F (gas mark 5). Put the beans and sauce in a heavy casserole, cover and bake for 20 minutes. Serve garnished with chopped parsley.

*Drunken beans

This dish is best prepared with a good British draught beer, or alternatively use bottled ale or Guinness. Keg and canned beers are not very satisfactory.

4 oz (½ cup) fatty bacon, diced
1 medium onion, sliced
2 cloves garlic, crushed
4 oz (1 cup) lean pork, cubed (¾ inch)
8 oz (1 cup) tinned tomatoes

1 lb (2½ cups) cooked kidney beans, drained
16 fl oz (2 cups) beer
salt and black pepper to taste

Heat a heavy frying pan and fry the bacon until most of the fat has been melted off. Add the onions and garlic and fry until softened. Put in the pork and brown the cubes on all sides. Transfer the mixture to a heavy saucepan and add the tomatoes. Bring to the boil, cover, reduce heat and simmer for 30 minutes or until the pork is just tender. Add the beans and beer and return to the boil. Cover, reduce heat and simmer a further 15 minutes. Finally season to taste with salt and black pepper and serve.

Kidney bean and cider casserole

2 tablespoons vegetable oil
2 cloves garlic, crushed
2 medium onions, sliced
1 medium green pepper, diced
2 medium courgettes (zucchini), sliced
   sliced

1 bay leaf
2 tablespoons tomato purée
½ lb (4 cups) cooked kidney beans
salt and black pepper to taste
8 fl oz (1 cup) dry cider

Preheat oven to 375°F (gas mark 5). Heat the oil in a heavy frying pan and sauté the garlic and onion until golden. Add the green pepper and courgettes, stir and gently sauté until softened. Pour the mixture into a casserole dish and add the remaining ingredients. Mix well, cover and bake for 40 minutes.

Refried kidney beans

This characteristically Mexican dish is now popular all over the southern states of the USA and the Caribbean islands. On a recent trip to New York I had the dish served with fried bananas. It was delicious but very filling.

1 lb (2½ cups) kidney beans, soaked
   overnight, drained
2 tablespoons vegetable oil
1 large onion, sliced
2 cloves garlic, crushed

stock or water to cover
salt to taste
4 fl oz (½ cup) vegetable oil
8 oz (1 cup) grated cheese

Heat 2 tablespoons of vegetable oil in a heavy saucepan and sauté the onion and garlic until golden. Add the beans and just cover with stock or water. Bring to the boil, cover, reduce heat and simmer very gently for 2 to 3 hours. Stir now and again and add more stock or water as needed. Finally season to taste with salt and cook a further 10 minutes. Drain the beans and reserve the liquid. Put the remaining vegetable oil in a large heavy frying pan and heat over a moderate flame. Add ¼ of the beans to the oil, heat through and mash with the back of a wooden spoon. Add more beans and some of the reserved cooking liquid and repeat the procedure. Repeat this until all the beans and liquid are used up. Keep stirring and heating the mixture until it is very nearly dry. Serve immediately topped with grated cheese.

★Chili con carne

Chili con carne is probably the world's best known bean dish. There are endless varieties although each chef usually believes that he or she has hit upon the perfect method. My own taste is not for very hot food so the recipe below may be a little mild for some palates. Do add more hot pepper sauce or chili powder if you wish.

1 lb (2½ cups) kidney beans, soaked overnight, drained	*or* hot pepper sauce
2 pt (5 cups) water	salt and black pepper to taste
2 tablespoons vegetable oil	2 teaspoons dried oregano
3 cloves garlic, crushed	12 oz (1½ cups) tinned tomatoes
1 large onion, diced	reserved cooking liquid
1 lb lean beef, cubed (¾ inch)	
2 teaspoons chili powder	

Cook the kidney beans in the water for 1½ hours or until just cooked. Drain and reserve any cooking liquid. Put the oil into a heavy saucepan and add the garlic and onion. Sauté until golden and add the beef. Brown the beef all over and stir in the chili powder, salt, pepper and oregano. Cook for a further minute and then add the tomatoes and 8 fl oz (1 cup) of reserved cooking liquid. Cover the pot and simmer for 1 hour or until the meat is tender. Stir in the cooked beans and simmer a further 15 minutes. Adjust the seasoning to taste and serve. Chili is excellent the following day. Just heat through and check seasoning.

Lentils

Whole lentil pilau

4 tablespoons vegetable oil	½ teaspoon allspice
8 oz (1 cup) brown rice	salt and black pepper to taste
24 fl oz (3 cups) boiling water	1 clove garlic, crushed
8 oz (1 cup) green or brown lentils, soaked 4 to 6 hours, drained	2 medium onions, diced
	8 fl oz (1 cup) yoghurt

Heat half the vegetable oil in a heavy saucepan and add the rice. Stir fry for 2 to 3 minutes and then add the boiling water. Stir in the lentils, allspice and season to taste with salt and black pepper. Cover the pan, reduce heat and simmer until all the water is absorbed and both the rice and lentils are tender (approximately 25 minutes). Add more water if necessary. Meanwhile put the remaining oil in a heavy frying pan and sauté the garlic and onion until golden. Put the cooked rice and lentils into a serving bowl, garnish the top with the fried onions and garlic and pour over the yoghurt. Serve.

Variations
The rice may be replaced by 8 oz (1 cup) bulgar wheat or 8 oz (1 cup) whole or pearl barley.

Lentil curry

2 oz (¼ cup) butter or margarine
8 oz (1 cup) brown or green lentils, soaked 4 to 6 hours, drained
2 medium onions, sliced
2 medium green peppers, diced

2 teaspoons curry powder
½ teaspoon dry english mustard
1 tablespoon tomato purée
16 fl oz (2 cups) water
salt to taste

Melt the butter or margarine in a heavy saucepan and add the lentils. Stir fry for 2 to 3 minutes and add the onions, green peppers, curry powder and mustard. Stir well and continue to fry until the onion begins to soften. Add the tomato purée and water and bring the mixture to the boil. Cover the pan, reduce heat and simmer until the lentils are tender (approximately 25 minutes). Toward the end of the cooking time season to taste with salt and add more curry powder if you wish. Add more water if needed.

Variation
Add or substitute 1 medium aubergine, cubed, to the ingredients.

Lentils with noodles

2 tablespoons vegetable oil
1 large onion, diced
2 cloves garlic, crushed
½ teaspoon ground cumin
½ teaspoon ground coriander

16 oz (2 cups) cooked lentils, drained
salt and black pepper to taste
8 oz noodles or spaghetti, cooked and drained
2 oz (¼ cup) melted butter

Put the oil in a heavy saucepan and add the onion and garlic. Sauté until golden. Add the cumin and coriander and toss in the lentils. Stir well and heat through. Season to taste with salt and black pepper. Add the freshly cooked noodles and gently mix. Transfer to a warmed serving dish and pour melted butter over the top.

Variation
Layer the onion mixture, lentils and noodles or spaghetti in a baking dish and pour over a tomato sauce. Sprinkle grated cheese over the top and bake in a pre-heated oven at 375°F (gas mark 5) for 30 minutes.

Lentil stew

2 tablespoons vegetable oil
1 medium onion, sliced
2 sticks celery, chopped
4 oz (½ cup) lentils, washed and
    drained
16 fl oz (2 cups) water

8 oz (1 cup) tinned tomatoes
2 medium potatoes, peeled and diced
½ teaspoon rosemary
salt and black pepper to taste
4 oz (½ cup) grated cheese

Heat the oil in a heavy saucepan and add the onion and celery. Sauté until the onion is softened and golden and then stir in the lentils. Pour in the water and tomatoes and mix well. Add the potatoes and rosemary and season to taste with salt and black pepper. Bring to the boil, cover, reduce heat and simmer until the lentils and potatoes are tender (approximately 25 minutes). Serve garnished with grated cheese.

Lentil stuffed courgettes (zucchini)

2 large courgettes (zucchini)
2 tablespoons vegetable oil
1 medium onion, diced
1 clove garlic, crushed
1 teaspoon cinnamon

¼ teaspoon nutmeg
12 oz (½ cup) cooked lentils
salt and black pepper to taste
2 tablespoons chopped nuts

Preheat oven to 375°F (gas mark 5). Halve the courgettes lengthwise and scoop out the pulp leaving a shell ½ inch to ¾ inch thick. Chop the pulp and reserve. Heat the oil in a heavy frying pan and sauté the onion and garlic until golden. Add the reserved pulp, cinnamon and nutmeg and gently sauté for a further 10 minutes. Combine this mixture with cooked lentils and season to taste with salt and black pepper. Stuff the courgette shells with the mixture and place them in a greased baking dish. Sprinkle chopped nuts over the top and cover the dish with a lid or aluminium foil. Bake for 25 to 30 minutes or until courgettes are tender.

Lima and butter beans

The following recipes can be followed using either lima or butter beans.

Arabian lima beans

1 lb (2½ cups) lima beans, soaked
    overnight, drained
2½ pt (5 cups) water
2 tablespoons vegetable oil or butter
2 medium onions, sliced

2 medium cooking apples, cored and
    sliced
½ teaspoon turmeric
½ teaspoon allspice
½ teaspoon cinnamon
salt and black pepper to taste

Put the beans and water in a heavy saucepan and bring to the boil. Cover, reduce heat and simmer until the beans are tender, about 1½ hours. Heat the oil in a large, heavy frying pan and sauté the onions until golden. Add the apple, turmeric, allspice and cinnamon and cook with stirring until the apple is softened.

Drain the beans and reserve the cooking liquid. Add the beans to the frying pan and enough cooking liquid to just wet the contents of the pan. Season to taste with salt and black pepper and simmer for 10 minutes. Serve. Unsweetened yoghurt and chopped dried apricots are an interesting accompaniment to this dish.

Yellow-topped lima beans

1 lb (2½ cups) lima beans, soaked overnight, drained
2 pt (5 cups) water or stock
2 tablespoons vegetable oil
1 medium onion, sliced
1 medium carrot, sliced

1 clove garlic, crushed
½ teaspoon hot pepper sauce
salt and black pepper to taste
1 tablespoon fresh parsley, chopped
4 oz (1 cup) breadcrumbs
4 oz (½ cup) cheese, grated

Put the lima beans and water or stock in a heavy saucepan and bring to the boil. Cover, reduce heat and simmer for 1 hour. Sauté the onion, carrot and garlic in the oil until softened. Add this mixture and hot pepper sauce, parsley and salt and black pepper to taste to the beans. Simmer until the beans are cooked, about another 30 minutes. Preheat oven to 375°F (gas mark 5). Turn beans into a casserole and cover with breadcrumbs. Top with grated cheese and bake for 20 minutes or until cheese is melted and slightly browned.

Bean succotash

This is another variation of the American Indian dish (see Vegetable succotash, p. 94).

1 lb (2½ cups) lima beans, soaked overnight, drained
2 pt (5 cups) water
8 oz (1 cup) cooked sweetcorn
2 tablespoons vegetable oil

1 medium onion, diced
2 teaspoons molasses or treacle
½ teaspoon paprika
salt and black pepper to taste

Put the beans and water in a heavy saucepan and bring to the boil. Cover, reduce heat and simmer until the beans are just cooked, about 1½ hours. Sauté the onions until golden in the oil. Drain the beans and reserve any liquid for use in soups, etc. Put the onions and oil in the saucepan and add the beans, corn, molasses, paprika and salt and black pepper to taste. Heat through with constant stirring. Add a little reserved liquid if the mixture is too dry. Serve with baked potato and a green salad.

★Ham and lima beans

12 oz (2 cups) lima beans, soaked overnight, drained
2 ham hocks, halved
1 medium onion, quartered
1 medium green pepper, sliced
2 bay leaves

8 oz (1 cup) tinned or ripe tomatoes, chopped
1 tablespoon tomato purée
½ teaspoon dried english mustard
pinch of ground cloves
salt and black pepper to taste

Put all the ingredients in a large, heavy saucepan and add enough water to cover. Cover pan, bring to the boil, reduce heat and simmer for 1 to 1½ hours or until the beans are tender and the ham is falling from the bone. Add more water as necessary.

★Persian lamb with lima beans and rice

For 6 servings

8 oz (1¼ cups) lima beans, soaked overnight and drained
1 pt (2½ cups) water
salt to taste
1 medium onion, diced
2 tablespoons oil
6 lamb chops
1 lb (2 cups) cooked rice

½ teaspoon salt
¼ teaspoon black pepper
½ teaspoon cinnamon
2 tablespoons fresh dill, chopped
or
1 teaspoon dill seeds
2 oz (¼ cup) butter, melted

Cook the beans in the water until tender. Salt to taste. Sauté the onion in the oil until soft and golden and put aside. In the same oil brown the lamb chops on both sides. Add the water, salt, black pepper and cinnamon and simmer until the lamb is tender. Preheat oven to 350°F (gas mark 4). Now place half the rice, half the onion and half the beans in the base of a casserole dish. Place on top the lamb chops plus cooking liquid and half the dill. On top of this put the remaining rice, onion and then beans. Sprinkle dill over the top and pour over the melted butter. Cover and bake for 30 minutes. Serve.

Mung beans

Chinese fried vegetables and mung beans

8 oz (1 cup) mung beans
1 pt (2½ cups) water
2 tablespoons vegetable oil
1 clove garlic, crushed
1 medium onion, sliced
1 medium green pepper, diced
2 medium courgettes (zucchini), sliced

4 oz (1½ cups) mushrooms, sliced
1 oz fresh ginger, peeled and grated
or
2 teaspoons ground ginger
1 tablespoon honey
2 tablespoons soy sauce
1 tablespoon cornflour (starch)

Soak the mung beans in the water for 2 to 4 hours and then simmer in the same water for 40 to 45 minutes or until tender. Drain and set the beans aside. Heat the vegetable oil in a heavy frying pan or wok and stir fry the garlic, onion, green pepper and courgettes until softened. Add the mushrooms and ginger and stir fry a further minute. Blend together the honey, soy sauce and cornflour and pour the mixture over the vegetables. Add the mung beans and mix well. Stir and cook a further 3 to 4 minutes and serve over hot boiled rice.

Dried peas

Pease pudding

This traditional north of England dish is an excellent accompaniment to fish and chips, sausages or bacon. The pudding is normally cooked by boiling but a baked variation, which I have called Pease roast (below), can be made more conveniently. Pease roast has a much firmer texture than Pease pudding.

12 oz (1½ cups) split green peas	2 eggs, lightly beaten
water	salt and black pepper to taste
2 oz (¼ cup) butter	

Put the peas in a saucepan, just cover with water and bring to the boil. Reduce heat, cover and simmer for 30 minutes. Drain the peas and reserve the liquid for later use in soups, etc. Purée the peas, beat in the butter and egg and season to taste with salt and black pepper. Form the mixture into a ball and wrap in muslin. Tie it closed with string leaving a loose end of string. Lower the muslin bag into gently boiling water and cook for 1 hour. Turn the pudding onto a dish and serve.

Variation
To add flavour to the pudding boil along with it in the same pan a piece of bacon or ham bone.

Pease roast

Ingredients as for Pease pudding.
Prepare the seasoned peas, butter and egg mixture as above. Preheat oven to 375°F (gas mark 5). Grease a loaf tin and spoon the mixture in. Bake for 30 minutes or until the roast is just set.

Split pea croquettes with apple rings

8 oz (1 cup) split peas	1 egg, beaten
1 pt (2½ cups) water	breadcrumbs or wheat germ
salt to taste	vegetable oil
1 small onion, finely diced	2 tart apples, cut in ¼ inch thick slices
1 clove garlic, crushed	

Put the peas into a saucepan and cover with water. Bring to the boil. Reduce heat, cover and simmer for 30 minutes. Drain, reserve liquid for later use in soups, etc., and purée the peas. Season to taste with salt, combine with onion, garlic and beaten egg and mix well. Chill the mixture and then form into croquettes. Roll in breadcrumbs or wheat germ and brown in hot oil. Drain on paper towels and keep them warm in a hot oven. Gently fry the apple rings light brown on both sides and serve immediately with the croquettes.

Mushy peas

For some people mushy peas are a must with fish and chips. In the north of England even the invading Chinese fish and chip shop owners haven't managed to kill the habit, and mushy peas appear alongside sweet and sour pork on the menu.

8 oz (1 cup) whole dried peas
1¼ pt (3 cups) water

Put the peas and water in a saucepan and bring to the boil. Remove from the heat, cover and leave overnight. Return to the boil, reduce heat and simmer uncovered until nearly all the liquid is absorbed or evaporated. Remove from the heat, cover and leave another few hours. The peas are now ready for reheating and serving. Season to taste at the table.

*Peas and beef stuffed green peppers

4 medium green peppers
4 oz (½ cup) split peas
½ pt (1¼ cups) water
1 oz (⅛ cup) butter
1 medium onion, finely diced
8 oz minced beef

1 tablespoon tomato purée
½ teaspoon dried basil
½ teaspoon cinnamon
½ teaspoon salt
¼ teaspoon black pepper

Lightly boil the green peppers for 5 minutes. Drain and cool. Cut off the tops and reserve, remove the seeds and set the peppers aside. Put the peas in a saucepan with the water and bring to the boil. Cover, reduce heat and simmer for 30 minutes. Drain and reserve the liquid for later use in soups, etc. Preheat oven to 375°F (gas mark 5). Combine the peas with the remaining ingredients and mix well. Stuff the peppers with the mixture and put the tops on. Place the stuffed peppers in a greased casserole and pour in a little water. Cover and bake for 40 minutes or until peppers and stuffing are tender.

Soya beans

Soya bean and vegetable au gratin

8 oz (1 cup) soya beans
2 pt (5 cups) water
1 medium onion, sliced
2 sticks celery, chopped
2 medium tomatoes, halved
2 cloves garlic, crushed

1 teaspoon salt
½ teaspoon cayenne pepper
1 teaspoon thyme
1 teaspoon parsley
4 oz (½ cup) cheese, grated

Soak the beans in the water overnight and then simmer them in the same water for 3 hours. Drain the beans. Preheat oven to 375°F (gas mark 5). Put half the onion, celery and tomato in the bottom of a casserole dish and sprinkle over half the seasoning, herbs and garlic. Put in all the beans. Cover these with the remaining vegetables, herbs, seasoning and garlic. Cover the dish and bake in the oven for 1¼ hours. Remove the dish from the oven, uncover and sprinkle the top with the grated cheese. Return to the oven and bake a further 15 to 20 minutes or until the cheese is bubbly and slightly browned.

Variation
Any combination of vegetables you have available may be used in this recipe.

Curried soya beans

Serve with hot boiled rice, chutneys and cucumber and yoghurt salad.

8 oz (1 cup) soya beans
2 pt (5 cups) water
2 tablespoons vegetable oil
1 clove garlic, crushed
1 medium onion, sliced
1 medium eating apple, diced

2 oz (¼ cup) sultanas (or other dried fruit)
½ teaspoon coriander powder
½ teaspoon cumin powder
½ teaspoon turmeric
curry powder to taste

Soak the beans in the water overnight and then simmer them in the same water for 4 hours. Add more water as needed to prevent them drying up. Heat the oil in a heavy frying pan and sauté the garlic and onion until golden. Add the apple, sultanas, coriander, cumin, turmeric and curry powder to taste and continue cooking until the apple is softened. Add the contents of the frying pan to the beans, cover and simmer a further 30 minutes.

Sunflower seed, nut and vegetable, soya bean casserole

8 oz (1 cup) soya beans
2 pt (5 cups) water
2 medium carrots, diced
1 medium onion, thinly sliced
1 tablespoon honey
2 oz (¼ cup) sunflower seeds

1 teaspoon dill seeds
2 tablespoons fresh parsley, chopped
2 tablespoons worcestershire sauce
salt and black pepper to taste
2 oz (¼ cup) chopped nuts (almonds or pine nuts are the best)

Soak the beans in the water overnight and then simmer them in the same water for 3 hours. Drain the beans, reserve the liquid, if any. Preheat oven to 375°F (gas mark 5). Combine the beans with the remaining ingredients except for the nuts. Put the mixture into a greased casserole and add 8 fluid ounces (1 cup) of reserved liquid or water. Cover and bake for 1 hour. Remove the casserole from the oven, uncover and sprinkle nuts over the top. Return to the oven uncovered and bake a further 20 minutes. Serve.

Soya bean creole

8 oz (1 cup) soya beans
2 pt (5 cups) water
2 tablespoons vegetable oil
1 medium onion, thinly sliced
1 clove garlic, crushed
1 medium green pepper, sliced
3 tablespoons wholewheat flour

4 oz (1½ cups) mushrooms, sliced
8 oz (1 cup) tinned tomatoes
1 pt (2½ cups) water or stock
1 teaspoon basil
2 bay leaves
2 tablespoons fresh parsley, chopped
salt and black pepper to taste

Soak the beans in the water overnight and then simmer them in the same water for 3 hours. Drain and reserve the liquid if any. Preheat oven to 375°F (gas mark 5). Heat the oil in a flameproof casserole and add the onion, garlic and green pepper. Sauté until softened. Stir in the flour and cook for 2 to 3 minutes. Add the mushrooms, tomatoes and the water or stock, using up the reserved liquid to make up the quantity. Add the beans, basil, bay leaves, parsley and season to taste with salt and black pepper. Cover the casserole and bake for 1½ hours. Serve with coleslaw salad and high baked crackers.

Soya beans with hot tomato sauce

8 oz (1 cup) soya beans
2 pt (5 cups) water
2 tablespoons vegetable oil
2 cloves garlic, crushed
1 medium onion, diced

1 lb (2 cups) tinned tomatoes
1 teaspoon hot pepper sauce
¼ teaspoon oregano
¼ teaspoon cumin
salt to taste

Soak the beans in the water overnight and then simmer them in the same water until cooked, about 3 to 4 hours. Add water as needed to prevent the beans drying up. Towards the end of the cooking time prepare the tomato sauce. Heat the oil in a heavy saucepan, add the onion and garlic and sauté until softened. Stir in the remaining ingredients, cover the pan and simmer for 30 minutes. Serve the sauce over the beans either hot or cold with a salad or as a side dish to a main meal.

Soya bean products

See page 176 for ways of using tofu (bean curd), miso and soy sauce.

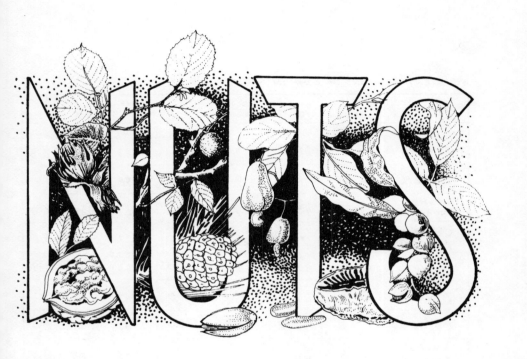

NUTRIENT CONTENT OF COMMON NUTS.

NUT	% PROTEIN	% FATS	% CARBOHYDRATES	VITAMINS IN mg (EXCEPT 'A' IN INTERNATIONAL UNITS)			
				A	B1 THIAMIN	B2 RIBOFLAVIN	B5 NIACIN
ALMOND	18·6	54·2	19·5	0	0·24	0·92	3·5
BRAZIL	14·3	66·9	10·9	0	0·96	0·12	1·6
CASHEW (ROASTED)	17·2	45·7	29·3	100	0·43	0·25	1·8
CHESTNUT (SWEET)	2·9	1·5	42·1	0	0·22	0·22	0·6
HAZEL. COBNUT. FILBERT.	12·6	62·4	16·7	0	0·46	0·0	0·9
PINE	31·1	47·4	11·6	0	0·62	0·0	0·0
PISTACHIO	19·3	53·7	19·0	230	0·67	0·0	1·4
WALNUT (ENGLISH)	14·8	64·0	15·8	30	0·33	0·13	0·9
WALNUT (BLACK)	20·5	59·3	14·8	300	0·22	0·11	0·7

ALL FIGURES GIVEN PER 100 g OF EDIBLE PART OF NUT.

Table 8

Nuts are the fruits of certain trees and bushes. They normally consist of a hard or tough outer shell which encloses the edible kernel. It is this kernel which we generally refer to as the nut. Although they are best known as a snack food, nuts are a delicious, highly concentrated food with a wide range of cooking possibilities. They are a valuable source of proteins, vitamins, minerals, fats and fibre and may be used as an alternative to meat, fish, eggs or pulses.

The snack-food type of nuts we are most familiar with are prepared by roasting the raw nuts after initially coating them in a saturated fat. They are then heavily salted. In this form nuts are not a particularly healthy food nor are they easily digestible. In the following pages we refer only to natural untreated nuts. They are best bought loose and not prepacked from a shop that stocks nuts in bulk. It pays to shop around since prices seem to vary considerably between stores. Also broken nuts, which are perfectly good for most cooking purposes, are often much cheaper than the whole variety.

Table 8 gives the nutritional composition of the most common nuts and this is followed by a description of each of these nuts listed in alphabetical order. The next section is on the preparation of nuts for cooking purposes followed by the recipes which are divided into savoury and sweet dishes.

Almonds

Almonds are possibly the most popular of nuts commonly available. They have been cultivated since very early times and they are mentioned a number of times in the Old Testament. Almonds grow on small trees belonging to the *Rosaceae* family and they are closely related to the peach. The tree appears to have originated in the Middle East and almonds were an important commercial product in Syria and Egypt in biblical times. They were later cultivated in Greece, and the Romans called almonds 'Greek nuts'. The tree spread westwards across Europe and from there to the temperate regions of America, Australia and South Africa.

In the spring the tree produces a beautiful pink and white blossom, followed by the formation of a green fruit which contains the seed or nut. The nut is coated with thin, dark brown skin. The skin can be eaten or peeled off after light blanching in boiling water.

Two types of almonds are grown. One is bitter and the other is sweet, and it is the latter variety we are most familiar with. Bitter almonds are broader but shorter in size than their sweet cousins and they contain small amounts of prussic acid, which is responsible for the bitter taste. The acid, although poisonous, is most volatile and can easily be removed by heating. Bitter almonds are most often used for the production of almond oil although occasionally they are called for in recipes in which a bitter flavour is required. Sweet almonds are used extensively in Middle Eastern and Indian cooking. They can be cooked whole or used ground in puddings, cakes and pastries (e.g. marzipan is a mixture of almond paste and sugar).

Almonds contain protein of higher biological value than any of the other common nuts. They are also a good source of B vitamins and unsaturated fats. Uncooked almonds are an excellent addition to salads, fruit dishes and breakfast cereals and a small amount of ground almonds will give an unusual flavour to regular soups and sauces.

Brazil nuts

Brazil-nut trees are native to the tropical regions of Brazil where the nuts are collected on a commercial scale. They are also found in the forests of Venezuela and Bolivia but not in commercially viable numbers. The trees, which grow very straight and tall, have never been successfully cultivated and the nuts are always collected in the wild. The familiar three-sided Brazil nuts grow on the tree inside a large woody coconut-shaped pod within which they are packed like segments in a grapefruit. A falling pod, which can be the size of a human head, could easily kill a man and the collectors who go into the Amazonian forests to gather the nuts need to wear protective helmets. The fallen pods, once found, are cracked open on the spot with a machette and the nuts still in their individual shells are extracted. From the forests the nuts are transported up the Amazon to the town of Para, a great marketing centre for Brazil nuts, and from here they are exported around the world. Surprisingly the Brazilians themselves do not consume many Brazil nuts and nearly all of the crop is exported.

Brazil nuts have been popular since Victorian times as a dessert nut, eaten either raw or salted, with a glass of port after dinner. In more recent years they have become popular in the manufacture of chocolates and chocolate bars. There are, however, a number of other culinary ways in which they may be used and they are also a rich source of protein, unsaturated fats and vitamin B_1.

Almond nut

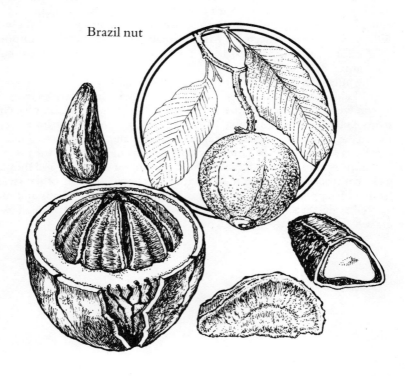

Brazil nut

Cashew nuts

Cashew nuts, as you can see from the drawing, actually grow on the outside of a pear-shaped fruit. This fruit is, however, not a real fruit and it merely serves to divert interest away from the cashew nut which is the real fruit of the plant. To add to the confusion the mock fruit is known as a cashew apple and in areas where the trees grow the apple is normally more popular than the nut. The plant in fact succeeds admirably in its plan to draw attention away from the nut.

The trees are native to Brazil and the name cashew is derived from the Brazilian Indian word *acaju*, which Portugese explorers mispronounced as *caju*. Portugese colonizers introduced the trees into Goa in India, from where the plant spread to other parts of the country. India now exports much of the world's cashew-nut supply, growing its own crop as well as processing other countries'.

The nut is enclosed in a shell which contains an acid fluid harmful to the skin and the nuts are always sold both shelled and slightly roasted to ensure all vestiges of the fluid are removed before consumption. Cashew nuts have a well balanced combination of proteins, fats and carbohydrates and they are a particularly nutritious food.

Hazelnuts, cobnuts and filberts

Hazelnuts, cobnuts and filberts are closely related nuts which grow on small trees or shrubs belonging to the *Corylus* family of plants. Originally they are native to the temperate regions of northern Europe and Asia but they are adaptable plants and these nuts are now cultivated in many parts of the world. The wild species were collected by the Romans and they were an important food source for marching armies. In Britain hazelnuts are still the most common of wild nuts.

The nuts occur in clusters of twos or threes and each is partly covered with a green helmet-shaped skin. Hence the name hazel which derives from the Anglo Saxon word *haesil* for headdress. In ancient Greek times the best hazelnuts came from Avella in the Campagna district of Italy and the specific botanical name for the tree is *Corylus avellana*. Filbert is probably derived from St Philbert whose saint's day on 22 August coincides with the ripening time of the nut.

The nuts may be eaten fresh, roasted, ground or chopped, and they are widely used commercially in the manufacture of chocolates and other sweets. They have wide application in the kitchen and may be used in salads and main dishes as well as desserts. They are a good source of proteins, vitamins, fats and minerals.

Cashew nut

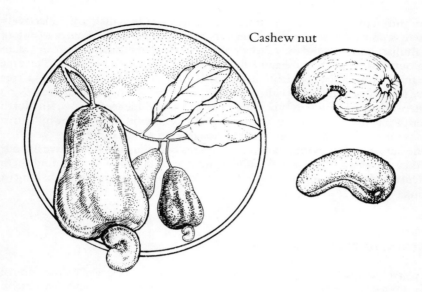

Hazelnut

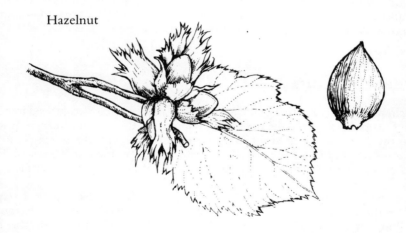

Pine nuts (pignolias)

Many different species of pine trees yield edible seeds which are collectively known as pine nuts or *pignolias*. The nuts grow inside the hard outer casing of the familiar pine cone and they grow unshelled. They are usually white or cream in colour with a soft texture and a flavour of turpentine if unroasted. The pine nuts most commonly available in Europe come from the stone pine, a tree native to Italy which is now cultivated all around the Mediterranean coast.

There are many different types of pine trees with edible seeds grown in North America but this food source has never really been exploited except by native Indians who collected the nuts as a traditional winter food supply.

Pine nuts if cooked with other foods impart a delicious and distinctive flavour and they are most popular in Middle Eastern and Italian cooking. I find them particularly delicious when sprinkled on top of a *gratin* dish just before baking or grilling.

Pistachio nuts

The pistachio nut is very popular in America where its pale green colour is most often observed gracing an ice cream cone piled high with pistachio ice cream. However, it has a venerable history and pistachios have been grown in the warmer parts of Asia for thousands of years. They are now cultivated in the Mediterranean countries of Europe, the Middle East, India and on a large scale in the south western states of America.

The nut grows in a thin shell which conveniently cracks open at one end when the nut is ripe. In Europe and America pistachios are normally eaten as dessert nuts or used for decorating sweets and pastries. In Middle Eastern countries they are used as important ingredients in savoury dishes. They are a good source of vitamin A as well as protein, unsaturated fats and minerals.

Sweet chestnuts

The chestnut tree is a native of the Mediterranean area but it was carried to northern Europe by the Romans and is now widespread throughout Europe. It was given the name sweet chestnut to prevent confusion with the horse-chestnut tree, a different species only introduced into Europe in the last 300 years. The seeds of the horse chestnut are not true nuts and they have a bitter unpleasant taste.

In southern Europe, particularly Italy, sweet chestnuts have been a staple food for thousands of years. They are eaten roasted, stewed or dried and ground into flour for bread and porridge making. Most of the chestnuts available for export are produced in France where they grow two categories, the regular chestnut called *chantaignes* and the best-quality chestnuts called *marrons*. It is from the latter that the famous *marron glacé*, a sweet glazed chestnut, are prepared.

Pine nut

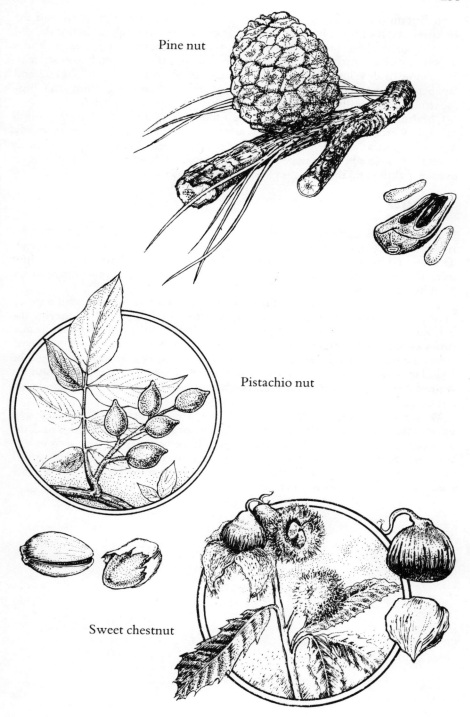

Pistachio nut

Sweet chestnut

In Britain the climate is too cold for the chestnut to ripen properly and the British have traditionally imported sweet chestnuts from Spain, hence the old term 'Spanish chestnuts'. In America, native sweet chestnuts have been almost wiped out by a parasite and their future in that country lies with botonists who are trying to develop a hybrid tree resistant to the disease. The Chinese and Japanese also cultivate chestnuts, and dried Chinese chestnuts bought at a Chinese store are generally much cheaper than their European equivalent.

Chestnuts are not such concentrated foods as other nuts and they contain much less protein and fat and more carbohydrates. They are, however, easily digestible and an excellent energy source. Serve them roasted or boiled with vegetables or salad as you may do rice or potatoes. Chestnut flour may be used in cake making and the purée is good in stuffings, sauces and desserts.

Walnuts

Walnut trees are native to Iran, but, as with many other plants, they were carried into many parts of Europe by the Romans and they are now widespread. The nut and its shell are the stone inside the green plum–size fruit of the walnut tree. The fruit appears in mid–summer, later turns brown and splits open, dropping its stone or walnut onto the ground.

The black walnut, which is different in shape and flavour and with a much harder shell than the ordinary variety, is native to America. In America the European walnut is known as the English walnut, whilst in Europe it's sometimes known as the Italian walnut. This seems a more suitable name since nowadays the walnut tree is rare in Britain. It was once very common and could be found in parks and gardens all over the country. However, a huge demand for walnut wood at the end of the eighteenth century resulted in many trees being cut down.

Walnuts, and particularly the black walnut, are a good source of protein and unsaturated fats. They also provide valuable amounts of B vitamins and the minerals iron, phosphorus and potassium. Black walnuts are also rich in vitamin A. The nuts are excellent in pies, stuffings, breads, casseroles, salads and as topping on *gratin* dishes and cakes. The unripe nut can be pickled and the raw nuts are good with cheese and fruit.

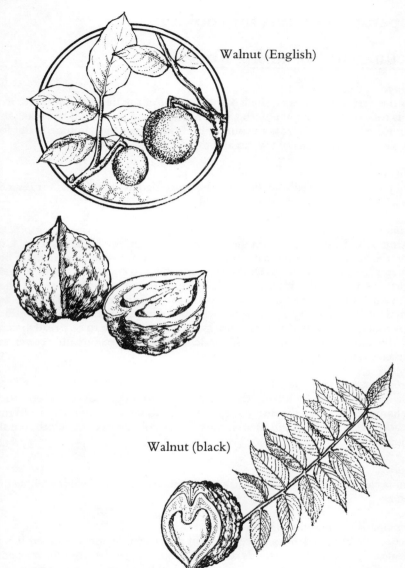

Walnut (English)

Walnut (black)

Preparation of nuts for cooking

Shelling and skinning nuts

Almonds
Almonds can sometimes be shelled with a twist of the fingers otherwise, if the
shell is too hard, a sharp tap with a hammer is normally enough to break it. To
remove the brown skin from the nut itself, drop the nuts into boiling water for 5
minutes, drain, rinse in cold water and the skin will just slip off.

Brazil nuts
Brazil nuts are most easily shelled after being chilled in the refrigerator for a day
or two. Use a nut cracker or small hammer.

Chestnuts
Chestnuts can be shelled and skinned more easily after boiling or roasting. Cut 2
slits in the outer casing on the flat side of each of the nuts and drop them in boiling water for 2 to 3 minutes. Drain and leave them to cool. The casing and skin
can now be removed with a vegetable knife. Alternatively place the slit chestnuts in a baking tray in a hot oven and cook for 10 minutes or until the slits start
to open up. Remove them from the oven and the casing and skin can be easily
removed with the help of a knife. Otherwise you may wish to buy ready peeled,
dried chestnuts from a Chinese store or delicatessen. To reconstitute cover with
water and soak overnight.

Hazelnuts, cobnuts and filberts
These can be shelled by hitting the centre of the rounded side of the nut with a
light hammer. To skin the nuts bake them in a moderate oven for 10 to 15 minutes, allow them to cool and then, if the nuts are rolled in a damp cloth, the skin
will just slip off.

Walnuts
Walnuts can be shelled easily by striking the junction of the 2 halves with a light
hammer.

Chopping, slicing and grinding nuts
For coarsely chopped nuts place them in an electric grinder and switch the
machine on for just a few seconds. Leave it longer to grind or mill the nuts completely. Otherwise put the nuts in a wooden bowl and chop with a sharp
vegetable knife and for fine grinding use a pestle and mortar. To slice nuts use a
sharp knife and slice each nut individually. If the nuts are very hard try boiling
them first.

Blanching nuts

Put the nuts in a pan of boiling water and allow to stand for 2 to 3 minutes
(longer for hazelnuts, cobnuts and filberts). Drain, rinse in cold water and rub
off the skins.

Roasting whole or chopped nuts

Preheat oven to 375°F (gas mark 5). Spread the nuts on a baking tray and place in the oven. Bake for about 5 minutes giving them a shake once or twice during this time. The nuts are ready when lightly browned. They may also be pan roasted on top of the oven. Put the nuts in an ungreased heavy frying pan and lightly toss about over a moderate flame. Some people add vegetable oil but it is not really needed.

For spiced roasted nuts sprinkle the roasting nuts with the following mixture just before you remove them from the oven.

For 1 lb of nuts

2 teaspoons salt

½ teaspoon ground cumin

½ teaspoon ground cinnamon

½ teaspoon ground ginger

½ teaspoon ground cloves

2 tablespoons sugar (less if you desire)

Weights and measure of nuts

1 lb unshelled almonds gives 6 oz (1 cup) shelled nuts
1 lb unshelled Brazil nuts gives 6 oz (1 cup) shelled nuts
1 lb unshelled hazelnuts gives 6 oz (1⅓ cups) shelled nuts
1 lb unshelled sweet chestnuts gives 10 oz (2 cups) shelled nuts
1 lb unshelled English walnuts gives 8 oz (1½ cups) shelled nuts
1 lb pine nuts equals 2 cups
1 lb pistachio nuts equals 2 cups
1 lb cashew nuts equals 3 cups
1 lb dried chestnuts gives 1½ to 2 lb of reconstituted cooked chestnuts.

Nut salads, soups and spreads

Almond cream soup

8 oz (⅓ cup) almonds
1 teaspoon coriander seed
8 fl oz (1 cup) milk
1¼ pt (3 cups) stock

2 oz (½ cup) fine wholewheat
   breadcrumbs
salt and black pepper to taste
8 fl oz (1 cup) cream

Combine the nuts and coriander and pass them through a fine grinder or crush them together with a pestle and mortar. Mix the milk and the stock together and bring the mixture to the boil in a heavy pot. Sprinkle in the breadcrumbs and mix well. Stir in the almond and coriander mixture, season to taste with salt and black pepper. Cover and simmer the soup gently for 10 minutes. Blend in the cream and remove from the heat. Serve.

Sweet and sour chestnut soup

2 tablespoons vegetable oil
1 medium onion, diced
1 lb chestnuts (parboiled and peeled)
1 teaspoon sugar

juice of 1 lemon
2 pt (5 cups) stock
salt and black pepper to taste
pinch of paprika

Heat the oil in a heavy frying pan and sauté the onion until soft. Add the chestnuts and fry very gently for 20 minutes. Put the onions, chestnuts, sugar, lemon juice and some of the stock in an electric blender and beat to a smooth paste. Alternatively pass the chestnuts and onions through a sieve and combine the purée with sugar, lemon juice and stock. Combine the chestnut paste with the remaining stock and bring the mixture to the boil. Season to taste with salt and black pepper and simmer gently for 10 minutes. Sprinkle the soup with a pinch of paprika and serve. For a richer tasting soup stir in 8 fl oz (1 cup) of cream before serving.

Walnut, banana and pineapple salad

lettuce leaves, washed and drained
4 oz (¾ cup) chopped walnuts
4 bananas, peeled and sliced
8 oz (1 cup) pineapple cubes, fresh or
　tinned and drained

4 oz (½ cup) cream cheese
2 tablespoons mayonnaise
juice of 1 lemon
salt to taste

Arrange the lettuce leaves in the bottom of a serving bowl and cover the top with the walnuts, bananas and pineapple cubes. Beat together the cream cheese, mayonnaise and lemon juice and add a little salt to taste. Pour (or drop) this mixture over the nuts and fruit. Chill and serve.

Lettuce and nut salad

1 large lettuce, leaves washed and
　drained
6 oz (⅔ cup) chopped nuts

french dressing
1 tablespoon sunflower seeds, toasted

Combine the lettuce leaves and nuts and toss in french dressing. Sprinkle with sunflower seeds.

Red-robed celery, apple and nut salad

3 stalks celery, chopped
1 apple, washed and sliced
4 oz (½ cup) chopped nuts

mayonnaise to taste
2 medium carrots, grated
2 oz (¼ cup) raisins

Combine the celery, apple and chopped nuts and mix with mayonnaise to taste. Put the mixture into a serving bowl and decorate around the edges with grated carrot. Sprinkle raisins over the salad and serve.

*Fennel, tuna fish and walnut salad

1 medium bulb fennel, finely chopped
8 oz tin tuna fish, shredded
4 oz (¾ cup) chopped walnuts

1 tablespoon vegetable oil
4 oz (1½ cups) mushrooms
salt to taste

Combine the fennel, tuna fish and walnuts. Sauté the mushrooms in the vegetable oil and add to the fennel mixture. Mix everything together and season to taste with salt.

Cauliflower in walnut and garlic sauce

1 small cauliflower, cut into
　flowerettes
2 tablespoons vegetable oil

Sauce
4 oz (¾ cup) walnuts, chopped
2 cloves garlic

2 slices bread (crusts removed) soaked
　in water
vinegar
vegetable oil
salt

Sauté the cauliflower in the oil until just softened. Set aside. Pound the walnuts and garlic together with a pestle and mortar. Add the soaked bread and mix to a paste. Put the paste in a bowl and add equal parts of vinegar and oil to form a thick sauce. Salt to taste. Pour over the cauliflower and serve as a salad.

Other cooked vegetables or fresh salads may be served with this sauce.

Chestnuts and sprout salad

¾ lb chestnuts
1 lb brussel sprouts

2 tablespoons vegetable oil
soy sauce to taste

Cover the chestnuts with water, bring to the boil, reduce heat and simmer for 30 minutes. Meanwhile sauté the sprouts in the oil until lightly browned. Add a little water, cover and gently simmer until cooked, about 15 minutes. Peel the chestnuts with a sharp knife and combine with the sprouts. Sprinkle with soy sauce to taste. Serve hot or cold.

Nut and tahini spread

4 fl oz (½ cup) tahini paste
juice of 2 lemons
2 cloves garlic, crushed

4 oz (½ cup) nuts (almonds, hazelnuts
or walnuts are best)
salt to taste

Combine the tahini paste, lemon juice and crushed garlic and blend to a smooth paste in an electric blender or beat vigorously by hand. Add the nuts and briefly blend, in the machine. If you are making the spread by hand finely chop the nuts before adding to the spread. Carefully season to taste with salt and serve with bread or as an accompaniment to cooked vegetables or salads.

Variation
Mix the spread with 4 fl oz (½ cup) natural yoghurt and serve garnished with chopped parsley.

Roasted nut and honey butter

1 lb nuts, roasted (see p. 235)
4 fl oz (½ cup) vegetable oil

4 tablespoons honey
1 teaspoon salt

Put all the ingredients in an electric blender and mix to a smooth paste. Add more nuts or more oil if the mixture is too thin or too thick. Store in a refrigerator.

Egg, cheese and nut spread

4 oz (½ cup) finely chopped or ground
   nuts
2 eggs, hard-boiled, shelled and
   chopped

4 oz (½ cup) cheese, grated
juice of 2 lemons
salt and black pepper to taste

Beat the nuts, egg, cheese and lemon juice into a smooth paste and season to taste with salt and black pepper. Serve on sandwiches.

Variation
Add 2 tablespoons of mayonnaise for a creamier spread.

Wine, nut and cheese spread

4 oz (½ cup) cream cheese
2 tablespoons dry red or white wine
2 oz (¼ cup) finely chopped nuts

Cream ingredients together and serve as a spread or dip for fresh salad vegetables.

Variation
Replace the cream cheese with a soft white cheese or even try a blue cheese or Camembert.

Savoury nut dishes

Brazil nut and rice rissoles

12 oz (1½ cups) cooked rice
6 oz (⅔ cup) milled or finely chopped
   Brazil nuts
1 tablespoon butter
1 medium onion, finely diced

1 teaspoon sage
salt and black pepper to taste
1 egg, beaten
oil for frying

Combine the rice and chopped nuts. Sauté the onion in the butter until soft and golden. Mix together the rice and nut mixture, onion, sage and salt and black pepper to taste. Add the beaten egg and form the mixture into oblong rissoles. Fry them golden brown in hot oil and serve with a cheese or tomato sauce or as an accompaniment to cooked vegetables.

Walnut and potato patties

12 oz (1½ cups) mashed potato
6 oz (1 cup) finely chopped walnuts
4 oz (1 cup) fine breadcrumbs
1 teaspoon mixed herbs
grated rind of ½ lemon

2 tablespoons finely chopped onion
salt and black pepper to taste
8 fl oz (1 cup) milk, chilled
oil for frying

Combine the first 7 ingredients and add enough milk to form a malleable mixture. Form into circular patties. Fry golden brown in hot oil or deep fry. Serve with béchamel sauce and a green salad garnished with tomatoes.

Pine nut roast

2 tablespoons vegetable oil
2 medium onions, sliced
6 oz (⅔ cup) pine nuts
4 medium tomatoes, skinned and
   quartered

4 oz (1 cup) breadcrumbs
1 teaspoon cinnamon
½ teaspoon allspice
salt and black pepper to taste
1 egg, separated

Preheat oven to 375°F (gas mark 5). Heat the vegetable oil in a heavy frying pan and sauté the onion until soft. Add two-thirds of the pinenuts and gently cook until the nuts and onion are lightly browned. Combine this mixture with the tomatoes, breadcrumbs, cinnamon and allspice and season to taste with salt and black pepper. Mix in the egg yolk and beat the egg white stiff. Fold the egg white into the mixture and put the whole in a greased baking dish. Sprinkle the remaining pine nuts over the top and bake for 30 to 40 minutes.

Courgette (zucchini) and hazelnut flan

1 lb courgettes (zucchini) sliced
4 oz (½ cup) chopped or ground
    hazelnuts
4 eggs, beaten

6 oz (⅔ cup) grated cheese
1 teaspoon dried basil
salt and black pepper to taste

Preheat oven to 325°F (gas mark 3). Put the courgettes in a heavy saucepan, add a little water, cover and steam until just softened. Combine the softened courgettes with the hazelnuts, beaten egg, grated cheese, basil and salt and black pepper to taste. Pour the mixture into a greased flan dish and bake for 30 to 40 minutes.

Variation
Line an 8 inch or 9 inch flan dish with 8 oz of shortcrust pastry. Pour the filling in and bake for 40 minutes in a 325°F (gas mark 3) oven.

Nut, corn and cheese casserole

8 oz (1 cup) sweet corn
8 oz (1 cup) tinned tomatoes
8 oz (1 cup) chopped nuts
8 oz (1 cup) cottage cheese

paprika and salt to taste
2 oz (½ cup) breadcrumbs
2 tablespoons butter

Preheat oven to 350°F (gas mark 4). Grease a casserole dish and put in separate layers of sweet corn, tomatoes, nuts and cottage cheese and season each layer with paprika and salt. Sprinkle breadcrumbs over the top and dot with butter. Bake for 30 minutes and serve.

Chestnut and vegetable casserole

4 tablespoons butter
1 medium onion, diced
1 medium green pepper, sliced
4 oz (1 cup) mushrooms, sliced
1 lb chestnuts parboiled and peeled

1 egg, beaten
2 tablespoons chopped fresh parsley
salt and black pepper to taste
2 oz (½ cup) breadcrumbs
1 oz (⅛ cup) butter

Preheat oven to 375°F (gas mark 5). Melt half the butter in a heavy saucepan and sauté the onion and green pepper until soft. Add the mushrooms and sauté a further 2 minutes. Chop the chestnuts in half and combine with the cooked vegetables. Add the beaten egg, parsley and salt and black pepper to taste and mix well. Pour the mixture into a greased casserole dish and sprinkle bread-crumbs over the top. Dot with butter and bake for 30 minutes.

Variation
Substitute 8 oz (1 cup) of chopped nuts for the chestnuts.

Red cabbage and chestnuts

Serves 6 to 8

2 tablespoons vegetable oil
2 medium onions, sliced
½ medium red cabbage, finely chopped
salt and black pepper to taste

6 oz (1 cup) parboiled and peeled chestnuts
1 lb apples, peeled thinly sliced
1 clove
juice of 1 lemon

In a heavy saucepan sauté the onions until golden in the oil. Add the cabbage, cover the pot and gently simmer until the cabbage is softened. Season to taste with salt and black pepper, cover again and leave to simmer for 5 minutes. Add the chestnuts, apples, clove and lemon juice and leave to simmer, covered, until all the vegetables are tender (about 20 minutes). Serve with baked potato and salad.

Variation
Add 8 fl oz (1 cup) fresh cream to cabbage and chestnut just before serving.

Turkish pistachio pilav

8 oz (1 cup) butter
1½ lb (3 cups) rice
2½ pt (6 cups) stock
1 teaspoon allspice

½ teaspoon cinnamon
salt and black pepper to taste
2 oz (¼ cup) sultanas
4 oz (½ cup) pistachios

Melt the butter in a heavy frying pan or saucepan and sauté the rice in it until each grain is coated with butter. Add the stock, allspice, cinnamon and salt and black pepper to taste and bring to the boil. Cover, reduce heat and cook until the rice is tender and all the liquid is absorbed. Stir into the rice the sultanas and half the pistachios, re-cover and set aside for 5 minutes. Meanwhile lightly toast the remaining pistachios. Pile the pilav on a serving dish and garnish with the toasted pistachios.

Black-eyed peas with nuts

1 lb (2 cups) black-eyed peas
3 pt (7½ cups) water
3 tablespoons olive oil
2 cloves garlic, crushed
2 medium onions, diced

3 tablespoons tomato purée
8 oz (1 cup) chopped nuts
1 teaspoon salt
1 teaspoon sugar
2 tablespoons chopped, fresh parsley

Put the peas in the water and cook until soft. Drain and reserve 4 fl oz (½ cup) of the cooking liquid. Heat the oil in a heavy frying pan, add the garlic and onion and sauté until golden. Combine the cooked peas, garlic, onion, tomato purée and nuts and season with salt and sugar. Return the mixture to the cooking pot and add the reserved liquid. Cook over a low heat for 15 to 20 minutes and serve garnished with parsley.

Chestnut soufflé

Serves 6

1 lb chestnuts, parboiled and skinned	2 oz (¼ cup) flour
16 fl oz (2 cups) milk	salt, pepper and cayenne to taste
2 oz (¼ cup) butter	4 eggs, separated

Put the chestnuts and half the milk in a pan, cover and gently cook until the chestnuts are soft and most of the milk is absorbed. Pass through a sieve, mouli or blend to a purée in an electric blender. Melt the butter in a heavy saucepan and stir in the flour. Slowly add the remaining milk to form a thick sauce. Beat the chestnut purée into the sauce and season to taste with salt, black pepper and cayenne. Preheat oven to 400°F (gas mark 6). Heat the chestnut mixture to boiling, remove from the heat and beat in the egg yolks. Whip the egg whites stiff and fold into the mixture. Put the mixture into a casserole or soufflé dish and bake for 30 minutes. Serve.

★Chinese chicken and walnuts

1 lb cooked chicken, chopped	1 medium onion, sliced
2 tablespoons sweet sherry	1 green pepper, cut in strips
3 tablespoons soy sauce	1 clove garlic, crushed
1 oz fresh ginger, sliced	8 oz (1½ cups) chopped walnuts,
4 tablespoons vegetable oil	lightly roasted

Put the chicken in a bowl. Combine the sherry, soy sauce and ginger and pour over the chicken. Cover and leave to marinate for at least 2 hours. Heat half the vegetable oil in a heavy frying pan or wok and add the onion, pepper, garlic and walnuts and stir fry over a medium heat for 4 to 5 minutes. Set this mixture aside and add the remaining oil to the pan. Drop the chicken pieces in but not the marinade and stir fry for 2 to 3 minutes. Now add the marinade and stir fry a further 2 minutes. Be careful not to burn the chicken since soy sauce tends to stick. Add the vegetables and walnuts and heat through. Serve over rice.

★Pine nut and chicken pilav

2 tablespoons oil	8 oz (1 cup) long-grain rice
1 lb cooked chicken, chopped	4 oz (½ cup) pine nuts
1 medium onion, diced	1 teaspoon salt
1 pt (2½ cups) chicken stock	

Heat the oil in a heavy frying pan and brown the chicken pieces. Add the onion and sauté until softened. Remove the pan from heat and allow to cool a little. Pour in the stock and add the rice, pine nuts and salt. Return pan to the heat, cover and simmer for 20 minutes or until rice is cooked and all the liquid is absorbed. Add more stock or water if needed.

Boiled rice with almond and pine nut sauce

1 lb (2 cups) rice
½ teaspoon turmeric powder
4 oz (½ cup) ground almonds
1 pt (2½ cups) vegetable or chicken
 stock
1 clove garlic, crushed

3 tablespoons chopped fresh parsley
1 teaspoon sugar
juice of 1 lemon
salt and black pepper to taste
2 oz (¼ cup) toasted pine nuts

Boil the rice by one of the methods given on page 60 and add the turmeric to the cooking water. Put the ground almonds and stock in a heavy saucepan and bring to the boil. Add the garlic, parsley, sugar and lemon juice and mix well. Season to taste with salt and black pepper. Simmer gently for 20 minutes or until the sauce is nice and thick. Add the pine nuts to the pot halfway through the cooking time. Serve the boiled rice piled high on a serving dish with the sauce poured over the top.

★Nut and bulgar wheat meatballs

8 oz (1 cup) bulgar wheat
1 lb minced beef or lamb
1 medium onion, finely diced
4 oz (½ cup) finely chopped nuts
1 tablespoon finely chopped fresh
 parsley

1 teaspoon salt
¼ teaspoon black pepper
1 teaspoon allspice
1 teaspoon mustard seed
2 cloves garlic, crushed
2 pt (5 cups) lamb or beef stock

Cover the bulgar wheat in cold water and leave to soak for 15 minutes. Drain and combine with the remaining ingredients except for the stock. Mix well and knead the mixture into a paste consistency. Wet your hands and form the mixture into walnut size (or a little bigger) balls. Bring the stock to the boil, reduce heat and simmer. Drop the balls 10 or so at a time into the stock and cook until they rise to the surface (about 12 to 15 minutes). Remove with a slotted spoon and keep warm in a moderate oven until all the meatballs are cooked. The meatballs may be served in the stock or on their own with unsweetened yoghurt.

Variation
Put the uncooked meatballs in a casserole dish cover with tomato soup (or seasoned, diluted tomato purée), cover and bake in a 350°F (gas mark 4) oven for 1 hour.

Vegetables stuffed with nut fillings

Several recipes for nut stuffings are given below and they are followed by description of the ways to prepare various vegetables for stuffing. Any of the stuffings may be tried with any of the suggested vegetables. They will provide a wide range of unusual and substantial vegetable/nut dishes. The fillings may also be used for stuffing poultry and fish.

Armenian pine nut filling

2 tablespoons butter
1 small onion, diced
8 oz (1 cup) rice
2 oz (¼ cup) pine nuts
2 oz (¼ cup) currants

12 fl oz (1½ cups) water or stock
1 teaspoon salt
¼ teaspoon black pepper
½ teaspoon allspice

Sauté the onion until golden in the butter in a heavy saucepan. Add the rice and pinenuts and sauté a further 2 minutes. Add the remaining ingredients, stir well and bring to the boil. Reduce the heat, cover and simmer until the rice is cooked and all the liquid is absorbed.

Brazil nut and bread filling

2 tablespoons vegetable oil
8 oz (1 cup) chopped Brazil nuts
1 small onion, diced
4 tablespoons finely chopped celery
  leaves

1 teaspoon salt
¼ teaspoon hot pepper sauce
12 oz (3 cups) breadcrumbs
2 tablespoons finely chopped parsley
4 fl oz (½ cup) hot stock or water

Heat the oil in a heavy saucepan, add the nuts, onion and celery leaves and sauté until the nuts are lightly browned. Add this mixture to the remaining ingredients and mix well together.

Chestnut stuffing

1½ lb chestnuts, parboiled and peeled
2 pt (5 cups) vegetable stock or water
2 tablespoons vegetable oil
1 medium onion, diced
4 oz (1 cup) breadcrumbs

2 tablespoons chopped fresh parsley
1 teaspoon salt
½ teaspoon nutmeg
½ teaspoon paprika
¼ teaspoon ground ginger

Simmer the chestnuts in the stock or water until very tender. Drain and reserve the liquid for future use. Chop up the chestnuts. Sauté the onion until golden in the oil. Combine the chopped chestnuts, onion and remaining ingredients and mix well.

Hazelnut and orange filling

2 tablespoons vegetable oil
1 medium onion, diced
2 stalks celery, finely chopped
4 oz (½ cup) chopped hazelnuts
1 lb (2 cups) cooked rice or other grain

1 medium orange, peeled and chopped
2 oz (¼ cup) raisins
1 teaspoon cinnamon
½ teaspoon salt

Heat the vegetable oil in a heavy frying pan and sauté the onion, celery and hazelnuts until the onion is golden. Combine this mixture with the remaining ingredients and mix well.

Walnut and cottage cheese filling

8 oz (1 cup) cottage cheese
4 oz (½ cup) chopped walnuts
4 oz (1 cup) breadcrumbs
1 tablespoon chopped fresh parsley

½ small onion, finely diced
1 teaspoon salt
½ teaspoon black pepper
1 teaspoon dried thyme

Combine all the ingredients and mix well.

Methods of preparing vegetables for stuffing

Stuffed tomatoes

Use large firm tomatoes. Cut ½ inch tops off them and carefully scoop out the centres leaving a ½ inch shell. Sprinkle the inside of each shell with salt and pepper. Stuff the tomatoes with the selected filling (adding if you wish some of the tomato pulp to the filling). Press the tops back in place, brush the tomatoes with oil, and pack them in a greased dish. Bake in a preheated oven at 375°F (gas mark 5) for 30 minutes.

Stuffed green peppers

Cut the tops off the peppers and remove the seeds. Dip the peppers in boiling water for 2 to 3 minutes. Drain and cool them under a cold tap. Stuff the peppers with the selected filling and pack them in a greased baking dish. Run in a little water, cover and bake in a preheated oven at 375°F (gas mark 5) for 30 minutes.

Stuffed cabbage leaves (dolmas)

Dolmas are traditionally stuffed vine leaves, and if you can obtain preserved vine leaves, do substitute them for cabbage leaves.

Wash a medium-sized cabbage and trim off the stalk. If you can, strip off the leaves from the cabbage intact. Wash them again and then dip them a few at a time in boiling salted water until they become wilted and pliable. If it proves difficult to remove the leaves from the cabbage whole, put the whole cabbage into a pan of boiling salted water and leave for 3 to 4 minutes. Lift out, drain and then peel off the leaves. Trim off the hard central leaf stalks, and cut the large leaves in two. Put a tablespoon of the selected filling into the centre of a leaf. Fold leaf corners into the centre and roll up, making a neat finger shape. Repeat this until all the filling is used up. Line a large saucepan with unused or torn leaves. This helps to prevent stuffed leaves sticking to the bottom. Lay the stuffed leaves on top, arranging each dolma at an angle so that it does not come into contact with the others. Cover with water and add the juice of 1 lemon and a little salt. Cover the pan and cook gently for about 1 hour.

Stuffed onions

Select and cook large onions in a small amount of simmering water for 20 minutes or until just soft. Drain, reserving the liquid. Cut a thin slice from the stem end of each onion and scoop out the centres, leaving a moderately thick wall. Stuff onions with selected mixture. Chop centre pulp of onions and place in a large pan with juice of 1 lemon and reserved liquid. Place the stuffed onions in the pan, cover, and gently simmer for one hour.

Stuffed marrow

Cook the marrows in a large pan of boiling water until pulp is just soft. Drain, allow to cool, and then remove pulp. Stuff marrow boats with selected filling, cover with a béchemal or tomato sauce and bake in a preheated oven at 375°F (gas mark 5) for 30 minutes.

Stuffed mushrooms

Choose large mushrooms. Remove stems and chop them finely. Combine stems with the selected filling. Place caps gill side up in a greased, shallow baking dish and add the filling. Bake in a preheated oven at 350°F (gas mark 4) for 25 minutes.

Nut breads, cakes, puddings and sweets

Basic nut loaf

8 oz (1 cup) walnuts, finely chopped
8 oz (1 cup) almonds, finely chopped
8 oz (1 cup) cooked rice
2 eggs, beaten
2 oz (½ cup) breadcrumbs

1 medium carrot, grated
1 teaspoon thyme
1 tablespoon chopped fresh parsley
4 fl oz (½ cup) water, stock or milk
salt and black pepper to taste

Preheat oven to 375°F (gas mark 5). Combine all the ingredients and mix well. Turn mixture into a greased bread tin and bake for 30 minutes or until a knife pushed into the centre of the loaf comes out clean. Serve hot or cold.

Variations
1: Add up to 1 lb of chopped cooked vegetables.
2: Add up to ½ lb lightly sautéed mushrooms.
3: Add 8 oz (1 cup) of cooked beans or cooked grains.
   Experiment with combinations of nuts other than those suggested.

Nut and cheese loaf

8 oz (2 cups) breadcrumbs
8 fl oz (1 cup) milk
8 oz (1 cup) chopped nuts
8 oz (1 cup) grated cheese
1 small onion, finely diced

1 tablespoon chopped fresh parsley
1 egg, beaten
½ teaspoon cayenne powder
1 teaspoon salt

Preheat oven to 375°F (gas mark 5). Soak the breadcrumbs in the milk and combine them with the remaining ingredients. Mix well and turn the mixture into a greased bread tin. Bake for 30 minutes or until the loaf is firm and lightly browned on top.

Nut and potato cakes

1 lb (2 cups) mashed potato
8 oz (1 cup) chopped nuts
1 small onion, finely diced

½ teaspoon salt
1 egg, beaten
oil for frying

Combine all the ingredients except the oil and mix well. Form the mixture into eight ½ inch thick, round cakes and fry brown on both sides in shallow oil.

Fruit-topped uncooked nut cake

8 oz (1 cup) oatflakes
4 oz (½ cup) finely chopped nuts
1 large banana, mashed
1 medium carrot, grated
juice of 1 lemon

1 tablespoon sugar
2 tablespoons treacle
water, milk or cream
fresh fruit in season for the topping (or tinned fruit, drained)

Combine all the ingredients except the water and fruit. Mix well and then add enough water, milk or cream to form the mixture into a moist sticky consistency. Press the mixture into a shallow serving dish and decorate the top with fresh fruit pieces. Chill and serve topped with fresh cream.

Uncooked fruit nut balls

8 oz (1 cup) finely chopped walnuts
8 oz (1 cup) finely chopped figs
8 oz (1 cup) finely chopped dates
8 oz (1 cup) raisins

1 tablespoon fresh orange juice
1 teaspoon grated orange or lemon peel

Combine all the ingredients and knead into a consistent mixture. Pinch off small amounts and form into small balls. Chill before serving.

Lyn's orange and hazelnut teabread

6 oz (⅔ cup) hazelnuts
1 large orange
8 oz (1 cup) cottage cheese
6 oz (1½ cups) brown sugar

3 eggs, beaten
6 oz (1½ cups) brown flour
1 teaspoon baking powder
1 tablespoon clear honey

Preheat oven to 350°F (gas mark 4). Reserve a few of the hazelnuts whole for decoration and chop up the rest. Cut two thin strips of peel from the orange and cut away any pith attached to them. Reserve these for decoration. Grate the remainder of the rind. Put the cottage cheese and sugar into a bowl and beat into a cream. Add the eggs and orange rind and beat again. Sift the flour and baking powder together and fold into the mixture. Stir in the hazelnuts and put the mixture into a greased bread tin. Bake in preheated oven for 70 to 80 minutes until nicely risen and golden brown on top. If the bread is correctly cooked the top will spring back when pressed. Turn the bread out of the tin and leave to cool. Meanwhile cut the reserved orange peel into shreds and place in a small saucepan, just cover with water and gently boil for 5 minutes. Drain and mix the softened shreds with honey. Brush top of teabread with the mixture and leave to cool completely.

Lyn's banana and walnut teabread

4 oz (½ cup) butter or margarine
8 oz (2 cups) brown sugar
2 eggs, beaten
4 bananas, mashed

8 oz (1 cup) brown flour
1 teaspoon baking powder
½ teaspoon salt
4 oz (½ cup) chopped walnuts

Preheat oven to 325°F (gas mark 3). Cream the butter and sugar together and then beat in the eggs and bananas. Sift the flour and baking powder together and fold into the mixture. Stir in the salt and the nuts, reserving a few for decoration. Put the mixture into a greased bread tin (smooth down the top and sprinkle over the reserved nuts). Bake for 1 hour or until the bread is nicely risen and baked golden brown on top. Turn the teabread out of the tin and leave to cool. Serve slices spread with butter.

Chocolate hazelnut cake

4 egg whites, beaten stiff
8 oz (1 cup) sugar
8 oz (1 cup) coarsely ground hazelnuts
1 teaspoon cinnamon
1 teaspoon vanilla essence
1 tablespoon cocoa
8 oz (2 cups) flour
4 fl oz (½ cup) milk

Filling
4 egg yolks
4 tablespoons sugar
4 oz (½ cup) melted cooking
  chocolate
1 tablespoon butter
whole hazelnuts for decoration

Preheat oven to 350°F (gas mark 4). Cream the egg whites and sugar together. Add the next 6 ingredients and mix well. Turn the mixture into a greased and floured cake tin and bake for 45 to 50 minutes. Cool. Turn the cake out and split it into 2. To make the filling beat the yolks with the sugar. Add this to the chocolate melted in a double burner and stir well. Soften the butter and stir it into the mixture. Cook and stir over a low heat until the filling thickens. Cool and then spread ⅔ of the filling between the 2 halves of the cake. Put together and spread the remaining filling over the top. Decorate with whole hazelnuts.

Nut cake with icing (frosting)

8 oz (1 cup) sugar
4 oz (½ cup) butter or margarine
1 lb (4 cups) flour
2 teaspoons baking powder
8 oz (1 cup) chopped nuts
8 fl oz (1 cup) milk or cream
4 egg whites, beaten stiff

Icing (frosting)
1 teaspoon butter or margarine
1 tablespoon milk, hot
8 oz (½ cup) icing (frosting) sugar
1 teaspoon lemon juice
Chopped nuts for decoration

Preheat oven to 350°F (gas mark 4). Cream the sugar and butter. Sift the flour and baking powder together and mix with chopped nuts. Combine the sugar and butter and flour mixtures and stir in the milk. Mix well and then fold in the egg whites. Turn the mixture into a well-greased cake tin and bake for 30 to 35 minutes. Meanwhile prepare the icing. Melt the butter in the hot milk. Add the sugar stirring continually. Stir in the lemon juice. Turn the cake out of the tin and allow to cool. Cut it in half and spread half the filling between the two halves. Put together and ice the top of the cake. Decorate with chopped nuts.

Hour nut pudding

4 oz (½ cup) butter or margarine	1 egg, beaten
4 oz (½ cup) sugar	5 oz (1¼ cups) breadcrumbs
4 eggs, separated	½ teaspoon salt
grated rind and juice of 1 lemon	½ teaspoon nutmeg
4 oz (½ cup) milled or finely chopped nuts	2 fl oz (¼ cup) cream or milk

Cream the butter and the sugar and beat in the 4 egg yolks. Blend thoroughly either by hand or with an electric mixer. Add the remaining ingredients except the egg whites and mix them together. Beat the egg whites stiff and fold into the mixture. Put the mixture into a greased pudding basin and steam for 1 hour. Serve with stewed fruit and cream.

Almond and chestnut pudding

¾ lb chestnuts, parboiled and peeled	3 oz (⅜ cup) sugar
12 fl oz (1½ cups) milk	1 tablespoon butter or margarine
½ vanilla pod or essence	2 oz (¼ cup) ground almonds
3 eggs, separated	1 tablespoon chopped nuts

Put the chestnuts, milk and vanilla pod in a saucepan and boil until the chestnuts are soft and tender. Remove the vanilla pod and purée the milk and chestnuts in an electric blender or pass through a sieve. Put the purée in a mixing bowl and add the 3 egg yolks, sugar and butter. Cream them together and stir in the ground almonds. Beat the egg whites stiff and fold into the mixture. Turn mixture into a greased pudding basin and steam for 1 hour. Turn pudding out and sprinkle with chopped nuts.

Tiny walnut crescents

8 oz (1 cup) butter	2 oz (¼ cup) raisins
1 lb (4 cups) flour	4 oz (½ cup) sugar
2 eggs	1 teaspoon cinnamon
4 fl oz (½ cup) milk	¼ teaspoon salt
4 oz (½ cup) chopped walnuts	

Preheat oven to 375°F (gas mark 5). Rub the butter and flour together. Add 1 egg and enough milk to form a soft dough. Knead the mixture and form into three equal portions. Roll each portion into a ball and roll them out into 8 inch to 10 inch circles. Combine the remaining ingredients. Cut each circle into 8 slices as though you were cutting a cake. Divide and spread the nut mixture over each circle of pastry and roll up each of the slices, starting from the broad end, to form filled crescent shaped rolls. Carefully transfer the cresescents to a greased baking sheet. Beat the remaining egg and brush it over the crescents. Bake for 30 minutes or until the crescents are well cooked and golden brown on top.

Baked apple stuffed with nuts

4 large baking apples
4 oz (½ cup) chopped nuts
½ teaspoon cinnamon

3 oz (⅜ cup) sugar
1 tablespoon butter
6 fl oz (⅔ cup) water

Preheat oven to 350°F (gas mark 4). Core the apples but do not peel. Make a slight incision with a sharp knife around the middle of the apples and arrange them in a baking dish. Combine the nuts, cinnamon and half the sugar and mix well. Stuff the apples with the mixture leaving a little mound standing proud of the apple top. Top each with a dab of butter. Dissolve the remaining sugar in the water and pour it into the baking dish. Bake the apples for 40 to 50 minutes. Serve hot or cold.

Spiced hazelnut macaroons

4 eggs
1 lb (2 cups) sugar
1 lb (2 cups) ground hazelnuts
1 tablespoon lemon juice

2 teaspoons grated lemon rind
1 teaspoon cinnamon
¼ teaspoon ground cloves

Preheat oven to 300°F (gas mark 2). Cream the eggs and sugar together for 15 to 20 minutes. Add the remaining ingredients and mix well together. Dip your hands in cold water and form the mixture into small balls. Place on a greased baking tray and bake for 45 minutes.

ENGLISH-AMERICAN FOOD AND COOKING TERMS

Food

English	American
castor sugar	granulated white sugar
demerara	dark brown sugar
icing sugar	confectioners sugar
treacle	molasses
biscuit	cooky or cracker
scone	biscuit
porridge	oatmeal
currant	raisin
french bean	snap or string bean
swede	rutabaga
spring onions	scallions
courgettes	zucchini
marrow	squash
cornflour	cornstarch
aubergine	egg plant

Cooking

to grill	to broil
to ice	to frost
to mince	to grind
tin	can
baking tin	cake pan
baking sheet	cookie sheet
frying pan	skillet

Oven temperatures

Temperature gauge	Oven temperature °F	Oven temperature °C	Gas mark
very low to low	200–300	93–148	¼, ½, 1, 2
medium low to med	300–350	148–176	3
moderate	350–375	176–190	4
medium high to high	375–450	190–232	5, 6, 7
very high	450–500	232–315	8, 9

Conversion of imperial measurements to metric

The following table may be used for the conversion of imperial to metric:

Grams or millilitres	Grams or millilitres (to nearest unit of 25)
1	25
2	50
3	75
4	100
5	150
6	175
7	200
8	225
9	250
10	275
11	300
12	350
13	375
14	400
15	425
16	450
17	475
18	500
19	550
20	575

English–American measurements

English	American
	fluid
1 pint = 20 fl oz	1 pint = 16 fl oz
2 pints = 1 quart = 40 fl oz	2 pints = 1 quart = 32 fl oz
1 fl oz	1½ tablespoons
	dry measures
flour	
1 oz	4 tablespoons (¼ cup)
2 oz	8 tablespoons (½ cup)
4 oz	1 cup
butter, sugar	
1 oz	2 tablespoons
2 oz	4 tablespoons (¼ cup)
8 oz	1 cup

GLOSSARY OF TERMS USEFUL TO BRITISH AND AMERICAN READERS

Bolt	to sieve coarse grain to remove the bran
Bran	the fibrous outer layer of wheat or other cereal grains
Bulgar wheat	wholewheat grains parboiled, dried and then cracked
Burghul	another name for bulgar wheat
Congee	a thin porridge or gruel made from rice or millet
Corn	English word meaning staple grain but also used more specifically for the cereal grain called maize in America
Corn on the cob	name used in Britain for fresh sweetcorn still on the cob
Corn dodger	type of corncake
Corn flour	white or yellow corn finely ground
Couscous	large grains of semolina. Couscous is also the name of a dish prepared by steaming couscous and serving it with a meat or vegetable sauce
Dark rye	flour made from the whole rye grain
Durum flour	variety of hard wheat used in the manufacture of pasta
Endosperm	the main part in mass of a cereal grain. It is principally starch with some protein
Extraction rate	describes the proportion removed of the nutritious outer part of the wheat grain before it is milled into flour. The lower the extraction rate the more has been removed and the less nutrient the resultant flour contains
Farina	flour made from the endosperm of cereal grains. Used for puddings, soups and cereal dishes
Germ	contained within a cereal grain it is the embryo of a new plant. It is rich in nutrients
Grits	coarsely ground cereal grain. The word normally refers to hominy grits
Groats	whole or partially milled grains of hulled cereal grain. Most often used in connection with buckwheat and oats
Hard flour	flour made from hard-grained wheats. Contains more gluten than soft wheat and is better for bread and pasta making
Hominy	whole kernels of corn soaked in alkaline solution, washed, boiled and dried
Hull	outer inedible covering of seed or cereal grain
Husk	same as hull
Kasha	mush made from buckwheat or buckwheat and barley mixture. Sometimes used to describe other boiled cereal grains
Kernel	whole grain, normally meaning wheat grain and also the soft part within a hard shell of a nut
Leavened	refers to bread or cakes made with a rising agent, normally yeast but also baking powder

Legumes	group of plants containing the various edible beans and peas
Light rye	rye with some of the bran removed
Meal	hulled grain coarsely ground into a flour
Mush	boiled meal, normally meaning boiled cornmeal
Oatmeal	coarsely ground oats
Paella	Spanish dish prepared with rice, meat, poultry, fish and vegetables
Pearl barley	produced by removing the fibrous bran layer from whole grain barley
Pilaff, Pilau, Pulao	all names describing dishes prepared by cooking rice with meat or vegetables. See index
Pulses	same as legumes
Samp	another name for hominy
Semolina	flour of various grades made from the starchy endosperm of wheat grain
Soft flour	made from soft-grained wheats. Low in gluten content and good for making cakes and biscuits
Unleavened	refers to breads made without a rising agent
Wild rice	seeds of an aquatic grass native to North America. Unrelated to ordinary rice
Wheat berries	hulled whole kernels of wheat

BIBLIOGRAPHY

BLAND, B.F., *Crop Production: Cereals and Legumes*, Academic Press, 1971

BROTHWELL, DON, and PATRICIA, *Food in Antiquity*, Thames & Hudson, Praeger, 1969

DE SOLA, RAPHL, and DOROTHY, *A Dictionary of Cooking*, Constable, 1971

DOGGETT, H., *Sorghum*, Longman, 1970

DRUMMON, J.C., and WILBRAHAM, ANNE, *The Englishman's Food: A History of Five Centuries of English Diet*, Cape, 1957

FINDLAY, W.M., *Oats*, Oliver & Boyd, 1956

GREEN, S., *Guide to English Language Publication in Food Science and Technology*, Food Trade Press, 1975

GRIST, D.H., *Rice*, Longmans, 1975

HAMMOND, W., *Rice*, Coward-McCann, 1961

JOHNSON, LOIS S., *What We Eat: The Origins and Travels of Foods round the World*, Bailey, 1972

KINSEY, C., *Oats*, HMSO, 1959

KENT, N.L., *Technology of Cereals*, Pergamon, 1966

LEANARD, W.H., and MARTIN, J.H., *Cereal Crops*, Macmillan, 1963

LOEWENFELD, CLAIRE, *Nuts (Britain's Wild Larder)*, Faber & Faber, 1957

MOORE, ALMA CHESNUT, *The Grasses*, Macmillan, 1960

MORITZ, L.A., *Grain-mills and Flour in Classical Antiquity*, Oxford University Press, 1958

MORSE, C.V., and PIPER, W.J., *The Soybean*, McGraw-Hill, 1923

NICKERSON, BETTY, *How the World Grows its Food*, Ryerson Press, Toronto, 1965

PLATT, B.S., MILLER, D.S., and PAYNE, P.R., *'Protein values of human foods'*, in *Recent Advances in Human Nutrition*, edited by J.F. Brock., Churchill, 1961

RAYNS, F., *Barley*, HMSO, 1959

ROBINSON, D., *Wheat*, HMSO, 1959

Rodale Press editors, *Nuts and Seeds, the Natural Snacks*, Rodale, 1978

TANNAHILL, REAY, *Food in History*, Stein & Day, 1973

United Nations Food and Agricultural Organization publications

Food Composition Tables for International Use, Washington DC Nutritional Studies No. 3, Charlotte (1949) Chatfield

Food Composition Tables – Minerals and Vitamins – for International Use, Rome Nutritional Studies No. 3

Legumes in Human Nutrition, Nutritional Studies No. 19, W.R. Aykroyd and Joyce Doughty, Rome, 1964

Maize and Maize Diets, Nutritional Studies No. 9, 1953

Rice and Rice Diets, Nutritional Studies No. 1, 1948

Rice: Grain of Life, World Food Problems No. 6, 1966

Wheat in Human Nutrition, Nutritional Studies No. 23, W.R. Aykroyd and Joyce Doughty, 1970

US Department of Agriculture publications

Composition of Foods – Raw, Processed and Prepared, Washington, 1975
Nutritive Value of American Foods in Common Units, Washington, 1975

Weatherwax, Paul, *Indian Corn in Old America*, Macmillan, 1954
Wilson, Constance Anne, *Food and Drink in Britain*, Constable, 1973

INDEX